"Who wants to hold a position of leadership in the context of decline? When 'change and decay in all around I see' is the norm, how can one talk about being a leader? [Harrison] has not only grasped the nettle of leadership in the seminary that he is currently serving but also used his manifold experiences and learnings to remind us that leadership is not a numbers game, nor a measure of outcomes dovetailed to societal expectations of success, but faithfulness and commitment to God's church."

—The Rev. Dr. Jayakiran Sebastian, H. George Anderson Chair and Professor of Mission and Cultures, United Lutheran Seminary

"It is a fact that churches and religious organizations are diminishing.... This remarkable book... deals with concrete issues. Harrison's approach is historically informed and theologically grounded, but above all it is pragmatic.... There are no simple recipes for institutional transformation such as Harrison envisions, for it depends on the transformation, personal commitment, and honest engagement of those who are willing to take the lead in moving hopefully through difficult times."

—The Rev. Dr. Charles Hefling, Theology Department, Boston College

"Harrison invites leaders to help churches learn to be small—faithfully, lovingly, and hopefully. If you are leading a shrinking religious community, this book will reassure you that this reality is likely not your fault, yet it is still your responsibility to respond. Through scripture, story, and practical exercises, this guide invites you to transform yourself and your organization, not through numerical growth, but through a vision to participate in God's reconciling work in the world."

—The Rev. Dr. Sarah Kathleen Johnson, Director of Anglican Studies at Saint Paul University and author of *Occasional Religious Practice: Valuing a Very Ordinary Religious Experience*

"'If the church were another kind of organization, I would recommend that we shut down.' [D]aunting words, but I wish I had had this study 20 years ago, as the diocese of which I was Bishop entered into major discussion and decisions about its future.... If your understanding of what it is to be Christian, and Church, is not changed by this study, then you haven't read it properly. Read it. Integrate it. Actively apply it.... and become an active participant in God's transformation of the world!"

—The Rt. Rev. James A.J. Cowan, 12th Bishop of the Diocese of British Columbia

"Harrison brings together sociological insight, lived ministry experience and his always thoughtful theological reflection, acknowledges where we are as a 'Shrinking Church' as simple fact, and then gives leaders ways to move forward faithfully and effectively. The discussion questions make it a valuable tool for church boards and a must-read for those preparing for ministry."

—The Rev. Dr. Heather McCance, President, Atlantic School of Theology, Nova Scotia, Canada

LEADERSHIP IN A SHRINKING CHURCH

Finding New Vision in Unlikely Places

WILLIAM H. HARRISON

Seabury Books
NEW YORK

Copyright © 2025 William H. Harrison

All rights reserved. No part of this book may be reproduced, stored in a retrieval system, or transmitted in any form or by any means, electronic or mechanical, including photocopying, recording, or otherwise, without the written permission of the publisher.

Unless otherwise noted, the Scripture quotations are from New Revised Standard Version Bible, copyright © 1989 National Council of the Churches of Christ in the United States of America. Used by permission. All rights reserved worldwide.

Seabury Books
19 East 34th Street
New York, NY 10016
www.churchpublishing.org

Seabury Books is an imprint of Church Publishing Incorporated.

Cover design by Newgen
Typeset by Nord Compo

ISBN 978-1-64065-717-5 (paperback)
ISBN 978-1-64065-716-8 (hardback)
ISBN 978-1-64065-718-2 (eBook)

Library of Congress Control Number: 2024947748

For Ken M,
for getting me started.
For Rita, Richard, and Charles,
for the journey.

CONTENTS

Introduction: What this book does and why ix

1. The First Step 1
2. The Good News in a Shrinking Church 19
3. The Organized Church in a Post-Church Age 29
4. Leadership in a Shrinking Church 51
5. How Church Leadership Became Too Big and Lost Focus . . . 75
6. Under Pressure 87
7. Finding New Vision for a Church Organization 99
8. Partner, Thoughtfully 137
9. Considering Closure 149
10. Vision in Unlikely Places 157

Acknowledgments 165
Notes 167
Index 185

INTRODUCTION

What this book does and why

In 2017, I flew to Saskatoon, Saskatchewan, on the Canadian prairies. My task? To meet with a demanding hiring committee concerned about the future of a deeply cherished, meaningful, valuable seminary serving the Western Canadian portion of a historic Christian denomination.

I was familiar with the place and its work. I'd previously taught at a partner school. I had a vision for the seminary. I met with the committee and the community from 8 a.m. until 9:30 p.m. I was excited and engaged. I gave a lively address about the history of ministry and the challenges of today's church, about the bright future for the seminary responding to those needs with training for leaders, lay and ordained. I preached about God's promise of eternal life, with its biblical sense of immediacy.

I got the job.

So, leaving my sons behind at school in Ontario, my wife and I moved to Saskatoon that summer. I dove into the work, full tilt.

I learned that I could anticipate a crisis of some sort more or less every day, issues that no set of policies could resolve. Some questions involved personalities; I discovered that managing emotions would be at the heart of my work. Some involved specific challenges that no policy could touch; I found myself in constant conversation with a whole variety of people throughout academic, church, and government structures. This wasn't just the usual kind of busyness that attends my sort of work.

We had a problem.

As is my usual approach, I kept doing high-level assessment of the situation even as I responded to a seemingly endless parade of challenges. I always ask questions about what's going on. I was familiar with (and, of course, I heard) all the usual explanations: We needed more money, this person or that hadn't realized this or that thing, some great course of action had been ignored, etc., etc. I wasn't buying any of it. There was a system-level issue here.

Turned out, the problem was not that difficult to find.

Problem Part 1: The school had become a small-sized Canadian seminary from being a medium-sized Canadian seminary, in a bumpy experience lasting roughly a decade and a half. In this case, by "small" I don't mean anything complicated and comparative; I mean that we had gone from having the resources and student body to maintain a full curriculum and range of student services all by ourselves

ix

to a point where we could no longer imagine doing these things alone. We simply were not large enough to continue operating independently.

Problem Part 2: Nobody had told the system that this was happening! So, parts of the school were still trying to function as if the change had not occurred. Convocation week was packed with events that needed a large staff to sustain, even though successive waves of layoffs had trimmed staff to a minimum. We were still trying to manage 56,000 square feet of building complex, including a residence that mostly served students from a larger university rather than our own school. We were acting as if we were a medium-sized school, only temporarily inconvenienced—as if a big turnaround could be expected at any time.

Problem Part 3: The seminary's leaders had not been trained for decline, for shrinking student numbers, graduating classes, volunteer pools, and potential hiring pools. Let's face it: almost nobody is trained for such a situation. All the management programs, all the business schools, all the books—they are all oriented toward generating and maintaining growth. The result was that the actual process of getting smaller happened in a somewhat disjointed fashion, with some curious results. That big building complex that I mentioned a minute ago? We simply did not have the staff to care for it, which meant that: Lots of preventable things went wrong and we didn't have resources to fix them properly; we were doing minimal annual maintenance, rather than the full renovation needed; and my job as president was mostly building management. So much for grand visions of reimagining leadership formation for the church!

Instead, my first big task was to tell the board that we were really a small school. Our job was to figure out how to be small, not how to get back to what we once were. The response was a sigh of relief followed by a sense of genuine enthusiasm. Rather than being all tightened-up and prepared for the next problem, the board could start to see its work as a challenge to which they might be equal—or, at least, as equal as anyone could be. We could focus on finding new ways to participate in God's transformative work in the world! The result was a whole process of reimagining the school, a process that continues today and likely will be ongoing for as long as our ministry continues.

The experience about which I have begun to tell you is the proximate cause of this book, though I suspect that its genesis goes back much further. I have lived a variety of church challenges over the past few decades. The congregation in which my wife and I were married no longer exists, a victim of multiple forces including demographic change and painful infighting that was in evidence when I was a member of the parish council, long before the parish closure. Both my wife and I have served as clergy in congregations that closed while we were in leadership.

This book is in answer to my realization that nobody is trained to manage shrinking organizations, including churches. I want to change that, by telling stories that come from me and others, along with the lessons that I have learned through living the challenges. In addition to various church leadership roles, my formation includes a PhD in theology, along with other degrees in theology, political science, and English literature, and a university certificate in professional leadership. Theology continually reminds me of the big picture, the reasons for doing what I do. Political science helps me to think formally and structurally about issues of order and disorder, as does some experience in practical politics in my younger days. English literature reminds me of the importance of exercising imagination in difficult moments, and always emphasizes people and their life complexities as part of the overall story. Leadership training keeps me aware that many people are studying the sorts of challenges that we will discuss; there are many helpful resources available, some of which may seem only tangentially related to church life.

I hope that this book will enable others to be prepared for the challenges of getting smaller, able to recognize what is occurring and respond helpfully in a timely way. Thus, we will engage both theory and practice as we move forward.

Our Journey Together

I interrupted my story about seminary leadership at the moment when the school was ready to think about God's transformative work in the world. Reimagining transformation, and the church's place in it, is the core purpose of this book. In that sense, the book is the rest of the story, as I process it in relation to the larger context in which I work. This means that we will be thinking both theologically and practically, all the way through.

Some straightforward and practical sociology will set the starting point. For too long, and in too many ways, the church has been committed to a vision of salvation built upon numerical growth. We have seen our task as increasing the number of people who are baptized, or who attend church, or who make a personal decision for Christ, depending upon our theological perspective and church experience. Today, the model of numerical church growth is dying in the core of that portion of the world that I am calling "the Anglosphere": Canada, Australasia, the United Kingdom, and the United States of America. People are no longer joining the church in large numbers. We are truly a shrinking organization, in nearly all denominations of substantial size. Interestingly, as we shall see, people are not joining other voluntary organizations and are skeptical of the numerical growth model in a variety of ways. The church, therefore, must be about something else, and so must church leadership.

To do that, we need to think theologically. I propose a turn to Paul's notion of Christians as ambassadors of reconciliation (2 Corinthians 5:16–21). As ambassadors, we are invited to participate in God's work of transformation. As we discern what this means, I will suggest a threefold movement: the transformation of the world (chapters 1–3), the transformation of the self (chapters 4–5), and the transformation of the church (chapters 6–10). I have chosen to follow this order because knowing the goal from the beginning can make the prior steps easier to understand and to undertake. That said, the existential development in our lives is commonly different: Usually, we need to be at least somewhat transformed before we can contribute to transforming the church, and the church must be at least somewhat transformed before it can participate in God's transformation of the world.

The result of my approach is that this book may not be exactly what you expected when you took it off the shelf or out of the delivery envelope. Leadership is not exactly the topic until chapter 4 ("Leadership in a Shrinking Church"), and some of the most specific tools for finding vision and moving the church forward appear in later chapters (6–10, with an important core in chapter 7). To me, this route makes sense because I usually try to identify both my destination (in this case, transformation of self, church, and world) and the conditions of my travel (the shrinking church, anti-institutionalism) before I propose solutions (Gospel Vision Statement and related tools).

There is another, perhaps deeper, reason that I have chosen this route: I believe that transformations that are internalized, becoming repeated patterns of behavior, are the kinds of transformations that are most effective. Most of us know the difference between passing fads and real changes in our lives. In some workplaces, changing theories of leadership, management, and education can feel like a succession of plagues. My hope is that this book will offer you and your organization vision and tools that will be with you and sustain you through the complex challenges that you face now and in the future.

Transformation and Exercises

This book is meant to be practical. My hope is that when you have journeyed through it, you will feel better equipped to face the challenges of leadership in a shrinking church. The only value in announcing the bad news (the church and other voluntary organizations are shrinking rapidly) is to prepare us to live into the good news: God's work continues, and we can be part of it! Moreover, this book is meant to assist you and your organization to understand more deeply what you are about and how you can be about it more truly, consistently, and realistically, in a challenging environment.

This book, therefore, is a both a reflection on the nature of leadership and a workbook. After every chapter, there will be a set of exercises, intended to help you to engage with the issues raised in the material that you have just read. In every case, there are three sets of questions. The first is focused on your life, with questions designed for personal reflection. The second is about your organization, intended to help you think through the situation of the committee, congregation, parish, seminary, denominational judicatory, or whatever church organization involves you. The third is focused on the world, for consideration of the big context of engagement, ministry, and mission. This structure follows the existential order of transformation: self, church, world.

The work of the exercises is intended to be cumulative. As you work through the book, earlier answers will be relevant to later ones, so having all your materials in one place will be helpful. Thus, I encourage you to record your answers in one place, a single book or computer directory or something similar. The point of the workbook structure is that it helps you and your organization to learn and to be transformed.

I invite you to take the exercises seriously. They are not really an optional extra to the book, in the way that some study guides are. Instead, they are integral to the purpose: fostering transformation. The questions are an invitation for you to engage with the kinds of transformation that I talk about. The more that you put into answering the questions, the more that you are likely to get from the book. Of course, some people will prefer not to do the exercises, perhaps because they slow progress through the book. I understand that perspective. After all, speed-reading is a basic academic skill; it is the only way to get through the quantities of reading that I need to do routinely. If time is an issue for you, or you find that the exercises are slowing your progress unduly, consider simply jotting some quick thoughts in point form. I hope that completing the exercises will enable you to reach the end of the book with a sense that: You have understood what I am trying to say; you know something more about yourself and are finding helpful ways to grow; and you have greater clarity about next steps in the life of your church organization.

A Quick Overview

The chapters in this book are meant to progress in a developmental sequence. Leaders might use them as a guide for personal growth or as a kind of road map for the organizations they lead. The first three chapters are preparatory for working directly on the complexities of leadership.

Chapter 1 names the core issue in the Anglosphere church today: numbers are shrinking. This is exactly where people in the pews tend to locate the challenge, and they are correct. In this, we move in a different direction from some contemporary approaches. Susan Beaumont focuses on churches that are in a "liminal space," unsure where they are going.[1] Beaumont speaks to a broad variety of contexts, including the shrinking church,[2] and provides leadership strategies. I seek to shift the conversation back a step, centering the experience of declining numbers. With that focus, I invite us to think about transformation that God accomplishes and in which the world (including the church) participates. This clarifies the purpose of the church as it shrinks, helping us to understand the meaning of life in a church that is disappearing in our day. My approach also emphasizes that leadership is not the reason for declining numbers, so that leadership strategies will not fix this problem.

This book differs from many other contemporary reflections on the church because my thinking is not based primarily in secularization theory (the belief that the Western world is growing less religious).[3] I do not deny that secularization is happening; it is, and resources that help us to think about its implications are helpful and important. However, that is not where I am going. Instead, I approach the question from the perspective of Robert D. Putnam's sociology, which points to a dramatic decline in engagement with volunteer organizations of any kind, a decline in traditional forms of social capital, from the 1960s onward.[4] The challenge that we face is not necessarily church, as such, but volunteer commitments in general and the membership growth assumptions that they tend to carry. We will see that Christianity, from its earliest beginnings, has been shaped by a numerical growth narrative that is no longer helpful because of the disinclination to join and because visions of numerical growth no longer have an uncomplicated grip on social imagination.

Chapter 2 focuses on the good news of Christ Jesus, emphasizing the link between God's transformative work in our lives and the invitation to serve as ambassadors of reconciliation. This understanding of salvation, taken in the context of a shrinking church, calls us to imagine the church as engaged with the world, rather than internally focused.

Chapter 3 invites the church to think differently, in a more nuanced way, about transformation, building on Bernard Lonergan's thinking about the kinds of changes that we humans need to see in order to serve God and the world as fully as humanly possible.

Our reimagining of salvation provides basic theological underpinnings for a shift to a church that serves God's transformation of the world, whether one assumes the secularization or the social capital dynamic. Instead of demanding a specific moment of conversion, a habit of some forms of Protestantism, or expecting people to make an explicit commitment to the church, common in all forms of Christianity, this understanding of transformation recognizes growth in all aspects of life, creating room for all people who respond to the touch of divine love: spiritual but not religious, those of other faiths, and atheists. To help us understand transformation more deeply, I will draw on some examples, especially the fictional presentation of transformation in the movie *Groundhog Day* and the real-life example of Sargent Shriver, as discussed in the work of James Price and Kenneth Melchin.

Chapter 4 begins to focus specifically on leadership, addressing a series of considerations. We will start by considering some of the qualifications needed for leadership in a shrinking church: a significant degree of transformation; an ambassadorial emphasis that centers on reconciliation; self-appropriation; a gospel focus; the capacity to lead through big changes; a capacity for vulnerability, honesty, and courage; and openness to ongoing education. We will find some resources in contemporary leadership theory, especially the work of Ronald Heifetz and that of Brené Brown.

Chapter 5 moves to address some of the history of church leadership over the past millennium, which has been largely a task-focused story of ever-expanding ministry of presbyters (pastors/ministers/priests), as the priorities of the church have shifted without losing any previous emphases. This chapter concludes with a discussion of leadership as it is emerging today.

Chapter 6 addresses a variety of pressures that affect church organizations during the challenge of shrinking: high levels of anxiety, the emergence of warriors, the tendency toward bias, and impacts of social media.

Chapter 7 speaks to the challenge of finding new vision for an organization facing the realities of a shrinking church. I will introduce the idea of a Gospel Vision Statement (GVS) that links our understanding of the good news with the realities of local situation, incorporating mission, location, identity, and resources. We will review some samples of what a GVS might look like and reflect on aspects of process that can aid in constructing a GVS. We will also reflect on helpfully working with a GVS.

Because creating a GVS and living it can often best be accomplished with assistance from others, chapter 8 addresses the possibility of partnerships. We consider ways that a common vision for mission and compatible resources enable a good partnership. We then address some ways in which partnerships take on new meaning in the context of a shrinking church that is rejecting the numerical growth model and turning to an ambassadorial church model.

One of the implications of a shrinking church is that closure is sometimes the healthiest, most God-serving direction. The church is seriously, viability threateningly overbuilt, with leaders exhausted from trying to sustain arrangements intended for many more people. Chapter 9 discusses the challenge of deciding to close, when closure is likely to be a good choice, and ways to make the process easier.

Chapter 10 concludes the discussion and reflects on some meanings of life in a shrinking church and ways that this book is intended to be helpful.

Taken together, this variety of elements provides an account of the good news that gets to the heart of God's transformative work in the world and links that vision with the specific work of God's transformation in individual persons. Individual persons serve as leaders, so the understanding of leadership that unfolds builds upon that story of personal transformation, with the addition that leaders invite and enable others to engage transformatively. Concretely, church leaders engage their organizations in the effort to envision transformation in their own lives and in the lives of people—and, indeed, all of creation—in the areas where they serve. Leaders enable reconciliation, which makes common vision and new partnerships possible. Leaders also speak hard truths, which may mean assisting an organization to close down, especially in a world where there are more congregations and other ecclesiastical structures than are imaginably sustainable. Ultimately, we will live our way into a church that is better suited to serve God's call to participate in God's transformative work in the whole world, regardless of our numbers.

Exercises: Introduction

Because we have only just begun, this set consists of preliminary exercises, based on (or inspired by) the issues that the introduction raises and that further chapters discuss. With these questions, I invite you to identify some of your current thinking, along with your expectations for this book.

A. Your Life
1. What do you hope to get out of reading this book? Is there a kind of framework or particular set of skills that you would like to develop? You may wish to record your hopes and return to the list as you read.
2. What leadership roles do you hold, both in the church and in other contexts? What leadership roles do you foresee yourself undertaking? Are there any understandings or skills that you have not already named but would be useful in these roles and might appear in this book?

B. Your Organization
1. Is your church organization feeling the pressure of shrinking church engagement? If it is not right now, is the pressure likely to come in the foreseeable future?
2. Do you see declining numbers in the church? If so, why do you think people are not joining?
3. What do you think the church is all about? What is its purpose?

C. The World
1. Do you sometimes wonder whether expansion (of any kind: money, power, resources, people) is a good model for the world? Why or why not?

CHAPTER 1

THE FIRST STEP

Sometimes, being church stinks. It isn't simple. It isn't easy. It isn't gentle. Today, the difficulties are all affected by—and often driven by—the experience of declining levels of participation. People don't come to church. Those who do attend are usually older, bringing the challenges of later life alongside their wisdom and commitment. Shrinking attendance means that ever fewer people are carrying increasing loads, as needs grow, buildings age, the organizational environment becomes more complex, and society professionalizes.

We adopt all sorts of strategies to fight numerical decline. Sometimes, they even work—at least, in some places and on limited time scales. Unfortunately, we're fighting the wrong battle. Possibly worse yet, we're fighting an unwinnable war.

Leaders face the stress and carry the responsibility. Even when they aren't blamed, they deal with the fallout. One result is that today's leaders are tired. Another is that fewer people want to follow in their footsteps.

The numbers problem is clear. People aren't joining any organization that involves significant voluntary commitments. This social shift is not really about the church. It's about society. We can't change the trend, or, at least, we can't do so by ourselves.

It's not you. Don't let people pressure you about it. You didn't create the situation. You can't solve it.

It is, however, still your challenge. A changing world means that the church in the Anglosphere is going through a massive transformation, part of which is numerical shrinkage.

The Numerical Growth Model

The challenge begins with our root narratives. There is a biblical and Christian growth narrative that we will address. However, in fairness to the whole story, we must recognize that the desire for numerical and geographical growth, while perhaps not applicable to every society, has a broad enough history to be regarded as something more than Christian and more than recent. The growth of empire is evident in many parts of the world from as early in history as we are able to reconstruct. Similarly, and sometimes in parallel, religious believers have tended to seek opportunities to share their religion with others. Buddhism, Islam, and Hinduism have such histories.

The church has its own specific view of growth, which is not universal to societies or religions. This may be most evident in the way that the author of the gospel of Luke and its (most likely) companion volume, Acts, constructs the story. The gospel of Luke is probably the first part of a history, with Acts as the second portion, together moving from the Jewish context through Pentecost and out into the whole world. This history tells the story of God's creation of the church—and God's blessing of the community—as a narrative of numerical growth. The blessing is evident in the numbers, which tends to suggest the corollary that the church is failing to receive God's blessing if its numbers are not rising.

Pentecost, described in Acts, is precisely about people with all sorts of national backgrounds hearing the gospel in their native tongues. Today, some Christians speak of Pentecost as the "birthday of the church" because the Spirit enters the Christian community and enables the spread of the good news beyond a small community of Jewish Christians. The celebration of success comes early in Acts. On the day of Pentecost, "about 3,000 persons were added" (Acts 2:41). In chapters 3 and 4, immediately following Pentecost, Peter and John speak to a great crowd, and though the two disciples are arrested for their preaching, the text triumphally announces the addition of 5,000 to the early church as a result of their testimony. In chapter 5, the apostles perform signs and wonders, and "more than ever" believers are added (Acts 5:12–16). In chapter 6, "The word of God continued to spread; the number of disciples increased greatly in Jerusalem, and a great many of the priests became obedient to the faith" (Acts 6:7). The text is punctuated with such remarks about growth. Whether or not the numbers are accurate is immaterial to our point, except that exaggeration would reinforce my suggestion that numerical increase is of the essence of the early Christian story. After all, why would the author overstate unless they wanted to emphasize the power of Christian preaching to increase the numbers joining the church? From earliest times, the church has taken its cue from the biblical command to "Go into all the world and proclaim the good news to the whole creation" (Mark 16:15). This command, which has resonated through the church's history, is drawn from the section that scholars call the long ending of Mark. This ending is a late addition to the text. Its inclusion emphasizes the church's understanding of the biblical texts as being growth focused: if the text is not as explicit about the priority as it should be (and Mark is complicated on this), then a growth focus gets added.

The church's earliest literature, the Pauline and other letters, is all focused on the shifts that come with geographic and numerical growth. The letter to the Romans expresses Paul's wish to visit them "in order that I may reap some harvest among you as I have among the rest of the Gentiles" (Romans 1:13). 1 Corinthians speaks to division among members of the church at Corinth, apparently rooted in them having received the gospel and baptism from different preachers. 2 Corinthians is partly Pauline travelogue and partly a call for Corinthian Christians to provide financial support to the church in Jerusalem. Galatians is an effort to speak to the relationship between the rapidly growing non-Jewish church to Jewish Christianity, which had a more obvious and direct connection to the nation of Israel.

For Christians, this is all very familiar material. Indeed, that is exactly the point that I am trying to make: Christians have a profoundly internalized narrative image of numerical growth. We find our religion very difficult to think in ways that do not focus on expansion in these terms. In fact, growth is what followed, as Christianity has spent two millennia becoming a world religion. "Christianity, a faith that began nearly 2,000 years ago in the Middle East, is now followed by 2.4 billion people, and is the primary religion practiced throughout the Americas, Europe, Australasia, and sub-Saharan Africa."[1] Followed by 31 percent of the world's population, Christianity is the world's largest religion, ahead of Islam (24 percent), Hinduism (15 percent), and Buddhism (7 percent).[2] Our religion continues to gain numbers at impressive speed in places such as Africa and Asia.

But Numbers Also Go Down

This narrative of numbers is a problem for us, because the church has stopped growing in some places where it has historically been large and powerful. The church is not alone in feeling the pressure: all voluntary organizations are in dramatic decline that may, for some, prove to be terminal. We see this in the core of a connection of countries that is sometimes called "the Anglosphere," including Canada, Australasia, the United States, and the United Kingdom.

We tend to think of the challenge of declining numbers as a church thing, rooted in a long trajectory of secularization that affects the countries in this category. The nature and meaning of secularization are subjects of a vast amount of literature. We will not go into it here, except to say that John Locke's late-seventeenth-century distinction between the civil polity, which directs everything to do with life in the world and has the power to enforce its rulings, and religion, which is focused on life after death and is entirely voluntary,[3] has been decisive for the way that Westerners view religion. Religion has become optional and, for many, irrelevant. When Friedrich Nietzsche declared that "God is dead" this is exactly what he meant: in the minds of many people, God has no impact on daily events.[4]

There is truth in the secularization narrative, but it hardly explains the decline in Lions Club membership. I was briefly a member of the Lions in a small town, before life circumstances moved me onward and I lost touch with the group. We raised funds for good causes and enjoyed social life together. After meetings, we would sit and drink scotch while the poker game began. I noticed nothing about this that could not continue without church. However one defines religion, the Lions did not depend upon it or incorporate it in their lives as a club, except with a simple grace at banquets.

However, there is another, more recent narrative that was identified in the United States and applies also to Australasia, Canada, and the UK, a story that I find more persuasive in accounting for the decline in voluntary associations. Robert D. Putnam, in *Bowling Alone: The Collapse and Revival of American Community*, traces a trajectory coming out of the Gilded Age in the nineteenth century. Putnam argues that, starting around 1890, Americans constructed an extensive system of organizations and became a nation of joiners. His focus is on something that he and others call "social capital," a reservoir of communal strength built on social relations.[5] His argument is that the Progressive Era at the end of the nineteenth century caused an eruption of social creativity meant to foster civic engagement and transform society.[6] Although there is significant scholarly criticism of aspects of Putnam's account, notably in relation to his assertions about the causes of the increases in civic engagement and his recommendations about ways to restore it from its declining state,[7] nobody disputes the decline in voluntary engagement that he traces.

We are not especially concerned with the causes of this decline; our focus is on its occurrence and consequences. However, I will enter a comment that I think important, because it shows both that a return of the era of joining is unlikely and that we might not want it again, at least in the form in which it previously happened. I suspect that Putnam underemphasizes, though he considers, the impact of war.[8] Two massive wars enforced organized social relations, by pressing everyone to share a common sense of purpose around care for the world, to function as a team for both work and leisure, and to stand united against common enemies. Christians should note that the extensive work of chaplains meant that religion was an integrated function of military life. The point carried over to popular culture: When the television show, *M.A.S.H.*, envisions the Korean War, the chaplain is a pivotal and respected figure. Even the nonreligious characters appeal to Father Mulcahy when life gets complicated. After World War II was over, the habits of communal activity, including religion, were not immediately shaken. In this context, the crusades of Billy Graham saw enormous results, as did radio and television ministries starring Rex Humbard and Oral Roberts, along with many others.

In a concerted effort to keep the trajectory going, a substantial body of church growth and congregational development literature appeared. Donald A. McGavran is commonly recognized as the founder of the church growth movement, with his 1955 book, *The Bridges of God*. In it, McGavran pioneers the use of sociological analysis to assess reasons that people choose to become Christians. McGavran has numerous successors, building on the social scientific methods that became important to many aspects of Western life in the twentieth century.

However, church membership peaked in the 1960s, as did membership in other organizations. The impetus to join, sustained on a more or less upward trajectory through the twentieth century, began to change. The youth counterculture of the 1960s rejected the tightly linked culture of parents and grandparents. If two world wars likely helped to foster a culture of joining, then war (Vietnam, Algeria, the Troubles in Ireland) and various revolutionary movements (Irish Republican Army, Black Panthers, Red Brigades, Baader-Meinhof Group, Front de Libération du Québec) may have contributed to that culture's decline. *M.A.S.H.* (a show of the 1970s and early 1980s) is, in its heart, both antiwar and critical of easy joining. The original movie version (with the theme song "Suicide is Painless") is even more so. *Hair: The American Tribal Love-Rock Musical* is an explicit (in every sense) attack on the hypocrisy of a world that emphasizes close community at the expense of honesty. The limitations on that close community were also revealed when Martin Luther King Jr. and others drew attention to the racism that underpinned the social order in the USA, and feminists such as Betty Friedan and Germaine Greer did the same for sexism. The 1960s and 1970s, which I think of as the post-postwar era, certainly gave numerous indications that the consensus was failing.

One reason that I think the two major wars of the twentieth century may be central to the growth and decline of volunteer organizations is that they are shared experiences of the whole Anglosphere. The important limitation in Putnam's work, from our perspective, is its focus on the USA. As we shall see, a similar pattern seems to be playing out throughout this family of countries.

In any case, our priority is not in understanding the reasons for the rise in these kinds of social capital or their decrease but in recognizing the significance of the cycle and, especially, the decline. For our discussion, the most important aspect of Putnam's work is that it highlights the universality of the decline throughout society. The book's title is well chosen and profoundly revealing; *Bowling Alone* is a reminder that people still bowl informally with friends but rarely join bowling leagues—once a popular pastime. The impact has been felt in every kind of organization. Putnam carefully assesses a variety of forms of social engagement: political, social, religious, and philanthropic. Patterns are consistent throughout American society. People no longer join in the way that they did in the earlier part of the twentieth century. Most important, from our perspective, the challenge is not only in the church! It is everywhere in the community.

I have been unable to find a study resembling Putnam's for other countries in the Anglosphere. However, evidence suggests a similar trajectory. This appears to be true in Canada. Service clubs are vanishing; the news sphere is full of stories from cities, towns, and villages where clubs are tiny and old or closing entirely. In 2020, the Lions Club, once very popular, admitted to a forty-year membership decline.[9] The Rotary Club dropped 14 percent between 2003 and 2013.[10] Political parties are shrinking, with small and aging membership.[11] Scouts Canada is in decline: In 1961, it had a membership of 270,000 which had shrunk to just over 90,000 in 2000, while the number of leaders shrank by 21 percent in the five years between 1995 and 2000.[12]

In the UK, the BBC commissioned a research project intended to increase understanding of social developments among the population, especially with reference to the areas covered by BBC broadcasts. Researchers found substantial increases in social fragmentation (rising "loneliness indices")[13] and decreases in political engagement.[14] In the 1950s, the Conservative Party had 2.8 million members, while the Labour Party had 1 million; today, the membership numbers combined are around 1 million.[15] Freemasonry is seeing significant decline: "On average, there has been a 2.5 per cent annual decline in our membership each year across England, Wales, the Channel Islands and the Isle of Man since 2008, taking us from around 200,000 members 10 years ago to a little more than 150,000 today."[16]

In Australia, participation in service and other volunteer organizations dropped by 8–10 percent between 2006 and 2019.[17] The Rotary Club's membership "has deteriorated significantly on the basis of members per 100,000 of population... The actual fall in the past 22 years is about 28 percent, but per capita membership has halved."[18] Freemasonry has seen a steady decline since its peak in the 1960s; many lodges are small, with aging members, and are either closing or in danger of closure.[19] Political party membership has been in decline for many years.[20] The developments that Putnam traces appear to be consistent across the Anglosphere.

A broad decline in committed volunteer social engagement does not disprove the assertion that secularization plays some part in church shrinkage, or that church sinfulness has had an impact. However, neither secularization nor sinfulness can be an adequate account of the total social movement of which the decline in church membership is only one aspect. If all, or nearly all, volunteer groups in society are aging and shrinking, then specifically church-related characteristics cannot be sufficient cause to explain the challenge. We can reasonably assume that Putnam is correct in arguing that church membership decline is merely one part of an overall social movement toward declining social engagement.

This is an important point for us. As a consequence of the narrative of numerical growth to which we are accustomed, we too easily assume that lack of this kind of growth is a moral or spiritual failing. The narrative of failure can easily be reinforced by biblical stories, from the moment that humanity is ejected from Eden (Gen. 4:22–24) onward, that connect wrongdoing with a failure to thrive. Similarly, we are well aware that the destructive acts that we call sin have destructive impacts, often sustained over time.

The church certainly has moral shortcomings to which such a narrative can be attached: accounts of colonial imperialism, sexual and physical abuse, slavery, racism, sexism, heterosexism... The list goes on. Declining numbers are also easily connected to narratives of theological error: Conservatives accuse churches that uphold various kinds of sex and gender equality of committing to a liberalism dictated by society rather than Christian principles, while liberals accuse conservatives of authoritarianism in service of power and inequality—again, at odds with Christian principles. There may be something in any number of these narratives, and in others also, but Putnam's point overwhelms all of them. The decline in church participation may hit different churches in different ways and at different times but overall, it is morally and theologically neutral. People simply are not joining anymore. They are not joining any organizations, including bowling leagues and, yes, churches. People may be finding other forms of social engagement—online life may provide social capital of a different kind—but people are not committing to consistent, long-term participation in traditional structures. Seeking to be true to God's call is meaningful; indeed, for a Christian, it is the basic constituent of true life. However, it is not necessarily a means to increase the number of attendees in a church congregation.

Not Working Anymore

For North Americans, as for people in the rest of the Anglosphere, the numerical growth model that has been integral to Christianity is no longer working. Indeed, for many, numerical growth—in the church and elsewhere—is not a helpful vision. Journalist Charles C. Mann, in *The Wizard and the Prophet*, distinguishes two approaches to the future of humanity, especially in relation to agriculture and technology: the wizard, who envisions continued population and economic growth through the power of technological innovation; and the prophet, who calls for limits on human expansion on the grounds that we are exceeding the earth's carrying capacity.[21] Mann describes himself as seeing both sides and going back and forth, which is probably the world's position except in one crucial aspect: population. In developed countries, including North America, people are taking the "prophet" route and having fewer children; indeed, Anglosphere countries are consistently below the replacement rate of 2.1 children per couple. Expressed bluntly, this means fewer children in church. Declining birth rates also reflect a skepticism about a growth model that is built around rising numbers of people.

Many Christians, especially but not only on the liberal side of the church, concur with the prophet. Ecotheology, exemplified by such thinkers as Jürgen Moltmann, Rosemary Radford Ruether, Celia Deane Drummond, the evangelical team of Daniel L. Brunner, Jennifer L. Butler, A. J. Swoboda, and Bill McKibben, and many more scholars of all theological stripes, tends to stand firmly with the prophet, viewing humanity's treatment of the Earth with horror and a demand for change. When the Lutheran World Federation met in Windhoek, Namibia, in 2017, one of its core themes was "Creation—Not for Sale," focusing on the impact of excessive consumption of Earth's resources by the wealthy and the consequences for poorer people around the world. Though it does not focus specifically on church membership, ecotheology calls into question the growth paradigm that fixates on rising numbers. The focus, instead, is on learning to care for the world within its limits, in partnership with others who may be Christian or not, "our brand" or not.

The growth model, so characteristic of Western civilization in general, has produced its own backlash as it places intolerable demands on participants.

Byung-Chul Han, a philosopher with a background in Roman Catholic theology, identifies today's society as an "achievement society," built on the notion that we can accomplish anything if we choose to do so and commit ourselves to it, as distinct from a more traditional "disciplinary society," which is built around the ideas of limitations—the notion that there are things that we should do and should not do.[22] The result is that "the *pressure to achieve*" causes exhaustive depression.[23]

Han's argument speaks directly to the challenge of leadership in a shrinking church. The church's narrative of numerical growth fits precisely with the contemporary emphasis on endless achievement. The point of the numerical growth model is that doing church right results in more people joining. If people are not joining, then we are doing it wrong. A major text on the decline in church participation is called *The Great Dechurching: Who's Leaving, Why Are They Going, and What Will It Take to Bring Them Back?*[24] One of its core calls to the church goes like this:

> Tens of millions of people may be leaving the church, and more than eighty-six churches may be closing every week, but if we have eyes to see it, there is actually much reason to hope. We need to come to grips with some hard realities inside the church, but there are ways to win many of these people back. Some things are outside of our control, but others aren't. Success will require fruitful engagement with the things within our control without compromising the doctrines we hold most important. To put an even finer point on it, it is in the appropriate application of our doctrines where the lowest hanging fruit lies.[25]

In other words, correctly being church will add members. The authors may be right sometimes, but Putnam's argument means that we cannot expect this to be true. The point of the study is that many people have left the church because of the church's failure to meet its own standards, often in deeply reprehensible ways. The church should, indeed, be more faithful. The problem is with the direct and causal linkage between faithfulness and increasing numbers. That may not hold. An increase in numbers as a result of good behavior is not inevitable. For reasons that we will consider, it is not especially likely at this point in time. More significantly, this narrative creates pressure to achieve numerical growth, rather than fostering an invitation to live the life to which God invites us.

Clergy, who are among the most obvious leaders in the church, are feeling the pressure. Clergy burnout is a significant issue today, and many of its roots are in the church's numerical decline. As Han's argument suggests, burnout tends to be a greater risk among people who seek to accomplish the kinds of endless achievement—in this case, numerical growth—that is held up as the definition of success. Leaders are being destroyed by the narrative.

Moreover, Christians engaged with issues of ecumenical and interfaith dialogue tend to be skeptical of the once easy assumption that Christians of our kind (whatever that might mean) are always right and others are usually or always wrong. We have alluded to this in the mention of ecotheology, and the point generalizes. We do not have anywhere nearly enough space in this context to address these themes. Suffice it to say that most denominations are in substantial conversations with other Christian groups and many actively cooperate. I am an ordained historically Anglican person serving as president of a Lutheran seminary, a product of "Called to Full Communion," an agreement whereby the Anglican Church of Canada and the Evangelical Lutheran Church in Canada do many things together, including hiring each other's clergy.

More radically and profoundly, many religious people are engaged in active dialogue and shared action with people of other religious views: Buddhists, Jews, Muslims, Sikhs, etc. These dialogues function on principles of mutual respect and shared desire to learn. Ordinarily, they begin from the starting point commonly drawn from Leonard Swidler's "Dialogue Decalogue": "Dialogue is a conversation on a common subject between two or more persons with differing views, the primary purpose of which is for each participant to learn from the other so that s/he can change and grow. This very definition of dialogue embodies the first commandment of dialogue."[26] In a fundamental departure from the numerical growth image, the focus is not at all on the conversion of the other. Instead, the emphasis is upon a deeper understanding of both self and other, so that all may grow.

Christians have also become aware of numerous—and very recent—examples of the destructiveness of the Christian inclination to prioritize numerical growth above other considerations. The terrible and irremediable damage done to Indigenous peoples, their world, and their belief systems stands out. In the United States, these wrongs are too rarely noticed, hidden behind the evils of slavery. However, in Canada, Australia, New Zealand, much of Africa, and elsewhere, Christianity's purposeful destruction of Indigenous peoples has been at the forefront of public and church reflection for decades. Christian churches have participated, both officially and unofficially, in efforts to destroy traditional societies and beliefs, eliminating the ancient dances, songs, and stories. Churches ran residential schools; in the Canadian context, these were purposefully assimilationist and often abusive. Behind much of the North American effort was the philosophy of R. H. Pratt (founder of Carlisle Indian Industrial School in Pennsylvania), "Kill the Indian in him, and save the man."[27] Many churches have apologized for this deeply evil work, and some have begun specific efforts to change their approaches to the world as a result. We cannot claim spiritual authority or expect everyone to join us when we have such sin in our lives. The numerical growth model has much for which to answer.

We are changing, moving away from that model. When I teach evangelism, I teach it in a way that differs dramatically from the training of my youth and childhood. In the evangelical (and fundamentalist) context in which I was raised, evangelism was essentially a one-way street: I was there to distribute biblical truth to a world in need of God, a world that was destined to find itself in hell after death if it did not find a personal relationship with Jesus Christ. I was trained in the four spiritual laws, an explication of the gospel composed by evangelist Bill Bright,[28] and similar, ostensibly biblical, renditions of the Christian message. The point was to share these words with others and bring them around to my perspective, as formed by my church community, increasing the numbers destined for heaven and decreasing the numbers destined for perdition.

Today, I teach evangelism as a very different movement, with a different goal. I distinguish three steps. The first is an appeal to God to enable the other to speak God's word transformatively to me, such that the other's story, heard attentively, becomes a way of changing my life and position. In other words, far from beginning with the assumption that I have something to teach, I begin with the expectation that the other has something to teach me about who God is and what God is accomplishing in the world. The skeptical reader is, of course, correct that I have a difficult time living up to this approach, which is entirely counter to both my instincts of self-assertion and my training as a scholar expected to defend my every thesis. Nonetheless, I believe that it is the right starting place. Only when the other has been heard and knows that they have been heard, will it be (step two) time to speak my story, with the prayer to God that I may truly be a transformational divine word to the other; importantly, this will not necessarily mean that the other becomes a Christian, let alone a member of my denomination. If there is some element of success in the first two steps, then we may pray to reach the third, which is the moment where together—in deed and word—we become shared participants in God's loving justice in the world. Again, this will not necessarily result in the other becoming a Christian; indeed, it may make me more engaged with the insights of some other religious tradition. However, both of us, if there is some success, will be more deeply religiously transformed, in the specific sense of having a somewhat recognized and understood encounter with the loving God. I will say much more about this in the chapter on leadership where we will discuss healthier goals for the church.

I ended this section on a note about my teaching for a specific reason: I wish to make certain that this book is not read as a disincentive to sharing the good news of Christ Jesus. I intend precisely the opposite: I encourage people to live and speak the gospel as and because it is good news. If that attracts people, then so much the better. My concern is with Christianity's unfortunate tendency to play the numbers game, to define itself in terms of a narrative image as a numerically growing body.

The numbers narrative, the focus on membership growth, has lost its impetus in many places. It is failing because people no longer join volunteer organizations. It is losing its power because it is no longer a credible expression of people's theological and historical beliefs. As we shall see below, that has created extraordinary stresses for contemporary church leaders, who are still in the grip of the numbers narrative and have responsibilities to traditional church structures that depend upon large—preferably expanding—memberships. In addition, the emphasis upon membership numbers has ceased to be a helpful way to define church goals for many Christians. Both the historical impact of the numbers narrative, with its destructive impact on Indigenous peoples especially, and concerns about the current human growth priority, tend to weaken the credibility structure of the story. We need to understand our situation accurately and we need to redefine success. The numerical growth narrative is not the only, not even the most important, account of what God is doing in and through the church.

Admitting We Have a Problem

The first step to responding to a problem is admitting that it is there. Denial does not help, either at local or broader levels. In fact, most churches in the Anglosphere are shrinking, some quite rapidly, and the few that are growing tend to be small. The mainline churches, where people seem to expect membership decline, are showing it. Numerous studies have provided evidence of decreasing numbers. We have already referred to Davis and Graham, *The Great Dechurching*, a study in the United States. In Canada, Brian Clarke and Stuart Macdonald have provided *Leaving Christianity: Changing Allegiances in Canada since 1945*, and Joel Thiessen has written *The Meaning of Sunday: The Practice of Belief in a Secular Age*. Grace Davie's *Religion in Britain: A Persistent Paradox* raises many of the same questions for the United Kingdom, and Peter Brierley has tracked UK numbers with Faith Survey. There are other relevant assessments, including in other countries. Declining numbers are a reality.

Warning: Lots of numbers ahead! In the next couple of pages, I'm going to offer a brief review of attendance shifts, largely from the records of churches themselves. This is different from usual statistical assessments, which tend to build on uniformly collected and directly comparable census data about religious allegiance. I do something unusual here, because I want us to see what churches say about themselves or, where that is impossible, what researchers who look at actual numbers of people attending church have to say. Our concern is less with self-identification than with concrete engagement. The numbers show that the church has real issues to face.

We begin with Canada, where declining attendance is evident.

- Total membership in the Anglican Church of Canada peaked at 1,365,313, in 3,602 congregations, in 1965; in 2017 membership hit 359,030, in 2,206 congregations.[29] A report from the church's statistics officer in 2019 indicated that the trend line, if unchanged, would mean no Anglicans remaining in Canada in 2040 (though, of course, the statistics officer is aware that trend lines almost always curve rather than going to zero in the social

sciences); a 2024 report showed accelerated decline during the most intense period of COVID-19, implying an earlier sunset date, with a significant drop in every category of participation except funerals.[30]
- The United Church of Canada reached its highest point ever in 1965 at 1,064,033.[31] In 2021, membership stood at 352,812, in 2,586 congregations.
- The Evangelical Lutheran Church in Canada was formed in 1986, with 202,465 members in 665 congregations; in 2025, it self-describes as having over 75,000 members in 459 congregations.[32]
- The Roman Catholic Church is seeing a significant drop in affiliation: In 2011, 12.8 million Canadians identified as Roman Catholic; in 2021, the number was 10.9 million.[33] As important, far fewer are attending mass: According to the Center for Applied Research in the Apostolate at Georgetown University, only 14 percent of Canadians who identify as Roman Catholic say they go to mass at least once a week, and the numbers descend to 2 percent in Canada's historically Roman Catholic province of Québec.[34]

The same issue is visible in the United States:

- In 1987, the Evangelical Lutheran Church in America was formed with 5,288,230 members[35]; in 2020, there were 3.3 million baptized members.[36]
- The Episcopal Church peaked at over 3.5 million members in 1965[37]; membership in 2022 was 1,584,685.[38]
- The United Church of Christ had 2,246,610 members in 8,184 congregations in 1960[39]; in 2023, there were 712,296 members in 4,603 congregations.[40]
- Ryan Burge tracks significant decline in Roman Catholic numbers in the United States, with a smaller percentage of the population identifying from about 2008 onward (even with significant Roman Catholic immigration).[41] Mass attendance has shown a steep drop on a more or less steady trajectory since the early 1970s, so that today only about 25 percent of those who identify as Roman Catholic also claim to be regular mass attendees.[42]

The challenge is also evident in the United Kingdom.

- In the Church of England in 2009, average Sunday attendance was 895,000; in 2022, it was 547,000. In 1962, there were 1,892,765 Christmas communicants[43] in 17,902 places of worship.[44] In 2009, Christmas communicants totaled 985,000, and by 2022, that number had dropped to 595,000.[45] Christmas 2022 was celebrated in 15,581 places of worship.[46]
- According to *Church Growth Modelling*, Methodist Church in Great Britain membership peaked between 1910 and 1950 at around 850,000, with steep decline since.[47] In 2023, the church stated a membership of 170,000,[48] although

we cannot be sure that this number is calculated in the same way that *CGM* reached its membership statistics.

Peter Brierley published estimates for church attendance in the United Kingdom from 1980 to 2015 with Faith Survey. For England, he saw significant declines.

- Anglican: 1,370,400 to 660,000
- Baptist: 286,900 to 226,000
- Roman Catholic: 2,064,000 to 608,000
- Independent: 239,200 to 170,000
- Methodist: 606,400 to 200,000
- United Reformed: 188,300 to 33,100
- Other Churches: 139,800 to 87,000

These declines are hardly balanced out by the small increases seen in a few places: New Churches (75,000 to 166,000), Orthodox (10,200 to 26,100), and Pentecostal (221,100 to 298,000).[49]

In Australia:

- The Uniting Church is coming to terms with significant membership and attendance decline. It has long imagined itself as a church with more than 2,000 congregations and communities.[50] The world has changed. "In the Uniting Church today there are approximately 1,672 local communities with a typical median attendance of 28 people and an average age of 68. Around 380 of these communities are part of clusters. 62 percent of our members are retired and 16 percent are employed full time."[51] There are fewer people, the majority of whom are older, and members—especially lay leaders—are exhausted and burning out; this is a challenge to energy for mission and to basic health.[52]

- In 2016, NCLS Research noted a steep drop in church attendance from 1991 to 2001, with a slowing decline following; numbers continue to fall among Roman Catholics and mainstream Protestant churches, though Pentecostal numbers are rising.[53]

These declines are the norm for Roman Catholic and mainline Protestant churches in the Anglosphere.

Many people do not realize, though, that many conservative churches are also seeing significant membership decline, though in some cases it is delayed in comparison to mainline churches.

- The Southern Baptist Convention peaked at 16,306,246 in 2006; after that, its decline has been consistent and substantial, hitting 12,982,090 in 2023.[54]
- The Lutheran Church—Missouri Synod (LCMS) had 2,788,536 members in 5,690 congregations at its high point in 1970[55]; in 2023, the LCMS had 1,708,125 members in 5,826 congregations.[56]
- The Canadian partner of the LCMS, the Lutheran Church Canada, officially came into being (organizationally separating from the LCMS parent) in 1988 with 90,944 members in 354 congregations[57]; in 2022, there were 47,607 members in 276 congregations.[58]
- The Christian Reformed Church in North America, covering both Canada and the United States, had 256,015 members in 1963, then peaked at 316,415 in 1992, and was down to 204,664 in 2022.[59]
- In the United Kingdom, we have seen that Brierley estimates a significant decline in Baptist numbers.

Drowning in numbers? Consider that this is only a snapshot, taken with rough statistics and without close analysis. I think, though, that the point is made. Any anomalies or changes in calculation and reporting are simply overwhelmed by the sheer consistent volume of statistics tracing declining numbers. Church numbers are on a downward trajectory. This powerful body of evidence is an important part of the reason that I believe Putnam's argument about the impact of people's disinclination to join. The statistics are from nearly all church contexts and from across the Anglosphere. Greater faithfulness is not going to change this when it is happening to the vast majority of churches all over the theological spectrum. Be aware that this does not mean the trajectory will continue. Assuming that a statistical trend will continue to its logical conclusion is fallacious reasoning; if trends ran forever, then churches would still be growing as they once did.

Life in most church organizations in the Anglosphere today is defined by rapidly declining membership, combined with slowly shrinking numbers of congregations, parishes, and other organizations. Different people posit different reasons for the decline. From our perspective, the important thing to recognize is that decline is affecting nearly all denominations, across whatever theological or sociological spectrum that anyone cares to assemble. Therefore, shifts in theology or worship style are unlikely to change the overall trend, even if they may have some short-term, local, impact. Also therefore, the work of current leaders, whatever its limitations, is not the problem.

Decline is Decline, But Not Only Decline

A word to church leaders: The shrinking church is not your fault! This point must be emphasized bluntly and repeatedly. Too often, we blame present, local leadership for a truly enormous and international phenomenon. This is not helpful. Leaders, please hear and internalize that it is not your fault. You did not cause it and you cannot fix it, at least in anything more than a limited, probably temporary, sense.

However, if you are a leader, then the shrinking church is a challenge that lands on your plate. Now is the time for "a long, loving, look at the real," to quote Walter Burghardt.[60] The odds are that your congregation/seminary/other church organization is shrinking. This creates tremendous stresses for leaders, for me, for you.

As I write, I'm serving as a seminary president in North America in the third decade of the twenty-first century. People familiar with the life of the church will recognize that one sentence as a brief way of saying all sorts of things about declining resources, shortage of students, growing needs of shrinking congregations and church structures, shifting organizational systems, changing approaches to communication, increasing governmental expectations, and a myriad of other pressures. The challenges are associated with the numbers issues that we have seen in the churches that seminaries serve. I also know the impact from parish life. In one of my prior roles, as a parish clergyperson, I helped a parish to close. My wife, also a clergyperson, has helped one to close. In class, I have students who will be called upon to participate in parish reorganizations and closings, and in larger church organizations whose resources are declining.

The life of a church leader has changed from fifty years ago. Now, there is a routine need to watch for signs of decline and to recognize them for what they are. Often the first place that we become aware of the challenge (or willing to admit its existence) is when decline starts to hit our income and paying the bills becomes difficult, necessitating hard choices. Unfortunately, if this is true, then we face an especially awkward situation because declining giving tends to be a lagging indicator. "Lagging indicator" is a term that economists use to identify a financial impact that we see only after the change has occurred. In other words, usually people do not stop giving and then cease to attend or participate. Instead, they give until they leave, or move, or die. This means that leaders need to watch Sunday attendance, ages of participants, and levels of activity. Leaders need to take note when groups can no longer manage tasks that were routine a couple of decades ago. Can leaders still be found for formal roles? Can the church council still find members? Are there still people able to manage building-related jobs? Are there people to look after worship equipment? Can the catering group provide funeral teas? Slowly but surely, in one congregation after another, these basics of internal operation are becoming impossible. Forget about significant outreach activities, many congregations are hard-pressed to manage ordinary Sunday morning worship.

We must admit, and remember, that this really is decline. The church community has less ability to accomplish even the most ordinary tasks. Commonly, even traditional habits of church hospitality, such as hosting events and catering for them, have become impossible. Leadership has become difficult to recruit. Internal tasks, such as managing worship, buildings, and finances, have become difficult for many amid extensive cutbacks and a paucity of volunteer labor. Income is shrinking, affecting the ability to hire ministers and other staff or to care for buildings and other resources. Preachers face the dispiriting reality that congregations grow smaller every year, and most faces are the same as they were decades ago. The preaching task is to share good news when there seems to be very little that is good and to call to mission when there is little prospect of mission. Indeed, as churches seek to look beyond their walls, serious and ongoing public engagement places demands upon congregations and other organizations that they are unable to meet.

Meanwhile, government and judicatory regulations expand, placing greater demands on shrinking church systems and, therefore, accelerating the process of decline. Regulations are commonly created for excellent reasons: they respond to issues of abuse, operational safety, inappropriate employment practices, and a host of other social concerns. In the process, such regulations place greater demands on the system, expanding legal processes, limiting what volunteers can do, raising insurance costs, and otherwise impinging on daily functioning. Already stretched church structures find that they need to become larger to manage traditional functions, affecting their capacity to respond to new calls to mission.

We cannot deny that this is decline.

However, we must also recognize that there is progress amid this decline.[61] We can see an example of progress in the Southern Baptist Convention (SBC) in the United States, which now includes Black people and congregations—on legally equal footing with White people. The SBC came into being in 1845 as a separate organization from other American Baptists in order to support slavery in the American South.

We can see progress in the work that many churches are doing to recognize both the valuable religious insights of Indigenous peoples and the harm that churches have done. The Anglican Church in New Zealand is now known as "Anglican Church in Aotearoa, New Zealand and Polynesia, Te Hāhi Mihinare ki Aotearoa ki Niu Tīreni, ki Ngā Moutere o te Moana Nui a Kiwa." It has three parts: Tikanga Maori, Tikanga Pakeha, and Tikanga Pasefika. Each of these serves a different ethnic group, while the prayer book is in English and Maori, yet all three live together on equal standing in one church.

Many churches are ordaining women and celebrating their leadership. Most Anglicans, Lutherans, Methodists, and Presbyterians in the Anglosphere do so, along with some Baptists and Pentecostals. At time of writing, the primate of the Anglican Church of Canada, the national bishop of the Evangelical Lutheran Church in Canada, the moderator of the 2024 Assembly of the Presbyterian

Church in Canada, and the moderator of the United Church of Canada are all women.

Although it remains controversial, many would insist that the acceptance of gender and sexual complexity represents significant progress. We see this, for example, in the Episcopal Church and the Anglican Church of Canada, in the Evangelical Lutheran Church in America and Evangelical Lutheran Church in Canada, and in the United Church of Christ and the United Church of Canada. In all of these, gay and lesbian people are welcomed, baptized, and wedded, and invited into leadership.

Moreover, churches have developed a strong mission orientation. The Church of England (CofE) emphasizes this in its information collection (dubbed "Statistics for Mission"), which includes worshiping communities and fresh expressions of church (both nontraditional forms of church life) as actual categories, and includes statistics for engagement with social action projects;[62] this is a very different report from 1963, which specifically reflects the CofE as an established church catering to the whole population from parish churches.

In short, the church is changing. There is progress in the midst of decline. This book is intended to help us to recognize the nature of the decline that is happening, and to continue to pivot so that we can see more progress. The indications of decline that we have seen are the challenges that call forth new leadership and a new sense of purpose for the church. In a shrinking church, leadership is about working through processes of change, in light of new visions of church. That is what we will be addressing in the chapters to follow.

Exercises: The First Step

A. Your Life

1. Has your life been affected by the numerical model of church growth? If so, how has it made you feel?
2. Are you attracted to the numerical model of church? Repelled by it? Indifferent to it? Some or all of the above? Why?
3. Do you see declining numbers in organizations in other parts of your life? If so, where?

B. Your Organization

1. What do the numbers in your organization indicate? Assemble the following statistics, or as close as you are able, for (1) the most recent year, (2) five years ago, and (3) ten years ago:

    (a) attendance or participation (this will be average Sunday attendance or similar for congregations, student numbers for seminaries, volunteer numbers for a variety of ministries),
    (b) average age of attendees or participants, and
    (c) total income and expenditure numbers.

    If measured by the numerical model, are you identifying decline, progress, or stability, or numbers that go in more than one direction? What is the significance of the trajectory that your organization is on?

2. Do declining numbers in the whole church affect your organization? If so, how? What do you find yourself called to do as a consequence of having fewer people engaged?
3. Do you see progress, defined in any way that makes sense to you, in your church? If so, what does it look like? If not, what would it look like?

C. The World

1. Does my suggestion of a three-step process of evangelism (inviting the other to help you grow, sharing your story so that they can learn from you, seeking to participate in God's work in the world together—with no expectation that the other will become a Christian) change how you feel about communicating your faith? If so, in what ways? Does this make talking about your faith easier?
2. Imagine a church that does not treat numbers as a priority. What would it look like? Is it desirable? Does it seem realistic?
3. What impact do you see on the world from fewer people joining organizations? Do you see other forms of public engagement growing? If so, in what ways do these forms seem to be healthy or unhealthy?

CHAPTER 2

THE GOOD NEWS IN A SHRINKING CHURCH

Today's church in the Anglosphere is a tough place to look for good news. In the context of threats from climate change, destructive nationalisms, reckoning with various racist histories, and significant wars that implicate the world, the church is growing older and smaller. Every year, there are fewer attendees, fewer people pursuing leadership roles, fewer resources, more organizational challenges, more financial challenges, more building challenges, and higher levels of stress for everyone. We have a definite sense of being in a cycle of decline; the indications of faithfulness that we've seen provide some encouragement, but they still fall short of a coherent message of joy from the divine.

The Good News

So, in and from a shrinking church, what is the good news?

The church is about participating in God's transformation of us and our world. In 2 Cor. 5:16–21, Paul gives a powerful account of the good news that speaks to our current situation. Paul had a complex relationship with the church in Corinth. He seems to have been its founder, but from there on, the church appears to have been plagued by cliques and partisanship. Into this mess, Paul inserts the following message:

> From now on, therefore, we regard no one from a human point of view; even though we once knew Christ from a human point of view, we know him no longer in that way. So if anyone is in Christ, there is a new creation: everything old has passed away; see, everything has become new! All this is from God, who reconciled us to himself through Christ, and has given us the ministry of reconciliation; that is, in Christ God was reconciling the world to himself, not counting their trespasses against them, and entrusting the message of reconciliation to us. So we are ambassadors for Christ, since God is making his appeal through us; we entreat you on behalf of Christ, be reconciled to God. For our sake he made him to be sin who knew no sin, so that in him we might become the righteousness of God.[1]

The encounter with Christ Jesus changes the way that we understand everyone; we no longer know people solely from a human perspective, but from the perspective of divine love, which is the perspective that has transformed our understanding of who Christ is. The impact of this divine touch on us is profound; in the next chapter we will discuss it under the label of "religious transformation." This is a transformation in the human as knower, in which we are given something of the divine capacity to understand.

However, the change in me might have limited value, might even be misleading or illusory, but for the next point that Paul makes: this is not simply about me, some sort of shift in perspective that could as easily have been accomplished by donning rose-colored glasses. Instead, the transformation in our understanding is a step to understanding what God is accomplishing in the Incarnation, life, death, and resurrection of Christ. "There is a new creation: everything old has passed away; see, everything has become new!" We need to take seriously the kind of change that this is. This new creation is not a replacement of all the physical stuff (a materialist reading) or a merely spiritualized account of history (an idealist reading). Instead, this is God expressing through the universe exactly what God intends it to mean. The world really is as it is known from the perspective of divine love: a context in which God's love is active transforming all things. The world, the universe, is a new creation, imbued with the life given by God, so that the death that human destructiveness imparts is not ultimate, not decisive.

Creation, being transformed by Christ's Incarnation, is being reconciled to God, by God. Instead of being defined by sinfulness, creation is being defined by divine love and the transformations that love engenders. We, as people of the Incarnation, are invited to be agents of God's work of reconciliation. In the context of the passage, being ambassadors of reconciliation means that we ourselves accept reconciliation to God, something that Paul enjoins on the church at Corinth. Though I cannot help but wonder whether there might be a touch of arrogance in Paul's entreaty, given his history of differences with the Corinthians, he is certainly correct about the general point: evangelism begins with our own transformation, our own reconciliation with God. God can speak through us even in the depths of our own wrongdoing; however, the whole process is simplified, eased, and made more pleasant for all if we are being reconciled to God as God is making God's appeal through us.

In the final sentence comes the kicker, the piece that I find people prefer to overlook: All of this is so that in Christ "we might become the righteousness of God." This line forces us to return to the challenge of reconciliation and ask what, exactly, it involves. The text has given us two pieces: knowing the world through the eyes of love, as God knows it, and becoming ambassadors, by word and deed, of the message that God sets the world right. This sets a clear task for the church. We are called to know the world in love and invite the world to love. We are called to become a people committed to living God's love and invite others to live God's love. We are invited to mean what God means in the world. Thus, we are invited into God's activity of "setting the world right."

This is easy to say and offends nobody, though some people would take this opportunity to remind us that the church often has not, does not, and will not live up to its message. Failure to do what we know that we ought to do is certainly a problem. However, in many cases the bigger issue is to distinguish the better course of action from the worse. In the next chapter, we will address the problems of knowing. At this point, we need to remember a specific challenge that goes to the heart of the kinds of difficult decisions that leaders are called upon to make in a shrinking church.

The problem is that decisions are usually more complicated than the simple choice between the loving option and various nonloving options. Recognizing the new creation does not make life easy; nor does it make the way of reconciliation obvious. In a shrinking church, many of the decisions that we make, even the ones that are clear and obviously right, have some aspect of sadness. Closing a congregation, moving out of a much-loved building, dropping ministries to people in need—all of these are destructive of something and likely to be somewhat divisive, even if they are part of a creative process of becoming for the church. Our life as a shrinking church does not always feel like we imagine being Christ's ambassador ought to feel. This may be the deepest meaning of the story of the fall in Genesis: the act of creation is often touched by pain. Nonetheless, we are called to be creative and to move into new possibilities, where new joys will be found.

In the Shrinking Church

This account of the good news has some important reminders for the shrinking church.

God Works with All of Humanity and All of Creation

God takes the initiative and undertakes a transformation that works as much for a shrinking church as for a growing one. The transformation is from God, accomplished through Christ. The work is eternal, including and encompassing all of creation in all of history. We are invited to participate, to serve as agents of divine transformation, to cooperate with God's grace in the task of love in the world. In this, we are invited to share with all of humanity and all the created order.

God works in and with all of humanity. That is part of the point of the transformation of all creation. Christians are not the only ones in and through whom God works. Love is not confined to the church; indeed, sometimes the church is not at all loving, so that people find a need to leave to reconnect to God. God is truly eternal, present in and to all people; this means that all people can be participants in God's love and agents of God's love, enabling others to know the transforming power of love. One reason that this has sometimes been difficult for us to recognize is that we have been gripped by the numerical growth narrative which, by its very nature, posits a superiority of our thinking over all other thinking, a superiority of our way over all other ways—even when our thinking and our ways do not demonstrate the love that God communicates in Christ. Another, connected, reason is that we tend not to have a very profound understanding of what transformation is, so that we focus narrowly on a commitment to Christ or joining a church. These can be good things, but they do not really get to the center of what God invites us into. In the next chapter, we will think more about the nature of transformation, considering it in four aspects: intellectual, psychic, moral, and religious. I hope that the process of thinking about the nature of transformation will also help us to recognize how others contribute to the life of grace, just as we seek to contribute.

There is a further point to be made about God's transformative work: it engages all of creation. All aspects of creation can be God's loving agents. Too easily, we assume that the only hands that God has are ours,[2] limiting God, the creator of all things, to being a God of humanity, subject to humanity's limited capacities. However, God is truly eternal, present in and to all things; this means that all things, consistent with their ways of being, can be participants in God's love and conveyors of God's love. Certainly, the capacities of trees are different from the agency of a human being, and the transformative work of God in them is different from the transformative work of God in us. However, we are not wise to overlook the gifts that the rest of creation contributes to our transformation.

Because God shares love with all people and all of creation, we can recognize the new creation everywhere. Sometimes, driven by the extent of destruction around us or by the desire for power or by some other impetus, we are inclined to write God out of the story, proclaiming God's irrelevance or nonexistence. That approach does not account for either the fact of love or the capacity to know the world in the light of love. In naturalist accounts, love is easily—perhaps inevitably—reduced to an expression of self-interest or group interest;[3] however, we have endless examples to show that this is an inadequate explanation that fails to ask and answer many of the relevant questions. Not only do people routinely show kindness to those who are near and dear to them, but we see daily examples of people caring for those who are competitors or even enemies, and to people upon whom punishment would more likely be expected. In idealist accounts, the world as it is ceases to be valued as it ought to be, ceases to be truly loved, though we know that God loves all that God creates. We end up with triumphs of human power that can prove disastrous.[4] A more complex and helpful answer points out that God heals our woundedness, restoring us to the humans we were created to be, and transforms us, enabling us to share something of eternal life—the life of God, who engages with the world in love.[5] In the next chapter, as we consider the importance of the church as organization, we will think more about the meaning and importance of love.

These Ambassadors Go to Their Own Home World

Casting us as ambassadors in a transformed world puts us in a perennially ambivalent and ambiguous position. Ambassadors always occupy an interesting outside/inside position. However, this kind of ambassadorship is a bit different from situations with which we might be familiar. Christian ambassadors are ambassadors in their own country. In the complex already and not yet of the Kingdom, God has made of the whole world a new creation and has reconciled the world to Godself, an accomplishment that we experience as the whole of creation being transformed and reconciled, incorporated into God's meaning.. As Irenaeus of Lyons emphasized in his understanding of salvation, the transformation encompasses all of creation and all of history rather than being simply about an individual me, here and now.[6] Because this is an eternal action, it touches all aspects of being. In theology, the word "eternal" does not mean a long time; instead, it means present to all things at all times, simultaneously. Thus, the work is already complete in God's reconciling action. However, because we live in time, experiencing the world sequentially, we know the Kingdom only in part, as something that God is accomplishing. The core of the good news is that we can participate in God's transforming work. We are invited to a station greater than the innocence of Eden, the role of ambassadors of God's reconciling work in God's new creation.

Therefore, we are not "resident aliens," as some Protestants suggest.[7] Our lives are not defined by a Christian colony, in which we care for one another and out of which we reach to others. Nor is the church the "barque of St. Peter," a ship of the saved, sailed on the world's storms at the direction of a church hierarchy—as some Roman Catholics would have it.[8] Instead, we are the precise opposite: as religiously transformed, we are ones who are being granted the capacity to know the world as a sphere of God's loving action and to know ourselves to be at home in it. This world is of God, and we are of God. The true aliens are those who do not understand the world from the perspective of love, who do not live out of love, who live destructively. These are the aliens, the alienated. Indeed, when we cannot know the world in love is the moment when we feel alienated. We can see this happen in others. When they desert love or believe that love has deserted them, they are alienated, dissatisfied. Knowing God and the world from the perspective of divine love overcomes alienation, creating a sense of reconciliation with the other.

This is tremendously important because it makes sense of the church in a way that notions of alien identity do not. I was raised with a radical version of the notion that I did not belong in the world. Indeed, one of the songs that we sang at church firmly declared, "This world is not my home / I'm just a-passing through." In this context, most of the activities of most churches made no sense to me. The only reason to live after one has been "saved" seemed to be so that one could get others to make a decision for Christ as their personal savior: the numerical growth narrative. On the other hand, as I came to know more of the Bible, I began to realize that the text does not seem to lean so heavily on such a decision as I had believed. Instead, there is a deep focus upon commitment to communal justice and individual care. One contemporary way of describing the church's ambassadorial role is to think of it as diaconal, rooted in the work of *diakonia*. *Diakonia* is the church's task of service, rooted in baptismal commitment. Many churches have thought deeply about the nature of this task. One helpful account is in "To Love and Serve the Lord: *Diakonia* in the Life of the Church."

> *Diakonia* takes the form of prophetic witness, advocacy and empowering action, as well as compassionate care.
>
> *Diakonia* means not only giving aid, but also confronting the concentration of wealth and power which is the cause of poverty. A diaconal church accompanies, bolsters and empowers the economically weak and vulnerable; with them a diaconal church resists abusive manoeuvres that deprive them of their basic human rights, including economic, social and cultural rights.
>
> *Diakonia* is political in as far as it exposes structural injustice that affects people due to sex/gender, class, geography, religion and ethnic origin. The church empowers the voiceless to speak and speaks in solidarity with and for them when they cannot. "Speak out for those who cannot speak, for the rights of all the destitute. Speak out, judge righteously, defend the rights of the poor and needy" (Prov. 31:8–9).[9]

In this description, the church's role is precisely ambassadorial, exactly the task of ambassador of reconciliation. This is very different from the common understanding of service, which focuses predominantly upon giving of time and talent, or charity, which emphasizes giving of treasure (money or items that can be purchased with money). Instead, *diakonia* is about providing assistance, which can be economic, while engaging vocally and politically with and in support of the disempowered, the vulnerable, the needy. Deacons, whose title is both rooted in and evokes the language of *diakonia*, are sometimes understood as being called to a ministry of word and service; this kind of ambassadorial role is exactly what is meant by such a ministry, because it involves both voice and action. An ambassadorial church is a diaconal church.

Ambassadors Can Be Few.

God invites us to participate as ambassadors, as ones with the ability to understand the world from the perspective of divine love. We are called to be ambassadors, which is a profound call, but it is not the only call. Ambassadors do not transform the world by themselves; they convey the news and assist people to live into the desired transformation. As ambassadors for Christ, we are communicators, people who share the good news. God transforms the world, working with everyone and all things. Relative to populations, there are always few ambassadors, but they often have many partners. The church is called to be sacramental, a meeting place between God and the created order. The key to understanding the meaning of this, however, is recognizing that creation itself is sacramental. John 1:1–3 reminds us that creation occurs through the Son, Christ Jesus. "In the beginning was the Word, and the Word was with God, and the Word was God. He was in the beginning with God. All things came into being through him, and without him not one thing came into being." Creation is a divine product, reflecting divine life. Indeed, all life is the gift of God, through the Son.

Sin mars that reflection but does not destroy it. The world continues to be God's world, the physical and spiritual being to which God gives life. As John 1:4 points out, "What has come into being in him was life, and the life was the light of all people." The Incarnation overcomes the power of sin and death, reuniting God and creation. In Christ Jesus, God and the created order are fully united, fully reconciled, and the meaning of history is fully announced. Irenaeus calls this "recapitulation" or "summing up" or "gathering up," the work of taking up all of history and transforming it, re-expressing its meaning as the story of God reconciling the world with Godself.[10] "The true light, which enlightens everyone, was coming into the world" (John 1:9). God is present in and to every place and time. In Augustine's language, God dwells in the "simultaneity of eternity," in and with all people, all things.[11] Creation is sacrament. The Incarnation is sacrament. The fulfillment of it all in absolute reconciliation, the Kingdom of God, is sacrament. Eternal life is life with God, knowing God as the one who creates, reconciles, fulfills all things (John 17:3).

The difference between church and not-church, therefore, is not the presence of God. The church is not somehow separate from the world, uniquely God's home. God is universally present and active. The difference is in knowing the presence and seeking to live in it. The difference is understanding what God means in and for the world, so that our lives can be full of the meaning that God intends in creation. The church is not the only community that knows something of the meaning and importance of God's ways of love. However, it is such a community. Therefore, the church sustains a sacramental life so that we may be reminded of God's active presence, God's transformative work, God's intended meaning, in all of creation. This is the truth that we know and are called to share, as ambassadors of reconciliation.

People who know the meaning of history do not need to be many. Knowing the meaning of history is a great source of joy and the root of true hope. However, a generalized knowledge of what history is all about does not mean that a Christian will always be helpful in the concrete circumstances of life or that only a Christian can be of assistance. I know what an internal combustion engine does and have a basic knowledge of its general workings. I grew up in a time when being able to gap a spark plug and check the points in an ignition were assumed to be necessary parts of male life (though why these should be male only, I have no idea). However, when our family car has trouble, we take it to an auto mechanic who knows what to do and has the appropriate tools, which are mostly computerized now (and have nothing to do with spark plugs or ignition points). I do not especially care whether the mechanic is a Christian and knows the meaning of history. The relevant questions are about the car and what its problems might be. Dorothy L. Sayers made the same point when asked about the performance of her plays, which are manifestly Christian pieces, specifically concerned with the larger meanings of God's engagement with the world and the purpose of it all. People tended to inquire whether she insisted that actors in the plays be good Christians. Sayers declared that she had no interest in that question. She wanted good actors because the purpose of their work was to act. Good actors would witness to God's truth by presenting the truth of the play well and faithfully.[12]

The point is that God is in everyone, inviting us and assisting us to know people who can live the meaning of the world; people who live in love, who seek to understand the world correctly and live out their accurate insights, are many. Good actors, like good mechanics, are participants in God's work of transformation. They are participants in the life of reconciliation. We might reasonably say that their contribution is limited, which is both a true and a fair thing to say. However, honesty would compel us to admit that everyone's contribution to reconciliation is limited and partial, even that of the greatest among us. Mine is definitely minimal; while I have my useful moments, I am deeply aware that even in my chosen work of theology and seminary leadership, my work is but a small part of the life of my organization and (at most) a barely noticeable piece of the larger history of the field.

Being good at one's work is not the whole story of human life, however. Even as she demonstrated its importance, Sayers recognized that part of being a good actor or mechanic involves living a life that enables good acting or good work as a mechanic, so that the work is not fully separable from the lifestyle that sustains it. In *Zeal of Thy House*, a play about the building of Canterbury Cathedral, Sayers shows the good work of an architect who is genuinely committed to, in love with, the work, and out of whose knowledge and commitment a beautiful building will emerge. Being a good architect is not dependent upon an extensive understanding of the good news.

However, the architect, William of Sens, is cut down in mid-play, injured as a consequence of his own destructive lifestyle, rooted in seriously mistaken beliefs. God will take up William's accomplishments and use them as a part of God's church, even as another architect will take over the work and finish it as something different from what was started. Thus is William's failure redeemed in God's transformation of the world. Nonetheless, we must recognize that William is seriously limited as an ambassador of reconciliation. His theology as it applies directly to his work is strong though imperfect, but he is wrong, even blasphemous, in other aspects of his thinking.[13] This reveals the importance of the church, in its role in reconciliation. All are participants in the life of reconciliation, even though finding creativity in the lives of the most deeply destructive among us can be very difficult. Not all are ambassadors.

The organized church—the institutional church, if you prefer—exists to participate in God's meanings and to prepare us to share those meanings in our roles as ambassadors.

Exercises: The Good News in a Shrinking Church

A. Your Life

1. I have described the good news as an invitation to know the world in God's love, to recognize that God creates and fulfills it in love. We are invited to live in the world as ambassadors of reconciliation of all people and all things with one another and with God. In what ways is this account of the good news a new understanding for you?
2. Does this seem like a true account of the good news? Why and/or why not?
3. How do you serve as an ambassador of reconciliation? In what ways could you live into ambassadorship more fully?

B. Your Organization

1. How does your organization live into ambassadorship? In what ways could your organization live into ambassadorship more fully?
2. How does your organization live into *diakonia*? In what ways could your organization live into *diakonia* more fully? Note that this answer may be the same as the answer to the prior question, because *diakonia* is an important part of ambassadorship.
3. After chapter 1, you assembled some statistics for your organization. What is the meaning of those numbers for your organization's ambassadorial mission?

C. The World

1. Does this vision of the good news change how you understand the world? If so, in what ways?
2. Describe an instance in which a non-Christian has shown God's love to you. How has this affected your understanding of God's reconciliation in the world?

CHAPTER 3

THE ORGANIZED CHURCH IN A POST-CHURCH AGE

Anti-Institutionalism

Today, many people are anti-institutional. That is part of the reason for the general decline in joining structured institutions. People are disinclined to commit to organizational involvement, even when the cause seems to be worthy. Sending money, posting to social media, debating in the comments section of online news media—all of these are eminently popular. Long-term organizational commitment? Not so much.

The same phenomenon is reflected in rising numbers of people with no explicit religious identity, sometimes called "nones."[1] These people are not necessarily atheists or agnostics. Commonly, their agenda is not particularly antireligious. Indeed, the catchphrase often used to describe many of them is "spiritual but not religious," which is a way of saying that they have a sense that there is a real spiritual aspect to life, but it is one that is appropriately discovered along individual paths and often by drawing from multiple religious traditions. These people reject the idea that any organized religion holds a monopoly either on truth as a set of assertions or on truth as a way of being. Incidentally, Burge has noted that the number of nones who attend any kind of religious service is on the decline (though it has always been a low number),[2] emphasizing that even the anti-institutionalists are becoming more so.

Organized religion does not structure communal life in the way that it once did. For example, Sunday, the traditional day of Christian worship, does not carry the same set of expectations that it did when I was young. I grew up in the Canadian province of Ontario, where the federal "Lord's Day Act" of 1906 and successive provincial laws severely limited business activity on Sundays. Hockey practice was on weeknights or Saturdays, with only the occasional tournament occurring on Sunday. Sunday was for church or, at the very least, for quiet family activities, with the country drive and walk being common. The Act was overturned in the courts in 1985, as a violation of the Canadian Charter of Rights and Freedoms,[3] after Christianity lost its formal hold on the day, while sports or other organized activities had become the norm. Undoubtedly, the busyness of Sunday contributed to declines in church attendance; equally certainly, the loss of

Sunday is more symptom than cause, as it occurred long after church engagement had begun to fall.

In the previous chapter, we raised the possibility of imagining the church as diaconal, as emphasizing service in the world. This is a communal form of life. However, much of our diaconal activity does not depend directly on the church as organization. In my house, the major diaconal project is my wife's work with a financial literacy program focused especially on helping people in challenging circumstances. Governments and other organizations in society make efforts to provide financial assistance, but do not necessarily help people to understand how to manage money; for a significant number, this leaves the root problem in place. The group with which my wife is involved is an amazing organization that educates people about debt and interest, investment, banking, and so on. As it happens, my wife is clergy, with more than twenty-five years of experience in the church. The skills developed in that context are always helpful, but her degree in education and experience in multiple teaching and academic advising roles are more immediately relevant. The group is certainly not a religious organization and the others working with it are not necessarily religious in any formal sense, let alone specifically Christian. One of the arguments that nonreligious people often make, with perfect fairness, is that they do not need to be formally religious to be good people. Although *diakonia*, in its richest sense, is a whole-church undertaking, many people serve in diaconal ways without church structures.

Today, church involvement is a lot of work for the people who continue to attend. Tasks related to everything from basic operations to outreach ministries are becoming more onerous. The labor involved in church life has risen because: 1) numbers are shrinking, so fewer people share a big load; 2) institutional religion is not especially valued, so that church work gets less communal support and approbation; 3) there are plenty of opportunities to be both caring and transformative without church, focusing society's and members' interests elsewhere; 4) Sundays are largely given over to sports and leisure activities (or to jobs), limiting attendance and the capacity to volunteer; and 5) society's legal and bureaucratic expectations have increased. In this kind of context, the church as organization gets little credit. Indeed, even people who consider themselves to be regular attendees are not present at worship as often as they were fifty years ago. The shrinking church is largely sustained by people whose habits were formed in the immediate post–World War II era, people who are now in their sixties or older.

For many others, the church is now a puzzle. Why commit to all the effort of stable, formal, sometimes uncomfortable and demanding religious community? Why not simply function as an individual, doing one's own thing? Aside from caring for the long faithful and managing the shutdown of an organization—both underrated tasks but somewhat lacking in excitement and high vision—why should we bother with the church? Because this is a book about leadership in a shrinking church, we cannot avoid the question of why we might wish to stay in a shrinking organization.

God calls us to be ambassadors of reconciliation. As we have seen, the ministry of reconciliation involves being creative and diaconal, seeking to live the meaning with which God imbues the world. In a broad sense, these characteristics answer the question of "why bother?". Quite simply, serving others creatively is most easily done in community, and with communal support. However, the community is not necessarily the church. The community might as easily be a construction site, as in Sayers's play. What does the church contribute that is specifically church?

The Transformational Church and Self-Appropriation

Rosemary Haughton defines the church as "an educational structure with room for explosions."[4] This is, of course, a partial definition that does not address all the ways that the church has functioned and will function—perhaps, even, ought to function. On the other hand, Haughton's definition precisely gets at the core around which this book is built and the core idea that I hope will help you: the church is present to help people be aware of and encounter God in ways that transform. The church helps us and others to be aware of the presence and transformative nudging of the power that Christians know as the Holy Spirit of God, even if we are not aware of or inclined to use that sort of language. The community in which transformation occurs might be any community; it might include many Christians or none at all. The purpose of the church is to prepare people to be aware of the inbreaking of God wherever and whenever it happens, and to be able to find ways to live out the meanings and implications of God's transformative work in our lives. This awareness depends upon multiple transformations—none of which requires that people become Christian. A thriving church, therefore, is one that supports the right kinds of transformations, which may be a kind of progress that does not easily fit the numerical growth narrative.

Precisely because people are skeptical of institutions, we need to avoid thinking about education as a kind of top-down, "the church says" activity. People do not respond to authority in that way. On the other hand, people are interested in learning and growing. Formation is a big part of what people seek in society, even online. Today, we tend to see ourselves as projects, seeking fulfillment. Everyone who reads has imbibed at least one book that engages the work of understanding and developing the self. Indeed, the self-help section of the bookstore tends to be a busy place. The leadership and management sections also tend to be popular. Even if they are not overtly philosophical or theological, all these books teach something about the nature of the self, about ways to develop and complete it.

Philosophy and theology have always grappled with these questions. Our world, though, handles them differently from the ways that they have been treated in earlier eras. There has been a radical shift to an emphasis upon the individual and what the individual can know, a move that has been called the turn to the subject because of its focus upon the interior operations of particular persons. This has complicated roots in a variety of modern thinkers and developments. In an important sense, Immanuel Kant played a defining role. He argued that the object of knowing (whatever the object might be) is something that is, in principle, inaccessible to us because our subjective process of knowing constructs the object in our minds, using our intellectual categories of time and space. In short, what you think is outside of you is not what is outside of you.[5] Sigmund Freud pushed the conundrum further by claiming that even our knowing is opaque to us because we are not honest with ourselves; our psychological needs and desires often prevent us from recognizing and engaging with the operations of our psyches.[6]

This shift has also, for many people, felt like a distancing from God; with the sorts of intellectual and psychic developments that Kant and Freud have argued, Nietzsche[7] and his descendants have forced us to consider the question of divine irrelevance, while suggesting that morality is nothing but a question of power and the desire for it. Postmodernity has moved us out of a situation in which the positions of one culture—the Christian West, for most people who are likely to read this—is understood as a kind of absolute yardstick of civilization and into a sense that various cultures offer different, helpful, answers to the questions that we raise, while proposing questions that we have not considered.

Do these sorts of intellectual developments define how everyone thinks? Probably not. I am reasonably sure that most people do not talk about these kinds of things around the dinner table. However, these issues do touch the ways that people think, the ways that they approach issues. If the church is an educational institution that invites people to be aware of God's presence and action in the world, then the church needs to be able to speak to the kinds of complexities around people's thinking. We must be able to address these challenges both in the work of discipleship, participating in God's transformation of church members, and in the work of *diakonia*, participating in God's transformation of the world. In order to develop this theme, I will draw on the thinking of Bernard Lonergan, who has thought deeply and written extensively on what he terms conversion or, in the terminology I have been using here, on transformation.

Lonergan provides us with a language that speaks to the contemporary emphasis upon ourselves as persons, as subjects in society. The core term for the transformation in which the church, as educational organization, is called to participate is "self-appropriation."[8] The task of self-appropriation is precisely not self-ownership, even if that might be what it sounds like. Self-appropriation is a commitment to self-transcendence, to understanding how we think and act so that we can move beyond the trap of being captured inside ourselves, our irrational impulses, and our appetites.

One key to understanding these transformations is to recognize that they are processes, rather than endpoints. Having engaged with this kind of work over many years, I honestly believe that I am somewhat transformed in each of the ways that we will discuss. On the other hand, I admit, to my chagrin, that I am a very great distance from being fully transformed.

We are going to consider four kinds of transformations: intellectual, psychic, moral, and religious. The purpose will be to focus on the multiple steps of transformation to which the church invites people, as we learn and grow. Instead of thinking about Christianity as an invitation to a single decision, whether that might be to attending church or accepting Christ as savior or any other one choice, this approach means considering our commitments as covering multiple aspects of life. In addition, we will see that the transformation that we seek in the world does not depend upon people joining us. The church's message of life is not about our numerical growth. The church's message is about the transformations that God is working in people's lives.

Intellectual Transformation

God's love affects us in multiple ways, even when we do not recognize it at work. Among love's consequences is that it inspires us to be genuinely curious, wanting to know the truth. The desire to know truth has become both a philosophical and a practical problem for people today, as Enlightenment optimism about science's ability to know washes away in a sea of postmodern suspicion, much of it warranted. The language of "objectivity," based in the idea of impartial scientific inquiry, has too often proven to be a cover for biases of one kind or another: racism, sexism, classism, self-interest, etc., so that people have become dubious about knowledge of any kind—even, or perhaps especially, expert knowledge. Many people turn to the internet, with a sense that their own research is as likely to produce a helpful answer as any formal authority.

Lonergan invites us to understand knowing in a way that explains the successes and failures of science, and the strengths and limitations of the do-it-yourself model of learning. For Lonergan, knowing is the product of asking and answering relevant questions. Understanding this point and internalizing it produces an intellectual transformation.[9] Asking relevant questions encourages us to collect data. A big part of the challenge with understanding is that we do not always ask all the relevant questions; we leave out questions that might not serve our views or interests. Another is that we work with insufficient data sets. Both of these challenges are part of the postmodern critique of knowing. The results of missing questions and using inadequate data have been that in the name of objectivity, of supposedly disinterested research, we have seen spurious arguments about the inferiority of people with darker skin colors, inaccurate medical conclusions because women are ignored in research, and many other failures. These challenges are also among the risks of asking Dr. Google, which has resulted in dangerous conspiracy theories, endless financial scams, inaccurate health information (such as ivermectin for COVID-19), and many other failures.

The beginning of Lonergan's answer is to invite us to be attentive,[10] ensuring that all the relevant data is assembled, rather than only the information that appears to serve a particular conclusion, and that we are truly collecting all the evidence needed to answer the questions correctly. Attentiveness also requires learning. How are we to know when we are asking the right questions and using the right data sets? Only by developing substantial knowledge of the topic area. One of my sons was struggling with an absolute value question in calculus. My wife has a degree in mathematics and has taught the subject at the postsecondary level. My wife and son have been trying to give me a basic understanding of what calculus is and does, a process of education that generates a combination of puzzled looks and outright laughter. I am good at arithmetic; beyond that mathematics is not my thing. To resolve my son's calculus problem, my son went to my wife and the two of them worked away at it. I washed the dishes, a task for which I am highly trained and well qualified—making for a good division of labor. They knew what data they needed, so they asked and answered the relevant questions; I had no idea what the questions might have been. We are all called to be attentive, but we cannot all be attentive to the same things all the time. Thus, we are invited to learn from the world and share with the world in the process of communicating the good news.

As the data is assembled, we try various possible answers to the questions. If we are asking all the relevant questions, we will know that the answer comes when we can answer all the questions satisfactorily. We have reached a condition that we can reasonably call "certainty" when we have asked and correctly answered all the relevant questions. Part of the challenge of life, however, is that we are often unable to answer all relevant questions as fully as we might wish; sometimes, we can only manage partial answers, while at other times we must leave some questions completely unanswered. This does not contradict the basic method. Instead, this situation affirms the value of the method because most of our knowledge is statistical—that is, less than 100 percent certain. Answering some portion of the questions provides us with an indication of the statistical likelihood of any given conclusion, while also providing us with starting places for further investigation. Statistically, we can say with a very high degree of likelihood that there will be sunlight tomorrow where I am; however, at time of writing the probabilities of precipitation range from 10–40 percent through the day (tomorrow). So, I will continue to ask questions, watching both weather reports and the sky outside, especially as I hope to take out my kayak and I prefer to keep the water under me when paddling, rather than having it both above and below. Lonergan invites us to be intelligent,[11] which is a way of saying that we must be willing to work at the activity of asking and answering questions, especially in the fields where the world is depending on us.

This sounds like a simple, deductive process. As we know, that is not what happens in reality. Instead, we attempt a variety of possibilities, commonly starting with the obvious ones. Ultimately, if the questions prove to be answerable, that is because we have grasped the relationship among the various pieces of evidence—a relationship that may not be obviously logical, not simple puzzle-solving. This challenge appears in every discipline. It occurs in detective and legal work. Assemble all the available evidence and the correct resolution may still not be evident. Detectives can be wrong, sometimes dreadfully so, because the world often does not fit together in obvious ways. We all face these sorts of challenges in our lives, needing to bring all our understanding and experience to an ongoing experimental effort to find the right answer. Have you parented a teenager? If so, you know what I mean.

Sometimes the answer is not available within the existing paradigms that we inherit and demands an integration at a higher level. We need to think in completely different ways about the issues at hand. One example is the nineteenth-century recognition that history affects our theological thinking, an insight commonly traced to John Henry Newman's work, *An Essay on the Development of Christian Doctrine*. We can no longer discuss theological ideas as if they come directly from the Bible or as if they have existed unchanged from the first century onward. The whole discipline has changed, which affects all our conversations about Christianity.

Our challenge of responding to the numerical growth narrative may pose this kind of problem. The theological narrative that we inherit says that faithfulness will deliver numerical growth but in many cases it does not, so that we need to find an understanding of faithfulness that can include numerical growth but can also include other forms of growth. We have tried rejigging the existing systems and messages to make sense of the church, without obvious success. This is the context in which I am suggesting that making self-appropriation central to the Christian message changes things. The "turn to the subject" has given rise to various forms of radically individualistic religion, which those of us involved in more traditional and structured religious traditions can easily criticize. At the same time, we recognize that there are many valid criticisms of the institutional structure and systems of our religious traditions. We have a bifurcation of Christianity, and neither side is sufficient by itself. Self-appropriation may help us to find the answer, serving as a way of moving beyond the binary.

Aside from specific problems like the numerical growth narrative, there is also a general question about our answers. We have already noticed that sometimes we are wrong, even when we seek to be attentive to all the data and intelligent in asking and answering all the relevant questions. How do we know that we are wrong? We ask the question ourselves, checking our own work. As in the calculus problem, my son does exactly what his math teachers have always insisted, reviewing his answers to see whether they make sense. In the case of careful detectives who come to particular understandings of the cases with which they deal, they ask whether they have truly considered all the relevant data, asked and answered all the relevant questions, so as not to push for the conviction of an innocent person. In other words, we have our own systems of confirming our answers.

Lonergan invites us to be reasonable[12] in our thinking, recognizing that we may misunderstand and need to correct ourselves. This is the aspect of our understanding that people tend to forget about or underestimate, to the detriment of our thinking. People fall into scams and conspiracy theories because they do not check sufficiently. One difficulty with the construction that we call (incorrectly, I think) artificial intelligence is that, at least in its early forms, the designers have not included any such effort. The story of Steven A. Schwartz, a lawyer who used AI in a legal case and the court discovered that it had invented a number of court cases to establish precedents, has become legendary.[13] The AI had no self-checking function, and Schwartz did not review the court submission with sufficient care to catch the problem.

We do ask and answer the question, "Is my understanding correct?" Life trains us to do so. Failing to double-check the speed of a car's approach might get us killed when we cross the street. Society also fosters this capacity. For my son's calculus problem, the larger discipline of math—represented by his professor—reviews his answers. For the detective who concludes that someone is guilty of a crime, prosecutors and then courts review the whole case as further safeguards. Our checking is not always sufficient: pedestrians get hit, calculus errors are missed, and innocent people are imprisoned. However, the remarkable thing is not how often we err; being wrong is easy. The amazing thing is our capacity to find answers that prove to be correct.

Intellectual transformation is what happens when we begin to realize that knowing is about asking and answering questions, and about exercising our capacity for self-correction. The actual work of questioning and of assessing our accuracy is work that we do automatically, every day. However, we do not necessarily stop to notice what we are doing; if we fail to notice it, then we do not necessarily take the time and effort either to recognize how amazing it is or to work on improving our performance at it.

I know that this can seem to be an odd thing for a theologian to focus on—and to ask the church to emphasize!—especially at such a critical moment in the life of the church. However, there is a reason for us to think about what learning to understand means for us and to discuss the process with others: In today's world, we cannot easily have a helpful conversation about other kinds of change, including religious transformation, if we are not also able to say something about the possibility of knowing.

At a personal level, I find that paying attention to the questions that I ask and answer is transformative. My questions tend to be driven by engagement with things that I love; the more that I truly care, the better my insights are. On the other hand, I also catch myself not wanting to know, refusing to address questions that do deserve my attention, precisely because I would prefer not to know the answer, for whatever reason. Sometimes, an admission that I am avoiding questions or conclusions will sit in my mind and nag at me. These are signs of progress in intellectual transformation because I am noticing my failures. These are signs of how far I have to travel because there are times when I avoid knowing things that I ought to know. In church language, I have left undone those things which I ought to have done.

Psychic Transformation

One of the reasons that these oversights happen is the complexity of feelings. Robert M. Doran, a Lonergan scholar, has introduced the language of "psychic conversion" to address the extent to which engaging with our deepest psyche is an important part of knowing. Our feelings can help to guide us to the true and the good, or they can get in the way.

In my personal reflection on my intellectual transformation, I omitted mentioning that sometimes the reason that I do not ask and answer questions that I ought to consider is that my gut rejects answers that I might reach, or I have desires that might be incompatible with my conclusions. I did, however, mention the nagging feeling (conscience, in theological language) that can push me to consider the questions that I would prefer to avoid.

There is more to the challenge than this, however. Freud positioned feelings as potentially obscuring the truth from us, treating them as often irrational forces that cause bias.[14] Freud's view has real currency in our world. Indeed, we often carry these views into daily life. We say that we are biased in a conversation about the truth of some assertion when we have a particularly loving relationship with someone involved. When we talk about competing arguments and one of them has been made by a family member, we are likely to say, "Of course, I might be biased." More deeply, we speak of "Freudian slips" when a turn of phrase hints at a knowing that has been obscured from ourselves and others, or reveals motives that we do not fully wish to admit to ourselves and the world.[15] These slips of speech suggest that our psyches have aspects that we do not fully know, even may not want to know; they are all the more powerful because we do not know them or we refuse to acknowledge them. Feelings have a power to direct us, including directing our knowing and deciding.

The point of psychic transformation is that we are invited to engage with our emotional life, seeking to understand and engage those aspects of ourselves that can influence our understandings and decisions without our full awareness. The point of modern psychology is that this is not as simple as pushing our feelings to match our most desired outcomes. There are deeper aspects to our selves, rooted in all that has happened to us and all that we have known.

One of Carl Jung's main contributions to psychology has been his emphasis on the role of symbols, images freighted with meaning, in our inner lives.[16] Because understanding is not a simple matter of deduction or puzzle assembly, but an activity of gathering data and then "getting it" in ways that can be surprising, we rely often on symbols—commonly in the form of images—to help ourselves in knowing. One of the benefits and challenges of our psyche is that it plays a big part in which symbols will emerge as we think, and our psyche will also have an impact on ways that those symbols function for us.

The father is one obvious symbol that has power for us as Christians, because of its biblical and Trinitarian references, so we use it liturgically and talk about it with others. In recent times, we have become aware that this symbol functions differently for different people. It may not be helpful in conversation, may not even be retrievable, because it plays a role in some inner lives that may suppress insights rather than encouraging them. Because people experience fathers as everything from loving and supportive through tyrannical and violent to entirely absent, the symbol is awkwardly ambiguous and potentially destructive. The symbol has too many meanings to say anything specific, and those meanings are usually connected to deep feelings and complex reactions.

Doran invites us to attend to our inner lives so that we can understand our reactions to different symbols.[17] Psychic transformation is the process of discovering the symbols that function fruitfully and creatively for us, and of growing awareness of the symbols that suppress insights or work destructively in our knowing.

There is a related function to feelings that is a basic part of ordinary operation. Feelings tend to be guides to our values, the things that we desire and the things that we reject. Indeed, feelings can often provide a more honest announcement of our commitments than our expressions of our thoughts. True psychic transformation involves learning to listen to our feelings and to be discerning about them.[18] We need to distinguish moments when they lead us in constructive directions from those times when they urge us to be destructive. Is a gut attraction to a particular food a response to our nutritional needs for protein, vitamins, and minerals, or is it an unhealthy craving for elevated levels of sugar, fat, and sodium? Is a move toward a closer relationship with someone a genuine desire for mutual good, or is it a product of unwise dependencies?

These responses are connected to our symbolic imagination because symbols give rise to feelings and feelings give rise to symbols.[19] Think about the example of "father." You may feel both movements. Likely, your gut reaction to the language will come from your own experiences in relation to fathers. You may also be able to recognize how some of the symbolic meanings of the term father—which cover a broad range, as we've seen—have emerged. This activity of being attentive to our feelings and seeking to understand the roles that they play in our lives can help us to be aware of the need for psychic transformation. Destructive experiences can prevent the emergence of helpful images. Psychic transformation is about growing to understand our feelings and identifying ways that they can serve predominantly creative, rather than mostly destructive, outcomes.

Again, this may seem to be an odd thing for the church to focus on encouraging because it is not obviously religious. The reason, though, goes beyond this being a helpful priority in people's lives. A focus on psychic conversion moves conversation into the specifically religious sphere. As our example of the father suggests, we communicate in symbols. If we, ourselves, are to understand our own acts of knowing and deciding, if we are to know our own faith, then we must recognize the impact that different symbols have on us. Evangelism begins with transformation of ourselves. Moreover, if we are to speak religiously to the world, then our communications will be much more effective if others are also deeply aware of their internal symbolic lives. A focus on psychic conversion will also encourage us to attend to our own emotions and the ways that they impinge on our understandings and decisions, internally, and our interactions with others, externally. Emotions affect what we value and how we value it; understanding our emotions and learning how to be informed and directed by them is important to the work of living creatively, rather than destructively. If we are to speak and show Christ to the world, and if we are to know the world as Christ communicating with us, then we must live into psychic transformation.

Moral Transformation

Being to a greater degree attentive and intelligent, and intellectually and psychically transformed, is a good thing. However, these developments gain greater significance for the world when they lead to a transformation in our decision-making. When we have judged that we have understood correctly, we face the—often challenging—question, "What should I do?" Moral transformation is about making practical decisions that are consistent with the answers that we reach, with our understanding of the world. One effect of understanding truth as the product of asking and answering questions is that we tend to move beyond ourselves, beyond the world as it relates solely to us. If we want to know whether a field is good for planting alfalfa, then we need to know something about soil science, something about alfalfa, and something about crop machinery (probably other things, too). We must begin to understand how things relate to other things. There is a further shift that is possible as we move outward with our questions: we start to consider the impacts that our decisions will have on other people and other things. The moral question is how far we are willing to permit our questions to reach. Do we stop questioning when it might threaten self-interest? Do we stop questioning when it might undermine cherished theoretical assumptions? Moral transformation means that we take this larger understanding seriously, so that we make decisions that transcend our own interests, treating concern for the other and the whole world—future, present, and past—as valuable.[20]

Moral transformation expands the ways that we ask and answer questions, especially at the levels of decision and action. We all have a tendency to focus upon ourselves and our own needs. Moral transformation shifts our concern to the larger set of relations. Asking the question, "What should I do?", we do not think only of our own needs but consider what is best for others in the world. The short answer to the alfalfa question might be, "Yes, that field can feasibly and profitably be used to grow that crop." Then again, the answer might be, "Yes, if we use excessive quantities of chemical fertilizers, then treat the crops with enormous quantities of pesticides and herbicides, the field can feasibly and profitably be used," while knowing that all these inputs will wash into a waterway bordering the field—a waterway that serves numerous vegetative, animal, and human communities, all of which/whom will suffer from that course of action. The first answer might result from limited questioning, focused primarily on ways that the decision will affect only me. It might be the product of attending to a very narrow horizon of concern (the area that we see and think about), addressing only those outcomes that serve my bank account. The second answer results from considering bigger questions about the sets of relations that would be affected by my actions.

Moral transformation calls us to consider the larger range of issues. Instead of being self-focused, we seek to attend to the effects of our decisions on more and more of the world. Then, we commit ourselves to making decisions and undertaking actions that are consistent with the greater knowledge that comes from asking and answering questions that touch on larger concerns. We answer the call to be responsible.[21] This is a process that is affected by our intellectual development; the more that we know, the better our decisions. More knowledge is not sufficient to produce superior outcomes, though. We must grow in our willingness and capacity to live out of the insights that we have. That growth in willingness and capacity is moral transformation.

Religious Transformation

Some readers of this book will find it odd that we come last to the change that seems most clearly to be the role of the church: religious transformation. Those readers are correct. We come last to that which is first and continually most significant. Religious transformation underlies all the kinds of growth that happens in our lives. Religious transformation is the encounter with love that enables us to engage in knowing, deciding, and doing in the deepest possible ways.[22] Without some measure of love, we are very unlikely to become intellectually, psychically, or morally transformed at all, because love is the motive power.

Why, then, does it appear last? The invitation to being-in-love[23] is, on the face of it, more problem than solution. We cannot make ourselves be in love. Love comes as divine gift, a gift that is fundamentally transformative. Love is not merely emotional; it engages every aspect of our personalities and transforms our lives. Under the influence of love, we know the world differently, inhabit it differently. Nonetheless, being loving includes an emotional component that we cannot generate in ourselves. Being loving is an orientation that occurs in our inner lives but is often connected to an other that is not us.

We are treating last what is methodologically first because the other forms of transformation prepare us to recognize love in action. Love is the motive force that draws us beyond ourselves. Love encourages us to ask and answer questions correctly and on a larger scale than simply as the answers affect us. Love enlarges our horizons of concern. The goal of love is self-transcendence, which is precisely the goal of self-appropriation,

We will see a real-life example of how the process of self-appropriation works when we discuss leadership. The case of Sargent Shriver, as seen through studies undertaken by James Price and Kenneth Melchin, will help us to understand the links between transformation and public life, engaging the challenges of ambassadorship and *diakonia* in ways that can help us to reimagine the church's life.

I tend to find, though, that a fictional case of transformation is helpful as people think through the process and its implications. I like to draw on my favorite movie: *Groundhog Day*, the story of Phil Connors (played by Bill Murray), a weatherman in Pittsburgh who becomes trapped in an endless repetition of Groundhog Day in Punxsutawney, Pennsylvania.[24]

You may have seen *Groundhog Day*. It has come to be respected as a romantic comedy, but you may not have noticed the depth of development in Phil's character. It is rather complex. Phil begins as an arrogant man, completely self-centered and career-oriented, with plans to move up the ladder of television stations. In his priority of self, he leans toward the opposite of being intellectually transformed: convinced of his own brilliance and committed to disregarding the wisdom and contributions of others. Phil forecasts that a major winter storm will bypass his weather area. He is, of course, wrong. An iconic moment of the movie occurs when Phil and the crew from WPBH-TV9 are caught in the storm; Phil jumps out of a warm van—shirt and tie, no coat—marches through the pelting snow to a police officer closing the highway and argues that the storm is supposed to miss them, going into his TV weatherman act. Phil has proclaimed the weather; the world is not free to vary. Put differently, the viewer recognizes that no amount of evidence can cause Phil to ask and answer further questions or reconcile him to the reality that his position is wrong.

One of the main themes of the movie is Connors's intellectual growth, demonstrated as a process of asking and answering questions. We do not see him take the step of recognizing the importance of this path and seeking to understand the operations of his own mind, an important step in intellectual transformation. However, we do see him shift to engaging in the questioning and self-checking task. To connect with Rita (played by Andie MacDowell), Phil begins to question her about her interests and choices. When he gets it wrong, as in choosing white chocolate for her, he records (in the list in his head) the indicated preferences, showing his self-correcting function in operation. This whole process of getting to know Rita serves as an indication of his method of moving forward with her. It is also a hint about the ways that Phil finds to make progress. He takes refuge from the weirdness of endlessly repeated days in a local restaurant; eventually (on the same day, a much later day) telling Rita that he knows everyone in the place. Indeed he does, introducing her to several people and speaking some of their most intimate secrets. With one of them, Nancy, we know that he has seduced her by asking questions, though she eventually rejects him. The point, however, is that Phil could only have discovered people's intimate details by questioning them attentively and listening carefully. The process contributes to Phil's education, also. Deciding that he needs to learn to play the piano, he takes himself to a piano teacher; he gets into lessons rather impatiently, by overpaying enough to force out the girl currently at the piano (the viewer feels sympathy for her) but displays the patience of endless listening and practice, self-correction and correction from his teacher, to attain mastery. Every time that I view the movie, I am struck by the extent to which the questioning process is central to Phil's transformation.

Intriguingly, Phil also undergoes psychic transformation, though the process is somewhat less evident. The psychic disorientation of endless repetition of one day eventually drives him to a therapist who is, unfortunately, unable to help him. The issue is clearly one of extremely abnormal psychology, far outside the range of a practitioner who usually does basic couples counseling and more mainstream therapy. However, we get clues that Phil is doing his own psychological work. Early in the movie, he says, almost in passing, "I don't even like myself." At the moment when we see him begin to turn around, changing the trajectory of his life, he suggests that Rita probably sees him as a jerk. "That's okay. I am a jerk." This is a kind of self-awareness that we cannot imagine in the Phil Connors of the movie's beginning. By the end of the movie, we see a Phil who is much more at ease with himself. We see this in his carriage. Much more, though, we see it in his treatment of others. Phil's initial self-dislike is reflected in the rude, sometimes brutal, way that he treats others. His immaturity in making fun of Rita's love of the groundhog, Punxsutawney Phil, is shocking. His insulting description of Larry's eating habits, delivered right in front of Larry, is even harsher and socially unacceptable. Late in the movie, Phil is gentle and kind with Rita, a shift that we observe occurring. More surprising, though, is his treatment of Larry, whom we have come to recognize as socially awkward. Phil shows up with coffee and pastries, making sure that Larry gets his favorite, accepts Larry's advice, and treats him with respect. Phil has come to understand that a big part of his challenge with others is his own opinion of himself and has done some of the work of self-acceptance—self-appropriation—needed to come to terms with his identity. He is now able to accept others as they are.

Phil's self-orientation is at the heart of the early phases of the movie. He attends to himself, his appearance, his own opinions, and, most of all, his career. He is so focused on who he is and where he is going that he informs people at his station (once right in front of his producer!) that he expects to be moving on to a position in a bigger market, and to be making the move soon. As anyone who thinks about workplaces will recognize, this is a highly aggressive move. Only someone who is quite sure of their value in the organization will risk taking such a position without another offer on the table.

We see the self-orientation begin to shift when Phil discovers that short-term fun behaviors, such as stuffing himself with junk food, do not satisfy. The reality, though, is that he is not genuinely interested in other people as and for themselves. Phil begins to ask Nancy questions about herself, seeking information, but he is not really seeking to understand her. His questions are all oriented toward obtaining information that he can use to get her into his bed. He observes Punxsutawney and how it runs. Again, this is solely with a view to his own benefit, both in his efforts to kill himself in despair caused by being trapped in an ever-repeating day and in his efforts to live out various fantasies without consequences. His first efforts with Rita are also marked by his own self-centeredness; he simply does not know how to love her for herself.

At the end of the movie, we see a morally transformed Phil. His final Groundhog Day is marked by a succession of other-oriented tasks. He is kind to the people in his bed-and-breakfast accommodations, shows up with coffee and pastries to meet Larry and Rita, discusses camera placement with them, provides a poetic and meaningful reflection of Groundhog Day for TV, catches a child falling from a tree, changes a tire for a group of women, saves the life of a street person by feeding him and caring for him, uses the Heimlich maneuver to save Buster from choking on a piece of beef, plays piano for the Groundhog Day dance, gets Wrestlemania tickets as a wedding present for Debbie and Fred, somewhere in there finds time to fix Felix's back and buy an enormous insurance policy from Ned Ryerson (whom he had previously detested), and produces a beautiful ice sculpture of Rita (displaying a minute knowledge of her features, in addition to ice sculpting skills). When he finishes the day in bed with Rita, once the goal of his life, he goes straight to sleep. "It was the end of a very long day," he protests next morning. Phil is a changed man, with profoundly transformed priorities—along with being a bit superhuman; the movie is a comedy, after all. In addition to being deeply pleased, Rita is confused; she starts the day knowing Phil in one way and ends knowing him completely differently.

At the root of all the development is the beginning of a religious transformation. In the movie, Phil discovers the emptiness of being self-centered. He goes drinking with a couple of guys (Gus and Ralph) and raises the philosophical question of his existence, "What would you do if you were stuck in a small dead-end town and every day was just the same?" Ralph provides the answer by downing another shot; Gus declares, "That says it for me." At the end of the boozing session, they go out in Gus's old Cadillac and Phil drives on the railroad tracks, straight at an oncoming train, then jumps off the tracks just in time, before wrecking various things with the car and being caught by the police when the car can go no further. Repeated efforts to commit suicide lead nowhere. He continues to be trapped. Fantasy fulfillment accomplishes nothing. It does not lead to a sense of joy or meaningfulness. We see Phil's life at a dead end. The endless pointlessness of the self-centered life is rarely made so obvious.

Only after Phil declares his love for Rita do we see him begin to work at accomplishing things for others. His questions are about how to help people. We observe him counting carefully, so that he can time his interventions. We watch him make repeated efforts to save an older homeless man. At the hospital where Phil takes the man, a nurse says, "He was old. Sometimes people just die." Phil's answer is "Not today!" Then he runs into the off-limits hospital space and checks the man's chart. Phil is now all about life for others, instead of benefits for himself.

The explanation is in Phil's admission that he has been a jerk and his declaration of love for Rita, made while she sleeps. He goes so far as to say that he has loved her since he first saw her. He says all this while he awaits another repeated day, but one in which he begins his commitment to change. He reiterates the point when she admires his ice sculpture of her. "No matter what happens tomorrow, or for the rest of my life, I'm happy now because I love you." Even though she is profoundly different from him, he loves her. I find myself wondering whether his love for her is partly because of their differences. They have invited him to become a changed person, one more committed to the kind of beauty for which she cares; her love of French poetry, attachment to the beauty of the world, and desire for world peace have become part of him, though they would, no doubt, have been far too saccharine for the old Phil. One suspects that sweet vermouth on the rocks with a twist (her favorite drink) might be a step too far, though!

The final clue to the change in Phil comes in his fundamentally transformed attitude toward the world. The overriding sentiment of the early and middle parts of the movie is that Phil hates Punxsutawney with a passion. He hates going there and keeps careful count of the number of times it happens, correcting a colleague on air when she undercounts. Much of the misery that Phil feels throughout the movie reflects life in Punxsutawney, even as we are aware that this is a profound dissatisfaction with life in the world; Punxsutawney is no worse than any other place and certainly has its own charms. Yet, when Phil presents for the camera on his final Groundhog Day, his attitude is precisely the opposite. "When Chekhov saw the long winter, he saw a winter bleak and dark and bereft of hope. Yet we know that winter is just another step in the cycle of life. But standing here among the people of Punxsutawney and basking in the warmth of their hearths and hearts, I couldn't imagine a better fate than a long and lustrous winter." This passage serves as something of a Shakespearean soliloquy, revealing the internal operations of the speaker. Phil has accepted that his fate is to be in Punxsutawney, yet he now finds real love and true meaning there, rather than the darkness and hopelessness that marked his earlier Groundhog Days. At the end, when Phil and Rita step out of the bed-and-breakfast into the bright winter sunshine, Phil has a genuine smile, in remarkable contrast to his earlier sneer. He proclaims, "It's so beautiful! Let's live here!" We see a complete turnaround from Phil's starting point.

Phil has been gripped and transformed by love. Now, he is capable of knowing Punxsutawney in some degree as God knows it: through the power of love. This is a limited religious transformation; Phil does not recognize God as the giver of Rita, of Punxsutawney, of the world, and as the one who transforms his knowing. Nor does Phil know God in God's fullness (I cannot claim to do so, either, which is a reminder of the limits of my religious transformation). This is a set of steps on the way, however. Just as Beatrice becomes Dante's guide to the spiritual life, so Rita has begun Phil's journey. Phil has become a true citizen of earth and knows something of heavenly citizenship now that he has been through the transformation process.

This example, though fictional, has some helpful things to say to the church as it responds to a new era in which the numbers narrative fails and a new way of imagining the meaning of church emerges. The process of transformation is complex; what we think of as religious transformation is more complicated than we have often understood and is not enough by itself. The church's task is to help people to understand the meanings of their lives and recognize the motions of love—including its implications for knowing, deciding, and acting—in their stories, which provide the data that they have. The church's task for Phil, then, would be to enable him to see the transformations that have occurred in his life, and then to engage him with the next step of recognizing God's place in all this change—fostering the foundations on which he can build a deeper understanding of what the world is all about. In traditional church language, this is what is meant by discipling.

Phil has undergone some measure of intellectual, psychic, moral, and religious transformation. We do not know how deep the transformations are, how well-rooted, or—perhaps most important—how well understood. The changes have happened, but they have happened in a very specific, highly repetitive set of circumstances. There is a very real advantage to undergoing transformation in such a controlled context: Phil gets lots of do-overs, so he can learn important things, such as the difference between asking questions with a view to self-interest and asking the relevant questions in order to understand. He is truly a changed person as a result. However, there are also limitations to developing in one place, with roughly one succession of events, and no consequences that last until he gets it right. If Phil gets offered a more highly placed, fast track–oriented job tomorrow—perhaps as a result of his brilliant performance in Punxsutawney—will he be able to repeat the operations? He was required to undertake a lot of hard work, presumably over the space of years (given evidence like his move from beginner piano to leading role in a jazz quartet), to become a transformed person. Is he willing to continue that work, now that he has reached his goal of connecting with Rita?

Important for our discussion about the place of the church in God's transformational work, Phil's transformation has occurred without mentoring from the community and with only limited participation from Rita. Can Phil continue without purposeful support from the community? On this last point, note the word "purposeful." Undoubtedly, the community prefers the new Phil and will, absent other pressures, provide the sort of approbation that communities do when they develop a liking for someone. However, the people of Punxsutawney do not know what has happened to Phil and we have no reason to believe that they understand the process. They cannot be expected to sustain Phil on his path in any formal way and the changeability of public opinion always endangers popularity.

This set of limitations may be most significant in the context of Phil's love relationship with Rita. In one way, Phil knows Rita very well. He is able to claim a thorough and intimate knowledge of her facial features, as is reflected in his ice sculpture—a bust of Rita as she appears on Groundhog Day, over and over again. In another way, Phil does not know Rita and Rita does not know Phil. They have not even worked together before. Phil has only come to know her in the carefully defined context of the repeated Groundhog Day, and Rita cannot even claim that level of knowledge; the conceit seems to be that Phil retains memories from his repeated days, so he can learn, but others do not. Phil's love for Rita may be deep, a product of years together, but it is narrow. He began the story with an inability to love. He has much to learn about love and about Rita in the years to come.

The church is an educational structure with room for explosions. If the church were somehow engaged in the life of Phil, or a "Phil," the church would be called to support him in the kinds of transformation that have occurred in his life. The church would foster, and seek to further, the changes that he has seen.

If we go back to our discussion of being an ambassador of reconciliation, we are reminded that the passage begins with an assertion of change in knowing. "From now on, therefore, we regard no one from a human point of view; even though we once knew Christ from a human point of view, we know him no longer in that way. So if anyone is in Christ, there is a new creation: everything old has passed away; see, everything has become new!" (2 Cor. 5:16–17) We are invited to know the world as it truly is: the context of God's loving transformation of all things. Beginning by talking about intellectual transformation and supporting Phil in the work of understanding how he has come to know people and place more deeply, more accurately, through the process of asking and answering questions gives him a starting point. Engaging his story with him, from this perspective, can help him to understand the way that intellectual transformation has worked in him and support him in moving forward on the same healthy path. Forecasting the weather, if we assume that Phil continues to do this, will serve as less of a vehicle of self-aggrandizement. Instead, his fundamental commitment will be to asking and answering the relevant questions, so as to produce as accurate an assessment of the possibilities as he can. This would represent a significant shift for Phil, given that the entire premise of the movie is that his forecast for Groundhog Day is both wrong and delivered with the absolute assurance of someone not sufficiently committed to the self-checking that comes with true care for the task.

At the core of our reading of 2 Corinthians 5 is the insight that Phil (like all people everywhere) is a new creation and part of a whole world which is a new creation. The church is invited to address psychic transformation and help Phil to see that the move from "I don't even like myself" to being a valued and loved member of the community is both important and worthy of further investigation. Without this insight, people cannot easily hear the good news. If all that is heard in society's treatment of a person or in the church's preaching is an assertion of the worthlessness or destructiveness of that person, then no conversation about love can be truly internalized. Thus, this is one of the key recognitions to which the church would invite Phil through reflection on his life story, whether solo or with a counselor.

The call to being an ambassador of reconciliation explicitly invites moral transformation, inviting Phil to think about the extent to which his life and world have changed for the better as he has committed himself to doing the right thing. The church's hope is that this could strengthen the pattern Phil is developing and help him to incorporate it profoundly and consistently in his operations. Reflecting upon his experience with the homeless man, for whom Phil really needed to dedicate himself to understanding the particular requirements and ensured that they were fulfilled, could enable Phil to continue repeating the activities so that they are the norm for him beyond the Groundhog Day context.

All this work is about helping people to understand their stories as accounts of love in action. In other words, we are not really delaying conversation about religious transformation. Instead, we are reimagining evangelism and catechesis, making of them a richer process, taken step by step. Evangelism continues to be what it always has been at its best: enabling people to see God at work in their lives, to know the meaning of their—and the world's—existence. The first difference between what I am suggesting and what some people may understand as evangelism is that this approach begins by supporting people in recognizing the sorts of transformations in their lives that we believe God accomplishes and desires to accomplish. God is there, engaging everyone's life, even if they do not see this. The next difference is that we focus on the transformative power of love, rather than insisting on naming that love as the gift of God as Christians understand God. This is the second step in helping people to know God as part of their lives, without needing to move immediately to discussion of church, Bible, councils, Trinity, and Incarnation. At some point, a church reaching out to Phil would focus on love as the power within the transformations occurring in his life. Love is what drives us to understand correctly, engage ourselves deeply, choose right courses of action, and act accordingly. Being in love is a basic condition for being deeply attentive, intelligent, reasonable, and responsible, and also a probable outcome. For the church, therefore, evangelism means helping people to understand their stories as occasions of divine inbreaking—explosions—where the transformations happen.

This approach to speaking the good news is based in an understanding of God as one who is actively engaged with the world, transforming it into the world that it can be: God's new creation, the context of life in love. Transformation is a function of God's grace. Moreover, recognizing the workings of grace without understanding them as grace does not prevent them from occurring. Recognition of love at work, living into it, and seeking to foster it in our lives and the lives of others. . . these things are contingent on our understanding. Recognizing that love at work is God at work is an important insight. Indeed, it is the religious insight that enables us to establish our own religious foundations. We can begin to move forward in understanding God's revelation of reconciliation and new creation. Only as we begin to understand these things do doctrines about Trinity, creation, Incarnation, and the reign of God attain real meaning as living statements about the order of things, rather than as dead orthodoxies that the church uses to police boundaries and impose discipline. Only in fostering transformation—of all the kinds that we have named—does the church undertake its real task, finding its way into the true narrative to which it is called and learning to thrive differently.

Exercises: The Organized Church in a Post-Church Age

A. Your Life

1. How do you feel about institutions? Have your feelings about them changed over years? Has your engagement with them shifted?

2. What are your reactions to our discussion of the four transformations (intellectual, psychic, moral, religious), in your gut and your head? What do you think are the root reasons that you respond this way? Do you think that what I have said is all true or partly true or fundamentally incorrect?

3. What lessons can you draw for your own life from our discussion of *Groundhog Day*?

4. Pay attention to your own knowing. When you tried to understand what I was saying about intellectual transformation, what did you do? What helped you to understand? What made it more difficult? Did the concrete example from *Groundhog Day* help? Did you feel differently at different times? What sorts of things help you to ask and answer questions? Do you think that you have asked and answered the relevant questions about intellectual transformation?

5. Pay attention to your own psychological state. We thought about the example of father as a symbol that gets used often in church; it is a standard name for the first person of the Trinity, who is not, of course, father in the same way that humans are fathers. If this is a safe example for you to reflect upon, then try repeating the experiment that we followed in the chapter. What are your emotional reactions to the language of father for the first person of the Trinity? What are your body reactions? Is father a helpful image? Does the symbol help you to see God as creative, as understanding, as loving? Is father a disruptive image, interfering with your capacity to know the world in love? What happens when you switch the image to mother? Does that affect your responses? Do you find that easier or harder to accept? Or is it simply different or even indifferent? Through the week, try to pay attention to your gut responses to images, where your responses seem to originate, and how your responses affect your capacity to know and love.

6. Pay attention to your own moral situation. This time, try remembering a moment that you are not proud of, a time when you either suspect or know that you did not meet your own moral standards. Try to determine where the failure occurred. Did you ask and answer the relevant questions? Did you make a decision that was inconsistent with your conclusions? How far did your horizon reach? Did you focus solely or almost entirely on yourself? Did you pay attention to larger contexts and, if so, how far did you permit yourself to question? Is this a way that you often make decisions? Does it match the image of yourself that you want to match in this situation? Did

your action match the person whom you believe yourself called to be? If not, what got in the way? Try to draw some lessons from this work that will help you to make better decisions in the future.

7. Pay attention to your own religion. Is love its central principle? In what ways does your religion help you to love others? In what ways does it uphold you in love? Does your religious belief system describe a story of love? Does love characterize your religion's approach to everyone or only to people who agree with your religion? Are there ways in which being more loving could strengthen the life and activity of your religious community? In the moments when you know yourself to be acting religiously (at worship, for example), ask yourself whether you are being loving. If the answer is no, then begin the process of asking and answering the relevant questions; try to discover why not. The answers may surprise you. Many sorts of pressures can interfere. On the topic of this book, the stresses that come with life in a shrinking church can often drive us off track, so that we lose the reasons that we made a religious commitment in the first place.

B. Your Organization

1. Does this vision of transformation change how you understand the purpose of the church? If so, in what ways? You may wish to return to your answers to some prior questions, including those following the introduction, where you did some thinking about the purpose of the church.

2. How does your organization engage with people to accomplish these transformations? Are there transformations on which your organization focuses particularly?

C. The World

1. Does our discussion of *Groundhog Day* change how you understand other people? What about people who are in other religions or no religion at all? If so, in what ways?

2. Describe an instance in which a non-Christian has shown God's love to you. How has this affected your understanding of God's reconciliation in the world?

CHAPTER 4

LEADERSHIP IN A SHRINKING CHURCH

If the church were another kind of organization, I would recommend that we shut down. The numbers simply are not there to support a reasonable business model. We cannot assume profitability. No bank would back us. No investors would commit, except perhaps out of nostalgia or as a memorial to their grandparents. This is exactly why no schools train people to provide leadership or management in a shrinking organization. There's no reason to bother. In business, if you are looking at these results, walk away and start something else.

We cannot and will not walk away. The changes in our organization are not, for us, ultimate.[1] Instead, we know that God continues to transform the world. We need to rethink our direction as an organization and, therefore, who we are as leaders, rather than dropping the project entirely. We need leaders who can participate meaningfully in our life as ambassadors of reconciliation, in a changed context. In some ways, leadership is a portable skill. Companies hire leaders from other companies, even other industries, all the time. Thus, we will engage with some leadership theory, notably from Ronald A. Heifetz's work on adaptive leadership. However, the church also brings some specific considerations. Precisely because of our God-oriented commitments, we are different.

Adaptive Leadership

The shift that I have been suggesting, calling for a move from the numerical growth narrative to a vision of complex transformation, is of the kind that Heifetz and his fellow thinkers call an "adaptive challenge" because it demands change that reaches beyond simple fixes to an existing way of being. I am asking the church to reconsider both its definition of the challenge that it faces (declining numbers due to secularization) and its criteria of success (getting people into Christianity), with all the shifts in goals, priorities, and expectations that such a change entails. I am attaching a different meaning to the notion of a thriving church. The core distinction is between a technical problem, which can be solved by a technical fix using the right kind of expertise, and an adaptive issue that requires a much deeper kind of change, touching on identity. "Adaptive challenges can only be addressed through changes in people's priorities, beliefs, habits, and loyalties."[2]

This kind of change calls for what Heifetz calls adaptive leadership. "Adaptive leadership is the practice of mobilizing people to tackle tough challenges and thrive."[3] He identifies six principles for adaptive leadership:

1) "Adaptive leadership is specifically about change that enables the capacity to thrive." Part of the challenge is in discerning what the word "thrive" means in a particular context.[4]
2) "Successful adaptive changes build on the past rather than jettison it." Helping people to discern what must be preserved and what can be changed is central to the work.[5]
3) "Organizational adaptation occurs through experimentation." We need to try different things, using each effort as a springboard for the next.[6]
4) "Adaptation relies on diversity." Value different viewpoints.[7]
5) "New adaptations significantly displace, reregulate, and rearrange some old DNA." Seek to recognize the losses that will occur and respond to the defensive responses that will emerge.[8]
6) "Adaptation takes time." Leaders must stay with the project, as challenging as that might be.[9]

The purpose of the first three chapters of this book has been to redefine the meaning of the word "thrive" for the church, building on our biblical and theological heritage while displacing an important, even defining, part of our DNA. Coming chapters will help us to think about living this out in concrete ways.

There is another reason that I have turned to Heifetz to help us move forward: I see important links between Lonergan's work and Heifetz's. Heifetz and his colleagues develop a problem-solving process that involves system-level diagnosis, then system-level action, followed by self-level diagnosis, then self-level action.[10] There is a back-and-forth between the levels, that Heifetz and his fellow thinkers call the view from the balcony (the system level) and the view from the dance floor (the level of self and of personal interactions). In fact, we have been following this approach from the book's opening moment, when I arrived at my seminary. I was doing high-level assessment of the challenges (balcony) even as I sought to work with specific challenges of daily operations and relationships (dance floor). Lonergan's ideas specifically encourage us to focus on the big picture (progress, decline, general and group bias) and the self (knowing, transformation, individual bias).

There is a deeper connection between Lonergan and Heifetz, however. The work to which Heifetz invites us depends upon the activities that Lonergan identifies as core method, though there is an important way in which Lonergan's approach is more helpful. Heifetz's three "key activities" are: observing (paying attention to events and patterns); interpreting (identifying a variety of ways to explain your observations, and choosing the one that seems most correct); and intervening (designing and employing interventions to address a challenge).[11] Lonergan's four steps are: experiencing (assembling the data); understanding (grasping the meaning of the data, often through multiple efforts); judging (checking to see whether the understanding is correct); and deciding (identifying the course of action that is most consistent with the correct understanding).[12] The two processes are nearly identical; the difference is that Heifetz's activity conflates identifying multiple hypotheses and determining which one is correct under the same label—interpretation—whereas Lonergan accurately names them as two distinct activities: understanding and judging. Following Lonergan enables us to be sure that we do not miss the self-checking step, which might be the most important characteristic of human knowing—simply because we tend to overlook it.

Insights from Heifetz will play a significant role in the chapters to follow.

Leadership and Self-Appropriation

Our short introduction to Heifetz's work reminds us that leaders in today's church need some specific qualities to live the gospel and provide leadership through the process of institutional renewal. We begin with a return to the invitation to transformation. We must accept it if we wish to share it with others.

If our discussions of reconciliation, transformation, and adaptive leadership are accurate, then leadership begins with interiority, with a significant degree of transformation. In other words, we need to be able to experience, understand, judge, and decide well. We need to be attentive, intelligent, reasonable, responsible, and loving.

Indeed, at best, a church leader (really, any leader) will be someone who recognizes the importance of intellectual, psychic, moral, and religious transformation. That is true because, as we saw in the previous chapter, self-appropriation provides important aspects of the foundation for our preaching to the world of today and because self-appropriation is the ground for all the skills that a leader needs and leadership studies address.

The skill of self-attention known as self-appropriation is exceedingly important in the work of church leadership. Ultimately, our conversation focuses outwardly; we address how we relate to others as church and as church leaders. This fits comfortably with a lot of the work of leadership scholars, who discuss organizational purpose and the ways that we can best treat people in order to fulfill the purpose, such as expressing empathy. However, there is a prior consideration that needs attention before we move to the treatment of individuals or the transformation of the world. That first concern is us—our selves—and the ways that we, as particular persons, understand and engage. I need to know myself, my ways of thinking and responding, so that I can be supportive of other people.

Let me give you a personal example. When I was (much) younger, I tended to focus especially on the words that people chose and the logic of their arguments when we were in debate. This approach had a very real strength: The words that people choose can be more revealing of meaning than people anticipate, while the logic of their arguments is important to the work of discerning the truth in people's statements. The thing I was trying to approximate (the image of myself that I would bring to those discussions) was roughly a disembodied ear that ignored distractions and attended carefully to the other person's position.[13] I expect that you can see the flaws. This meant that I did not give sufficient attention to other cues, especially emotional, that were conveyed by facial expression and physical stance. I was not collecting all the data that the other person was providing. Moreover, focusing on the words in a context where people are not especially careful about verbal expression could lend to something of an overreading of their intended position, an unbalanced presentation. I was not consistently understanding what other people wanted to say; others would push back against my misunderstandings, but I could not correct myself without more development in ways of knowing. I could not understand the frustration that other people displayed. I needed to learn to ask and answer a greater variety of questions to be able to understand what other people were saying. To change the image, I needed to be something more like a full-bodied receiver, using every aspect of my being to hear the other. By recognizing the need to change the image that I hoped to match in conversation, committing to attend to more data for a richer understanding, and assessing bodily cues as either affirming or rejecting my understanding of other peoples' words (judging my own understanding), I became more self-appropriated and, thus, more intellectually transformed.

Intellectual Transformation

A core mark of leadership capacity is the willingness and ability to enter into this process of self-appropriation, attending to one's own levels of transformation and committing to further growth. This applies to all kinds of transformation. Today's church leader needs to be both intellectually transformed to an advanced degree and committed to further intellectual transformation, delving deeper into the work of understanding both their field and the extent to which their own intelligence can be developed by paying attention to the work of asking and answering relevant questions. A genuine desire to understand God, the good news, the world, society, people, systems, all as these things are touched by God's love, is central to leadership in a shrinking church. A person engaged with intellectual transformation is concerned about meanings; in this case, we are focused on the meaning of church. A church leader seeking intellectual transformation wants to understand the meanings of church and world, in order to rethink the way that church is lived.

Concretely, this matters because of the kinds of shifts that we have discussed in earlier chapters. The church is no longer able to cruise on previous insights or structures. Instead, every congregation, every ministry, every committee, every judicatory, every aspect of church is in the process of reimagining what being church means and how the meanings can be incarnated in a world where they have few benefits and minimal resources. All of this is happening in an immensely complex regulatory environment. Ignoring the complications will only lead to irrelevance or worse, and ultimately to disappearance. Leaders must be prepared to engage with situations in which carefully developed rules are not helpful. Instead, the direction will be defined by a gospel commitment, which will differ from community to community. Contemporary approaches to reflecting on the ministry of congregations and other church bodies, such as asset mapping (AM), emphasize asking and answering questions about the communities that we serve.[14] AM specifically focuses on accurate assessment of both the capacities of one's organization and needs of the community that the organization wishes to serve. Missional[15] and neighborhood mapping[16] work similarly. We will discuss the nature and expression of gospel commitment in greater depth in a later chapter. For now, we need to be clear about the importance of curiosity, driven and defined by love.

Conversations about politics, social media, online and telephone scams, and international disinformation operations have placed the question of truth at the center of contemporary society. The problem of how we discern right answers is not an obscure matter of discussion among dusty academics, pursued in unreadable journals. Instead, it is immediate, urgent, and on the plate (or, more often, the screen) of everyone today. Anyone who has received a scam email, or viewed a faked picture, or read a dubious article—in short, anyone with an online life—knows that asking the question, "Is this true?" is a basic part of everyday life.

We know that this is a leadership issue. Leaders who do not ask and answer all—or, as many as possible—of the relevant questions, including doing the self-correcting work of considering the possibility that they might be wrong and may need to confirm their understandings, and who do not recognize that asking and correctly answering *as many as possible* of the relevant questions is the criterion of truth, can cause serious errors. The point is true for everyone, but it has greater power in the leadership context. As I write, Russian President Vladimir Putin is at war in Ukraine, having invaded based on a whole selection of false assertions about Ukrainians supporting invasion, Ukrainians working with NATO to invade Russia, and other matters. The result has been massive loss of life, both Russian and Ukrainian. Indeed, an invasion that was originally intended to be a quick overnight affair has now dragged out over years, so that it is a failure on its own terms, in addition to producing longer term destruction for little evident benefit. Even if Russia makes permanent territorial gains, the costs have certainly been greater than planned and may be greater than Russia can afford. Insufficient intellectual transformation can be costly. In more specifically church-oriented contexts, a failure to pursue intellectual transformation has meant that numerous questions about the relation between the gospel and the views of Indigenous peoples were not asked and correctly answered. Too often, the church has simply (and simplistically) assumed that the beliefs of Indigenous peoples were false, even antithetical to the gospel;

now, we are starting to realize that many such belief systems have much to teach us about God at work in the world, while many of the beliefs adopted by Christians of the past three centuries or so have been deeply destructive.

Leaders engaged with intellectual transformation are, therefore, potentially better leaders. They are open to new possibilities and are more likely to make intelligent choices of paths for their organizations. They ask the relevant questions, assemble the relevant data, increase the likelihood of having accurate insights, and check their work carefully. The risk, as is probably obvious, is that being gripped by a desire for absolute accuracy can lock us into a refusal to reach a conclusion and make a decision. Life requires us to make decisions even when we are not yet ready, when the best that we can do is choose the likeliest option, without certainty that it will be the best. The reality of human knowing is that it is inherently statistical: our conclusions are more or less likely, based on the quality of the evidence that we have and our capacity for understanding it. Awareness of this is precisely what underlies the necessity for self-checking. The statistical nature of our knowing is also one of the reasons that further transformations are important. Inaction is also a course of action, and often a destructive one; moral and religious transformation, therefore, often call us to conclude, decide, and act, even without reaching satisfactory answers to all the relevant questions.

Psychic Transformation

Before addressing the importance of those transformations, we must recognize that today's leader ought to be significantly developed along the path of psychic transformation and open to further such change. I note that this tends to be a real priority of seminaries, which are often deeply aware of the psychiatric situation of students and the extent to which this affects their development in leadership preparation. Understanding our own motivations, some of which are not always obvious to us because our own psyches obscure them, enables us to benefit from the strengths that we bring. Psychic transformation enables us to understand something more of what we really mean when our expressions diverge—in unintended ways—from our positions as we believe them to be. The world is full of systems to foster awareness of our own psyches: the Myers-Briggs Type Indicator, Gallup's Strengths-Based Leadership, the Enneagram. . . . These and other measures are available; each has its own controversy. There are therapists, each following an approach that has supporters and opponents. The point about all these options is that they encourage us to ask and answer questions about aspects of ourselves that we may not recognize otherwise. I do not have the psychological training necessary to discern the value of particular tools, although I have made use of a variety of them and have found them to be beneficial to self-understanding.

As a leader and seminary president, I commend routine meetings with a leadership coach. A coach can contribute to psychic transformation, along with other forms of development. A good leadership coach will support your efforts to understand yourself, specifically as your personality affects your leadership role. Often a coach will recommend some of the personality indicators that I have mentioned, or others with which they are especially familiar. In addition, the coach will assist you to think through particular leadership situations, informed by the aspects of yourself that you are coming to know. At the same time, the coach will help you to ensure that you are asking and answering the relevant questions, encouraging you to probe your own reflections and fostering your intellectual transformation.

Left to ourselves, we do not always do an adequate job of understanding our psyches. The issue of insufficient psychic transformation is a challenge that we see in leadership all the time. I hesitate to mention the example of Donald Trump because it raises all sorts of issues and causes strong disagreements. Nonetheless, I turn to him as a particular case because he is one leader whose level of self-awareness is widely recognized as being limited, often in ways that damage himself and even his own interests. He gives no indication of being cognizant of the emergence of psychological issues in his public proclamations, as in his comments about women and their appearance and his repeated lies about crowd sizes. These are not rational choices; there is little evidence that insulting the looks of women whom he does not like or commenting on their bodies genuinely helps him electorally in any way. Similarly, insisting that his crowd sizes are always bigger, often of history-making dimensions, only undermines trust in his word. Instead of redounding to his benefit, these behaviors suggest that something psychologically deeper is in play in Trump's personality—at very least, significant insecurities. Trump is something of an extreme example. However, we all have insufficiently resolved issues that affect our public personas and, perhaps more important, our decisions and actions. In any organization, including the church (as we now know all too well), power can be mishandled. If we are unaware of important motivations, we may be prey to fears and desires that adversely affect our capacity to ask and answer the relevant questions correctly or to follow our conclusions with responsible actions. We have all known leaders of this kind and are aware that their irrational decision-making leads to unnecessary inconsistencies and uncertainties, with an increase in levels of organizational anxiety. We are generally happier and more productive when leaders are at least somewhat aware of the complexities of their own psyches and consider these things in efforts to understand and to make decisions. This is always true; it may be especially significant in a world where limited resources mean that we do not have large organizations to cushion the impact of individual personalities, nor multiple opportunities for a "do-over" when we fail.

Moral Transformation

Leadership serves the good of others. That is its meaning, the core of any helpful definition. If my priority is serving myself and my interests, then I am not a leader.

Therefore, leadership is best exercised by people whose moral transformation is substantial, and who are committed to further moral transformation in their lives. The leader of any organization has a variety of greater goods to consider: the organization, as a means to fulfill a larger purpose; the communities that the organization is intended to serve; and the people within the organization. Leaders in church organizations have the added priority of cosmic ends: participating in God's transformation of the world and carrying the good news to others. Precisely because the reason for the church is to participate in creation as ambassador of reconciliation, moral transformation takes on greater meaning. Moral self-appropriation, the task of ensuring that our decisions and actions are consistent with our confirmed insights, is more than usually important when we seek to share the good news with what we say and do.

The moral transformation necessary for church leadership is not the same as perfection. As far as I can tell, the world does not contain any perfect people. Because part of being church is recognizing our imperfections, and another part of church is welcoming other imperfect people, we will never reach the ideals that we tend to set for ourselves. That is why we find the good news of God's love, the assertion that God loves us freely and generously, so welcome.

More to the point, though, the moral transformation needed for church leadership is not necessarily the same as common understandings of perfection. What constitutes sin or inappropriate behavior in any given society is not always consonant with Christian priorities. The issue here, as in many aspects of life, is in the meaning of the actions. The purpose of Christian living, of the church in all its expressions, is to be an ambassador of reconciliation. Sin is action that does more to destroy the possibility of reconciliation than to create it. This may sound like a simple calculus. However, it is anything but, precisely because love rarely permits simple calculations. Jesus's parable of the shepherd who left the ninety-nine sheep in the fold to chase down the one lost sheep is a reminder that Jeremy Bentham's "greatest good for the greatest number" may be interestingly rational but it is not Christian. There is no easy route to the kinds of decisions that moral transformation produces. There is only the long and hard road of growing to understand one's field—in this case, leadership and church—and seeking to live as an ambassador of reconciliation, so that one develops a *habitus*, a way of life, as such an ambassador. This enables one to make the decisions for the good of others when such decisions are needed, and the world is unclear or even wrong.

Having noted the complexity about moral judgment, we must also recognize that leadership does get compromised by real moral shortcomings, failures to live the priority of the other. We are familiar with many stories of political leaders who have compromised their countries by spending great quantities of wealth on themselves to the detriment of the general populace; the shoes of Imelda Marcos have attained iconic status (though there may have been fewer pairs than popular legend suggests). Church leaders sometimes do something similar. In recent years, however, public acts of destruction by church leaders have tended to involve various kinds of abuse, along with efforts at cover-ups. Part of moral transformation in church leadership is in calling people to account for their failings. Another part is in changing destructive systems.

One of the major challenges in contemporary leadership—indeed, in contemporary society—is finding balance points between individual and corporate responsibility. Ever since Karl Marx (followed by various schools of Marxism) drew our attention to the role of systems and structures in moral existence, we have been in a conversation about where to locate responsibility for both creative and destructive outcomes. We cannot settle this question here, at least partly because it may be unanswerable in a general sense. I must emphasize, however, that moral transformation is not intended to be, and must not be, understood in an individualistic sense. Acts of understanding and deciding are functions of self-appropriation; they are, definitionally, interior to persons. We can think of our efforts to focus on them as attending to interiority. However, there is a dynamic to them. Understandings lead to decisions, and decisions lead to actions. Our actions have an impact on the world. Moral transformation, therefore, involves the recognition both of the significance of our individual actions and the impact of the systems in which we are implicated, in which we participate. Systems include biases that undercut people's abilities to come to correct conclusions and act appropriately. More will be said about biases when we discuss the pressures that church organizations face as they shrink.

Religious Transformation

While we commonly insist upon religious transformation as a characteristic of our church leaders, we do not always think seriously enough about what constitutes religious transformation or in what ways it might be helpful in our contemporary situation. An easy way to clarify what the average churchperson means when they talk about religious transformation is in the way that we test for it. These tend to follow the language that we use to address church engagement: believing, belonging, and behaving. So, we ask a series of questions. Do they believe as we do? This, we can test with courses, examinations, and concurrence with statements of faith. Do they belong to the church (or, more usually, "our church")? Attendance and participation records can settle this one. Do they behave appropriately? Inquiries with congregations and other church leaders, followed by criminal records checks, provide us with a reasonable amount of information.

All of these are good and useful ways of examining potential church leaders. More important, they are all clearly measurable—a characteristic that committees always find helpful. These are all, however, only indirect indicators of religious transformation, at best. Indeed, they may be entirely inappropriate to the question. We all know of people who can loudly proclaim the right words, who always attend church and participate extensively, but whose growth in love is insufficient for a leadership role—to state the case as politely as I can. In 1 Corinthians 13, Paul is clear on the issue: "If I speak in the tongues of mortals and of angels, but do not have love, I am a noisy gong or a clanging cymbal. And if I have prophetic powers, and understand all mysteries and all knowledge, and if I have all faith, so as to remove mountains, but do not have love, I am nothing. If I give away all my possessions, and if I hand over my body so that I may boast, but do not have love, I gain nothing" (1 Cor. 13:1–3). Paul's point is important: religious transformation is not about these kinds of outward signs, but about interiority, a change in our selves. Thus, we cannot use the usual markers of church involvement as anything more than hints of its occurrence in the lives of church leaders. Measurability is useful, but only in response to specifically intellectual questions; measurements do not reveal much, if anything, about a leader's growth in love.

In a book on evangelism, primarily oriented toward an evangelical audience accustomed to focusing upon religious transformation as a single decision to follow Christ, John Bowen suggests that emphasizing that one decision is a bit like inviting people to move from 49 to 50 on a scale of 100; it is movement, but it neither begins nor ends the process of transformation.[17] Bowen is right. I would add that many Christians are never specifically aware of a moment when they make such a decision, though the moment of baptism serves as a public marker for some. To an evangelical mindset, preparation for such a decision is often especially focused on the change in belief that leads to it. Evangelicals, following significant Protestants such as Martin Luther and John Wesley, also talk about a change of heart, an increase in receptivity to God, that accompanies the change in understanding. I have suggested that there is a change in understanding, though the focus on belief misses out on the most profound shift with which biblical and theological reflection invites us to engage. I have suggested also that there is a change of heart, though the church is not always clear on what that means.

If we recognize that there is a whole process of preparation that leads us to accept some understanding of Christian belief and seek to grow in it, then we need to think about what that process of preparation—religious transformation—looks like and how it affects church leadership. Following Lonergan, I have suggested that religious transformation is about growth in love. We have seen this kind of growth in the character of Phil Connors, in *Groundhog Day*. The limitation in that example is the lack of any explicitly "religious" reference. O. Henry gets closer to our point in his short story, "The Gift of the Magi," in which a wife sells her hair to buy a chain for her husband's watch even as he sells his watch to buy her combs for her hair. The story ends on a powerful note that never ceases to touch me, and which neatly illustrates the point.

> The magi, as you know, were wise men—wonderfully wise men—who brought gifts to the Babe in the manger. They invented the art of giving

> Christmas presents. Being wise, their gifts were no doubt wise ones, possibly bearing the privilege of exchange in case of duplication. And here I have lamely related to you the uneventful chronicle of two foolish children in a flat who most unwisely sacrificed for each other the greatest treasures of their house. But in a last word to the wise of these days let it be said that of all who give gifts these two were the wisest. Of all who give and receive gifts, such as they are wisest. Everywhere they are wisest. They are the magi.[18]

The experience of love between two people gives them the wisdom of the magi. The foolishness of those who live the generosity of love is greater than the wisdom of those who live by the profit-making rules of the world. Their love for each other prepares them to hear and know that love is of God. After all, the wisdom of the magi was precisely in their ability to see God at work, where others might see only a baby in a barnyard.

This is precisely where the church enters, as a community of people tasked with knowing the world as God's and, therefore, being prepared to see "explosions": the impact of love, as it reveals the meaning of the world. A church leader, therefore, is one who can both live the gift of love and recognize its presence, and who can help the community to form itself—in every aspect—as a vehicle for love.

Fostering this capacity is, or ought to be, the focus of all the church's practices. Prayer, sacraments, study, proclaiming and hearing proclamation—all should be oriented toward enabling us to identify and engage with the movements of love. Indeed, tracing the movements of love is exactly the purpose of creeds and doctrines, as Charles Williams has helpfully argued.[19] The church's belief commitments are meaningful as far as they enable us to recognize and participate in God's loving action in the world. Therefore, we hope, anticipate, and pray that our leaders will be so far formed by the life of the church that they will be able to support the community and extend its ministry as an expression of love, the ministry of ambassadors of reconciliation. This is leadership that can help the church to thrive.

A particular practice that our seminary and many church judicatories encourage is for leaders to work with a spiritual director. The role of such a person is exactly to support one in identifying the moments and modes of God's action in their life. Routine spiritual direction enables us to reflect on life, its joyful times and miserable, so that we are trained to know God at work. Modernity has been skeptical about the notion that God is active in the world (technically called the doctrine of providence). Philosophically, the Enlightenment committed itself to a theory of knowledge that recognized only the physically measurable and repeatable as real. Consequently, divine engagement with the world was ruled out *a priori*—at least, as something that can be known and affirmed by humans. As Christians, we are open to the idea of providence. However, God can usually be explained away by those who will not see. Spiritual direction takes the opposite assumption as its working hypothesis: our understanding of God is such that we can reasonably expect to find God at work if we know how to look. Life in spiritual direction is life in the effort to review the evidence of God's love in life, to understand the meaning of this evidence, to ensure that we are understanding it correctly, and to ensure that we are living life in a manner that is consistent with God's self-communication.

The world contains numerous examples of people who seek to live in religious transformation. Great countercultural figures stand out. Dietrich Bonhoeffer opposed Hitler and the Nazi campaign against Jewish people, serving as an unofficial theological educator and a founder of the anti-Nazi Confessing Church. Despite several opportunities to live outside of Germany, he deliberately stayed and was ultimately imprisoned and executed.

Another approach that some churches take is to honor particular people as saints. One benefit of this way of celebrating transformation is that it helps us to recognize that manifestations of love change over time. Today, St. Francis of Assisi is much appreciated. His status as patron saint of animals and ecology reflects contemporary priorities. Francis's dedication to a life of poverty is, perhaps, less welcomed and emulated.

We can find powerful examples of religious transformation outside Christianity. Mahatma Gandhi is an outstanding figure. His thinking about nonviolence was lived out in nonviolent action against oppressive British imperialism in India.[20] Both his thought and his actions influenced Martin Luther King Jr., so that Gandhi was a pivotal actor in the transformation of India and the United States, and an important teacher for many Christians.[21] Gandhi's life manifested a deep commitment to love, living it and learning it, even to the point of a martyr's death by assassination. The current (fourteenth) Dalai Lama, Tenzin Gyatso, has also had an international impact. He has been a teacher, focusing on truly religious priorities such as joy and compassion, and a diplomat, seeking peaceful ways forward. As a religious leader, he has brought his Buddhist priorities to interreligious conversations, deliberately seeking out leaders from other religions—including numerous Christian denominations. As a diplomat, the Dalai Lama has consistently sought peaceful resolutions of conflict, earning a Nobel Peace Prize for his commitment to nonviolence. Truly, these leaders are ambassadors of reconciliation.

The world has an unfortunate plenitude of Christian (and other religious) leaders who show few signs of commitment to religious transformation in their lives. We can follow the terrible history of Christians who have used lies of all kinds, including theological, to support brutal treatment of Jews. This goes back more than a millennium, found a strong advocate in the German Christian Movement under the Nazi regime, and may not be altogether gone today. We can review the roles of Christian leadership in efforts to subjugate, even obliterate, Indigenous peoples in the era of European colonialism and beyond. The list goes on. One contemporary, and very public, example is Patriarch Kirill of the Russian Orthodox Church. His firm commitment to Vladimir Putin's authoritarian regime, which Kirill has described as "a miracle of God," is evidence of a commitment to power rather than reconciliation. Kirill shocked the world with his vocal and consistent support for the Russian invasion of Ukraine, support which he framed in theological terms as a "metaphysical struggle, positioning Russia as a spiritual and holy nation in opposition to the sinful and devilish West. He has linked the war to a cosmic battle of good versus evil, elevating Russia's role to a divine mission."[22] Kirill's support of violence against a neighboring country, without so much as reference to any kind of just-war theory or any expression of concern for his coreligionists, suggests that subjugation holds greater meaning for him than reconciliation.

Diakonia and Ambassadors of Reconciliation

The examples of religious transformation that we have seen are helpful because they give us several useful pieces: evidence that religious transformation happens in the lives of people; indications that this sort of transformation, in substantial form, happens in people who are not specifically Christian or committed to Christian doctrines; and some suggestions of what religious transformation might look like in particular historical circumstances. My references to various examples have been necessarily brief, intended only to help readers to understand what I mean. Now, we need to make a shift to considering what a Christian leader with a significant level of religious transformation, along with substantial levels of intellectual, psychic, and moral transformation, might look like.

Kenneth R. Melchin and James R. Price have suggested Sargent Shriver as an example of a public figure living the kinds of transformations that I have been addressing.[23] Both scholars have access to the public story of Shriver's life; Price had a personal relationship with Shriver and holds an important role in continuing Shriver's work, giving Price important insights into Shriver's development of interiority. Nonetheless, all the usual caveats apply: undoubtedly, Shriver had a human level of inadequacy, failure, and sin.

I am drawn to the story of Shriver because it is exactly the kind of life that a shrinking church needs: It is a story of one person who engaged in a life of self-appropriation that was also a life of *diakonia* and of being an ambassador of reconciliation—lived by one who knew, in an exact sense, what being an ambassador means in today's context. In *The Call*, Price picks this up as Shriver's personal story, investigating Shriver's choices after the 1960 US presidential election. Shriver returns to Chicago, his beloved home where he has significant work to do, then receives a call from President John F. Kennedy. Shriver is Kennedy's brother-in-law and had been an active part of Kennedy's election campaign but is now ready to return to his regular job (managing the enormous Merchandise Mart building in Chicago for the Kennedy family) and other activities, including providing leadership towards integrating Roman Catholic schools in his role as board chair. Shriver is a successful businessman. He is also an active and dedicated Roman Catholic in the United States when Roman Catholicism was deeply suspect generally and specifically questionable in national leadership.

Kennedy calls Shriver with a request to lead the Peace Corps, an election idea that takes on a life of its own as it grips the imagination of university students. As an idea, the corps has very little content; at the time of Kennedy's phone conversation with Shriver, it is little more than a powerful invitation to American young people to engage with the project of world peace and care by volunteering their skills in countries with limited resources. Shriver has a difficult decision to make. In Price's retelling of a conversation with Shriver about the phone call, expressed in a dialogue with a fictional interlocutor named Didymus (DYD), Shriver (RSS) responds to Kennedy with a choice based in a sense of spiritual call.

> RSS: But when I picked up the phone, I was fully prepared to say no.
> DYD: Yet, you didn't.
> RSS: No I didn't. When the President offered me the role of leading a task force charged with designing the Peace Corps, I felt called to let go of my other plans and say yes to the challenge.
> DYD: What do you mean you felt called?
> RSS: I mean I felt spiritually called.
> DYD: Spiritually?
> RSS: Yes.
> DYD: That's surprising.
> RSS: It always is.[24]

Shriver's language of surprise is the same as Haughton's language of explosion. In both cases, the focus is on the inbreaking of the spirit, the power that Christians call the Holy Spirit. Shriver can recognize this precisely because he has been part of the educational structure that is the church. He goes on to speak of Mary as "the perfect example of spiritual openness," demonstrated in her meeting with the archangel Gabriel.[25] In the story, Mary is "consciously present to the spirit" as Shriver was aware of being in his conversation with President Kennedy.[26] Shriver is sufficiently religiously transformed that he is able to participate in a phone discussion while listening for God's voice and is able to change his life trajectory because he hears God's invitation.

We might, of course, simply reject Shriver's own reading of his choice. Shriver is aware that some people might do so on the grounds that a secular explanation is more acceptable, but that is not his assessment. Similarly, he recognizes the possible sectarian, specifically Christian, reading and insists that everyone has a form of spiritual common sense; others' spiritual senses may differ from Shriver's, but the differences can be transcended precisely because the spirit has freedom and is always active.[27] At a later point in the book, in the context of reflection on a different decision, Shriver will note that the spirit is always present, "Present as a call to recognize and transcend your blind spots... present as a tug to reach for your noblest aspirations... present as an invitation to be your best self."[28] This pneumatology is at the basis of Shriver's approach to the world as fundamentally religious.

On its own, religious transformation carries numerous risks, including the possibility that one might hear the spirit's voice when the spirit is not speaking—or, at least, not saying that which is being heard. Shriver brings a significant level of intellectual transformation to the conversation. Taking the apostle Thomas, commonly known as "doubting Thomas," as his model, Shriver asked the questions that he regarded as relevant, until he found himself satisfied with the answers.[29] As far as he is concerned, the core problem is that he does not know anything about a Peace Corps. Reassured that nobody else does either, and that he is free to follow the spirit in developing the vision and in building the organization, Shriver feels ready to assent.

We have an instance of listening to the spirit, while asking and answering the relevant questions; indeed, listening to the spirit drives questioning. We still have the question of moral transformation. If we accept that God calls people—which is a basic aspect of the Christian narrative, as Shriver points out—then the only reason for refusing Shriver's conclusion that he is listening to the spirit is an insistence that he accepts Kennedy's invitation out of self-interest. Such an argument likely fails on its own terms because Shriver agreed to give up the comfort, happiness, and profitability of life in Chicago, along with the fulfilling and valuable work there, for an uncertain and financially unremunerative public service role in a place that he did not especially like. Shriver's analogy to Mary is significant precisely because it entails a recognition that the tasks of God's reign often entail discomfort, in places that we would not choose, and with little obvious benefit to ourselves. More directly to Shriver's own point, he is aware that his choice could prove to be, in his words, "a false projection of my own aspirations and desires." He responds to both with the previous question about the nature of the role. He also asks Kennedy whether there might be reason to appoint someone else, perhaps a political ally; Shriver has names to suggest. Kennedy's response is that the whole thing could be a complete flop, in which case Shriver would be more easily fired than a non–family member! Self-interest seems to be ruled out as a motivator. Shriver does, indeed, seem to be responding from a stance of concern for the common good.

In *The Call*, Price uses conversations between people (himself and others) and Shriver to construct Platonic-style dialogues, resulting in a representation of the reality that Price has come to know over years of conversation with Shriver. This is hardly a standard academic presentation. Then again, seeking to understand a person's own self-appropriation is not a common academic task. As evidence, Price's work is a bit complicated to use. As example, however, it is outstanding, and Price intends it as indication and invitation: a suggestion that this is the way that interiority worked for Shriver and that, perhaps, if we engage in the life of transformation, we may find some similar realities in ourselves.

We can see an important difference between the example that we have in Phil Connors's life in *Groundhog Day* and the instance of Sargent Shriver (beyond the fact that one is fictional and the other historical): In the movie, we watch the transformation occur in Connors while he lives the change, whereas with Shriver, we are able to learn from his own self-assessment. Shriver is making an effort to be attentive, intelligent, reasonable, and responsible about himself being attentive, intelligent, reasonable, responsible, and loving, in a way that goes beyond the kind of self-awareness that Connors brings. We see that specifically in the quotation about spiritual calling. Shriver is aware of the feelings that he is having and the values that they reflect. He is aware of the meanings he attaches both to the words that he is hearing and to the acts of feeling and valuing that are happening in his personal processes.

For the benefit of all—and, perhaps, especially for those who find *The Call* unsatisfying in its unusual rhetorical device—Price and Melchin provide the larger historical narrative in *Spiritualizing Politics Without Politicizing Religion: The Example of Sargent Shriver*. Shriver was a peacebuilder and a Christian, committed to the work that we have identified as *diakonia* and to being an ambassador of reconciliation. He purposefully and thoughtfully brought his Catholicism to his life and work. In the 1950s Shriver spoke in especially Roman Catholic terms, as is reasonable for someone who became chair of the Catholic School Board in Chicago and worked in relation to the church hierarchy. A shift happens with the work to which Kennedy invited him. He knew that love could change people, moving them from destructive life to constructive.

> In the early 1960s, the years of the Peace Corps, we observe Shriver focusing resolutely on these transformative experiences of love, but now in the transposed language of "spirituality" and "compassion." Moreover, Shriver structured the policies and procedures of the Peace Corps to help create conditions for these transformative experiences.[30]

In creating the corps, Shriver emphasized spiritual values, the kinds of things that we are discussing in the context of religious transformation. He called participants to a spirit of openness to local cultures, fostered by a set of guidelines that emphasize relationship—"learn the language, commit personally to development work, embrace local customs, live at or near local standards of living, cultivate personal integrity, humility, and determination."[31] The key, for Shriver, was to live a life that reflected the kinds of transformations that we have seen and to design organizations that foster them.

This is *diakonia* in operation, the effort to recognize the world's needs and respond to them both individually and structurally. As Shriver envisioned it, the

Peace Corps would be about living the life of service so as to learn the life of service. In this, it becomes an offspring of church, its own kind of educational structure with room for explosions. In building the corps, Shriver served as an ambassador of reconciliation, creating a whole organization of ambassadors of reconciliation. Neither the participants nor the people whom they served would be expected either to be or to become Christians. Nonetheless, Shriver anticipated that they would have experiences of love, experiences of the spirit, experiences of God.

Gospel Focus

The heart of leadership in a shrinking church is found in the desire that others might have, and reflect upon, experiences of God. Leadership demands the ability to form an organization so that it fosters such experiences and enables reflection upon them, along with a willingness to live one's life on the same path. This is the source of the focus that we need. We cannot be about anything and everything. Nor can we simply be about shuffling along well-trod pathways. In a shrinking church, we need to be clear about our purpose, about what we are invited to accomplish. Too easily, leaders can fall into a mindset that focuses upon the basic tasks that come with church leadership roles. For presbyteral clergy, this has tended to mean "the three Ps": preaching, presiding, and pastoral care. Following inherited patterns has the virtue of matching most expectations, including the anticipations of existing church members.

This may have been a satisfactory approach to leadership in the past, or it may have been a mistake and a contributor to present challenges—quite possibly, both. The answer does not really matter. In a shrinking church, this will not suffice. The church's activity must be focused on the gospel task of being ambassadors of reconciliation—a task of which preaching, sacramental life, and engaging with a congregation's needs are no more than parts. We are invited to engage with the whole world in intellectual, psychic, moral, and religious transformation, the life of *diakonia*. This is why Sargent Shriver is a helpful example for us.

The gospel focus is the reason that our next chapter will discuss a specific tool for an organization that seeks to live transformatively. A Gospel Vision Statement (GVS) is a straightforward means of identifying and sustaining the gospel focus of an organization, whether it is a congregation or some other part of a church structure.

Leading Through Big Changes

The gospel focus connects with recent thinking about adaptive leadership. As we have seen, Ronald Heifetz defines leadership as focused on helping people to move forward, tackling difficult challenges. In discussions about the gospel, we have focused on what the church is called to accomplish. Bernard Lonergan and related scholars have helped us to think about some core characteristics that are both goals of the church and aids to leadership—both in the church and elsewhere. From the perspective of leadership theory, what we have done is situated most closely to the transformational leadership model of James MacGregor Burns. Burns argues that leadership is inescapably about morals; its goal must be the moral transformation of people and society, built around "lofty public principles."[32] Otherwise, leadership may motivate, but it will only move an organization toward destructiveness. One major criticism of Burns's approach, raised by Heifetz, is the difficulty of reaching transcultural agreement about the moral goods toward which organizations should be moved. This is a problem that Lonergan has solved for us by establishing a methodological protocol for identifying goods: we ask and answer questions of fact until all relevant queries have been answered, then make moral decisions based on our understanding and on our commitments to love—which reminds us that we would add intellectual, psychic, and religious transformation to Burns's emphasis on moral transformation. This is no cookie-cutter system for producing answers and decisions, but we know that systems generating results of machine-made uniformity will eventually fail to provide helpful outcomes, sometimes disastrously.

Turning to the example of Sargent Shriver and a consideration of some aspects of contemporary leadership theory, we are considering the specific place of leaders in a shrinking church, people whose task is to engage the whole church with the kinds of changes that are necessary at local, national, and international levels. For this, Heifetz's way of thinking about leadership is helpful. Heifetz focuses on leadership as accomplishing adaptive work.

> Adaptive work consists of the learning required to address conflicts in the values people hold, or to diminish the gap between the values people stand for and the reality they face. Adaptive work requires a change in values, beliefs, or behavior. The exposure and orchestration of conflict—internal contradictions—within individuals and constituencies provide the leverage for mobilizing people to learn new ways.[33]

The shrinking church consists of many people who are accustomed to the numerical growth narrative, and to a kind of structural stability provided by denominational and congregational capacities. These expectations and priorities are colliding with a changing reality. This shift does not mean dispensing with our core commitments to transformational life. Instead, the shift is precisely about faithfulness to our fundamental purpose, a point that Heifetz makes in his work. The complex reality is that we can expect challenges in the changes the church is facing precisely because long-treasured patterns are shifting and things that we hold dear are falling away. Adaptive leadership is about connecting new situations and new possibilities with core values of the church.

Heifetz takes us in a direction that should sound remarkably familiar: his approach sets a priority on continuous evaluation. Adaptive leadership points to "the pivotal importance of reality testing in producing socially useful outcomes" and evaluating "leadership in process," rather than waiting until outcomes are clear.[34] Exactly as Lonergan has suggested to us, the question of reasonableness, testing one's conclusions as part of every process of knowing, is paramount. We are invited to ask and answer questions constantly, and to engage in processes of reality checking, and to do so as groups rather than merely as authoritative or authoritarian leaders.

The reader will note a real transition in the book at this point. Our first chapter helped us to think about the church's situation, the core problematic (a confluence of a variety of questions to be resolved) that this book addresses. The second and third chapters focused on what the church says and does that is relevant to our circumstances. Now, we are shifting to direct practical advice for the adaptive work of leading in a shrinking church. As we continue to think about the future of the church, Heifetz's work will serve as an important reminder of the role of leaders in change.

Vulnerability, Courage, Honesty

Brené Brown emphasizes the importance of vulnerability in leadership, not only for Christian organizations, but everywhere. This is one of the places where our discussion of personal transformation and organizational life meet. Brown regards love and belonging as "the catalyst for courage, compassion, and connection," grounds for the possibility of relationships that allow for daring leadership.[35] Love and belonging are the antidotes to shame, the emotion that compromises our ability to take risks. Taking risks means that we will fail or, at least, take actions that produce less than optimal results. The challenge is to cultivate organizations in which risk-taking is encouraged.

Brown understands vulnerability as "the emotion that we experience during times of uncertainty, risk, and emotional exposure."[36] The point of Brown's work is that leaders need to be vulnerable, opening ourselves to uncertainty and being prepared to take risks. If we take Heifetz's work seriously, then we must be ready to engage with real changes that can be tumultuous and may not produce the desired outcomes. This means that we need the community, sustained by mutual love and the sense of belonging fostered by love, that enables risk-taking.

Fostering a capacity for vulnerability and, therefore, for courage in an organization is about developing psychic transformation at a communal level. Brown's point that love makes this psychic change possible is a reminder of the extent to which religious transformation functions as a condition of other transformations. Heifetz frames the challenge in an intriguing way, inviting us to "fall in love with tough decisions"[37] while holding people through their emotions.[38] "When you are leading people through adaptive change, it is their hearts (not their heads) that hold them back. And they will not let you into their hearts if you are not willing to let them into yours."[39] Vulnerability enables an environment of psychological safety, a fundamental condition of a healthy organization; Amy Edmondson describes psychological safety as "a climate where people feel safe enough to take interpersonal risks by speaking up and sharing concerns, questions, or ideas."[40] This is a climate in which communal growth can happen, where opportunities for progress can grow.

One of the implications of intellectual and moral transformation is that it should lead to public honesty, one of the most evident expressions of vulnerability and courage. Public honesty is not the same as saying everything to everyone; privacy is both necessary and legally required for many tasks of leadership. However, in the case of a church challenged by declining membership and resources, there will be a need to speak hard truths. A willingness to face them and communicate about them is decisive in today's church leadership. Some characteristics of true leadership only emerge when an organization is under considerable stress. This may be one of those times. Similarly, some characteristics of faithful discipleship—including the prophetic aspect—only emerge when the church is under significant stress. This may be one of those.

One of the church's resources in challenging times, like these days when long-standing models are breaking down, is the Easter story. This story reminds us of both the pain that can accompany faithful living and the power of God's transformative work in overcoming death. Our annual celebration of Easter reminds us that the Christian story has a narrative of death and resurrection at its core. Christ died and rose again, announcing that God's love is victorious.

We, the church, are called to live into the Easter story. In an important sense, death is always with us. We bring our organizations into existence to serve God's transformative work in places and times. Our organizations can die because God's transformation of the world does not ultimately depend upon us, as much as particular ministries and people might need us. God has ways of working with us even when our cherished organizational bodies have died. Moreover, God has hands and feet that are not ours. The church will continue even if my seminary/congregation/synod/diocese/denomination should cease to exist. God would continue to transform the world, engaging with all of creation in divine love, even if the whole formal structure of the church were to cease existing. The resurrection of Christ Jesus did not depend upon my capacity to change my world.

As Christians, we must be ready to live with death. This applies to us personally, of course; it also affects us institutionally. We must be ready to see our church organizations—including our whole denominations—die. We cannot live into biases, seeking to live in ways that are focused on ourselves and our needs. We are invited to see God in action in the world even as we see shrinking numbers in our pews, even as we close institutions.

Theologically, this places a responsibility on the shoulders of leaders to proclaim death and resurrection, saying the hard things that must be said about impending death. Pep talks will not serve. The pulpit is there for challenging and prophetic words, not merely for words of comfort. If our commitment to being ambassadors of reconciliation goes missing or becomes brittle because we are averting our eyes from the implications of shrinking resources, leaders bear the load of announcing this.

That said, as a church we must also remember that the point of Easter is not that church leaders, notably clergy, are expected to suffer on the cross for us. News of congregational challenge is often left to the clergy, which is entirely appropriate in some denominational systems and less so in others. However, responses that blame the clergy or insist that younger or livelier or something-er clergy would have changed the outcome are commonly unfair. Such grumbling misses the point that this book seeks to make: The church is shrinking, and that is not the fault of leaders. Instead, the community needs to take to heart challenging words about death and resurrection and find better answers, whether that involves different directions or straightforward closure.

Commitment to Ongoing Formation

One of the joys of being a Christian, formed in stories that are thousands of years old, is that we can and do look to different places and times for examples of how to live today. There are some remarkable similarities between the life of the early church and the circumstances that we are living into. The most obvious is that the early church was not at the center of society; it was essentially countercultural. Although Christianity still has far more influence in the core Anglosphere world than we tend to recognize (especially in the USA), our shrinking numbers are slowly letting the air out of that tire. In the longer term, we will probably be small, somewhat scattered, and no longer a fundamentally defining characteristic of Anglosphere nations. Declining numbers in churches, combined with a growing commitment on the part of broader society to inclusive politics, will increase our experience of life on the margins and remind us that the gospel may ensure that we belong in this world but always in a transformative way.

However, though there are ways in which our experience of church begins to resemble early church life, we also live with profound differences, ensuring that we cannot easily adopt their models. The most obvious change is that we now have two millennia of being church behind us. The world is familiar with aspects of our history, both creative and destructive, so that other people already have expectations and fears that we must navigate. Related to this is extensive theological development. We now teach theology historically, because the questions that we raise and the equipment that we have available to answer them are different from the early church's questions and tools. Another big shift, one that affects all of us daily, is that we live in a highly complex, continually developing regulatory and legal environment. The sorts of informal structures, with limited oversight, little or no professional guidance, and no insurance, that were normal possibilities even

100 years ago are no longer an option. Can you imagine a church with no recourse to insurance, lawyers, or accountants? Even the thought evokes a painful visceral response. That would be an organization just asking for trouble.

These are not the only changes. I am certain that you can identify others. One important consequence of these shifts is that church leadership today has become a very large and very complex task. One of the criticisms that a seminary president hears is the one about how education has changed. "Students are not learning as much about [fill in the blank] as they did in my day!" This tends to reflect a failure to notice how many other things our students now need to learn. People who teach prospective church leaders today are a dedicated lot; generally, they could have a much more comfortable life if they had taken up some other discipline or activity. Similarly, today's students preparing for church leadership are, on the whole, interested and committed; mostly, people do not seek to be church leaders today because they are seeking an easy life, high salaries, or respect and deference in the world. The challenge for today's students is that they need to master an exceptionally broad range of skills, both because of the adjustment to a world in which the church is shrinking and because of an accumulation of tasks focused on church leaders—especially presbyteral leaders (pastors, ministers, priests).

One consequence is that many leaders are not fully equipped for the roles that they are expected to fulfill. That is normal. Many religious organizations, whether congregations or other bodies, are led by people whose primary training is the Master of Divinity (MDiv) degree, which is broad in its coverage and designed as preliminary preparation for congregational ministry. There is far too much material to cover, with 2,000 years of historical and theological development and a complex contemporary environment for ministry. Moreover, even specialized MDiv programs rarely teach people how to help an organization get smaller and more focused or take the drastic steps that may be necessary. Mobilizing people to tackle tough problems that directly contravene the inherited and prevailing narrative of numerical growth is not the first priority of the MDiv degree or, indeed, most degrees.

This is where lifelong learning and abilities development becomes a priority, especially in relation to nontraditional skills. Many clergy focus their continuing education on preaching. This makes sense because preaching is important. However, clergy and other church leaders need to be adventurous about educational growth. True intellectual transformation means a willingness to ask and answer questions that we have not asked before, aware that we might get answers that we have not considered and may not like. Are attendance numbers down in your congregation(s)? Are volunteers becoming difficult to get? Does your congregation lack energy or direction? Better preaching may not be enough. Today's leaders need to focus on developing capacities for understanding congregations and communities, for thinking about and leading through change—including when change may be disruptive, even painful, for the church.

One response to this situation that we are seeing in the seminary context is the growth of advanced degree programs, especially the Doctor of Ministry (DMin). The DMin degree is designed to enable people who are in church leadership to develop higher level skills and to undertake research that helps to move the church forward on practical issues in church life.

Other church leaders are undertaking MBA (Master of Business Administration) degrees or related certificate programs. These may be among the most valuable options in continuing education for clergy. More and more often, church leaders whose training is for preaching, presiding, and pastoral care find themselves in management roles. They have little or no background in the complexities of today's management, human resources, public relations, conflict resolution, financial operations, and government relations fields. Intellectual transformation always happens in relation to specific fields, where we ask and answer specific questions; organizational theory has become a complex area with all kinds of specialized knowledge about psychology, systems theory, innovation, coaching, etc. Although college and university courses may not fit church situations precisely, a lot of material can translate. Indeed, because governments and the public have very high expectations of churches and other nonprofits today, and failure to meet expectations can have significant legal and other consequences, church leaders are wise to focus seriously on skills development in management areas.

Working in teams is now a necessity, in addition to being a blessing. Church leaders can benefit from learning team training and leadership skills. Becoming a trained leadership coach is a great way to develop capacities for team and organizational leadership.

The key priority is continued growth, both in self-appropriation and in understanding of the world, driven by curiosity and a sense of (personal and) the church's need. There are many skills to be mastered and many challenges to be faced. Continued personal growth is very likely to lead in unexpected directions, rather than simply refining age-old skills.

From the perspective of church organizations, including congregations, this may mean a significant shift in how people treat continuing education. Every part of church structures needs to take ongoing education seriously, as a priority that affects the capacity of the church to serve its mission. Indeed, continuing education is now needed for sheer survival. The church is an organization composed of many organizations—definitionally, a complex system—along with being many other things. We are not immune from the pressures, both internal and external, that organizations face. At the same time, we are shrinking, rapidly, limiting our available resource base. Church leaders need a sophisticated array of skills, along with our traditional commitments to worship, proclamation, and pastoral care.

And, when I say "church leaders," I don't mean only clergy. . .

Exercises: Leadership in a Shrinking Church

A. Your Life

1. In places in your life where you show leadership (not just church), identify ways that the four transformations (intellectual, psychic, moral, religious) could be helpful.

2. Imagine that you are in Sargent Shriver's place. How would you respond to President Kennedy? Are there other questions that you would ask?

B. Your Organization

1. Heifetz defines adaptive leadership as "the practice of mobilizing people to tackle tough challenges and thrive."[41] From our discussion, what aspects of adaptive leadership seem to be most important? Does Heifetz's model sound appropriate and helpful for your organization today? Does this sound like something that you could do? Are there other people in your organization who can do this?

2. Does caring for people's emotions seem important to adaptive leadership? Why and/or why not?

3. How can your organization identify leaders who can work in an adaptive leadership context?

4. What are the tough challenges in your organization?

5. Are significant changes happening or soon to happen in your organization? If so, identify them and indicate whether they are connected to numerical shifts in the church.

6. Does your organization have a sense of purpose that is consistent with what we have said about transformation and *diakonia*? If leaders followed the adaptive model, would they be facing challenges in meeting existing goals, or would part of the work be identifying new goals?

C. The World

1. Suggest some ways that adaptive leadership could help your organization to foster transformation and *diakonia* in the world.

CHAPTER 5

HOW CHURCH LEADERSHIP BECAME TOO BIG AND LOST FOCUS

We need to address the history of church leadership because it is what we inherit. We have developed a church structure that is built around the presbyterate—leadership by people who are variously called priests, pastors, or ministers. As a consequence, expectations of the presbyterate have become excessive and the church now finds the work of naming its task and living into it very difficult. This chapter is an effort to tell something of the story—in broad brushstrokes—of how we got here, with a consideration of the last 1,000 years of church organizational development, so that we can begin to imagine our way out of this challenging corner.

The Presbyteral Church

Predominantly, church leadership has been presbyteral. This form of leadership has tended to be defined by tasks, such as preaching, presiding, and pastoral care. Task definition is a way of imagining leadership that I am rejecting. Precisely the point of Heifetz's emphasis upon enabling people in an organization to make major change is that it focuses upon what the organization is called to be, rather than the basic tasks of day-to-day operation. The other thing to be noted is that even as denominations have emphasized different aspects of presbyteral leadership (and, therefore, developed differently), history has generally been marked by the accumulation of tasks, rather than choices among them. In this section, I will outline a rough set of clergy models, as I understand them, beginning in the eleventh century.

Please remember, therefore, that I am not presenting these models as if some of today's presbyteral clergy belong specifically to one model, while others belong to another. My point is precisely the opposite, in fact. The priorities of presbyters have changed multiple times over the past millennium, which is a good thing because the priorities of church have changed also. However, the role of presbyters has not, generally, moved from one model to the next. Instead, presbyters have commonly been expected to keep the old role while adding the new. Differences among presbyteral job descriptions are often about emphasis, rather than overall expectation; most, perhaps all, are required to function in multiple models, if not every one. The result has been a destructive transformation by accumulation, in which the responsibilities of presbyters have increased until they are simply untenable. In short, presbyteral leadership in the church has become too big a task for anyone. A shrinking church has revealed the failure of this approach.

We will also see an interaction between specifically religious expectations (the relationship with God), and broadly cultural intellectual developments (which might or might not have an obviously religious side). This interaction is present in every model and every shift to a newer model. It is, however, most evident in more recent developments—twentieth century onward—as secularization has taken hold in society.

The core focus of a priest, in the High Middle Ages (roughly 1000–1300 CE) was sacramental. The primary job description of a priest was to perform baptisms, masses, and burials[1] enabling the people to remain safely within the sacramental system by which they were saved and sustained. In theory, the high medieval world was understood as defined by a carefully constructed order, although sources differ on how that order was understood. God was understood as reigning over all, with the angels immediately below. Beneath God and the angels, in some arrangement (accounts differ because of local realities and great debates) were the pope, kings, lords, bishops, and abbots; beneath them were members of religious orders, then secular priests, then ordinary laypeople. While there is a lack of clarity about the higher orders, there is certainty about the superiority of clergy to ordinary laypeople, i.e., anyone not of the nobility.[2]

The Gregorian reforms of the eleventh century sought to reduce the power of lay rulers (kings and lords) over priests, emphasizing the extraordinary priestly capacity to undertake the act of transubstantiation, by which bread and wine are understood to become the body and blood of Christ.[3] The basic task of a priest became the work of saying mass, ensuring that people could view the elements that reminded them of the presence of the holy and powerful among them in the church. By this means, the priest connected the (powerless or nearly so) vast majority of the population to God and to the larger meanings of the religious and political community, thereby helping to sustain the overall order. People (and peoples) could be disciplined with excommunication, so that they would not be able to see a valid mass—and were, by definition, outside the divine order and in danger of hellfire. Baptism enabled people to enter into the church community, where they would be sustained by seeing mass; Christian burial conveyed people safely to a God-sustained afterlife. Functionally, priests also served as an educated class, especially participating in legal roles related to matters such as property on the strength of the literacy skills that priests were more likely than laypeople to possess,[4] but this was more a byproduct of education than a specifically priestly role; any educated person could do this. Priestly activity, specifically defined, was about standing in the presence of the holy and making it manifest for the people, who would then be reassured of their place in the divinely established order.

Perhaps the most purely priestly activity was the votive mass for special intention, in which a priest said a mass—commonly a private mass—for someone who had donated a sum of money to pay for the service. In the late medieval period, chantries emerged in England as chapels dedicated to masses for the souls of the dead; although some chantries provided some social benefits (such as occasional alms for the poor and rare examples of attached schools) until their destruction in the sixteenth century, their real purpose was simply saying masses meant to limit time in purgatory by ensuring that the souls continue to be held in the holiness that the church brings to the human order.[5]

Along with the priority of sacramental life stood, quite literally, an emphasis upon the buildings where the sacraments were enacted. Between the eleventh and fifteenth centuries, Europe was engaged in a massive exercise in church construction, which one author has dubbed "the Gothic enterprise."[6] One estimate suggests that, by 1350 CE, "there was one church for every 200 inhabitants of France and England, and that the English cities of Norwich, Lincoln, and York, with populations in the range of 5,000 to 10,000, each had forty to fifty churches."[7] These were commonly in the Gothic style, employing pointed arches, flying buttresses, and vaulted roofs to accomplish the magic of bright, colorful interiors and a vertical orientation soaring and gesturing toward the heavens. Such an extraordinary building spree, with structures that required skill to construct, along with care and attention to maintain, ensured that a significant part of presbyteral work was building-related. In an important sense, the sacramental life, because it emphasizes the visible and physical as an expression of the invisible and spiritual, may be taken to imply a preoccupation with church buildings. They serve as sacramental announcements to the world of the sacraments unfolding within. For many Christians, this is part of their enduring power, which we shall note into the present day. At the same time, we do well to remember that such buildings were not necessarily created with the church's needs in mind. Their excessive number, along with the spectacular quantity of architectural ornament and sheer size of many structures, are reminders that the glory of monarchs, nobles, and leading churchmen played a significant part in bringing these places into being.[8] This is another way of saying that considerations other than the gospel defined the building creation and care responsibilities of ordinary presbyters, who might be proud of the new structures or might find them merely troublesome but who definitely had the long-term task of serving the building along with the God it honored.

The purely sacramental way of imagining the presbyteral role ended with the Reformation, for both Protestants and Roman Catholics. The medieval worldview collapsed, while other visions came to the fore. However, for many Christians, the sacramental life remained central, with the Eucharist as the act that routinely renews the bond between believers and the divine order in heaven and on earth, or it has been rediscovered as having this meaning in nineteenth-century church transformations and the liturgical renewal movement of the 1970s and 1980s. Liturgical renewal in the twentieth century was sparked by a combination of growing historical scholarship, including the 1945 publication of *The Shape of the Liturgy* by Anglican scholar Dom Gregory Dix,[9] and by the post–World War II burst of ecumenical activity.[10] The result has been the emergence of a variety of liturgies built around similar principles and rooted in early eucharistic development. One consequence is that eucharistic leadership is still central to church life, with the result that presbyteral leadership—which is required for the Eucharist by most Christians—remains at the heart of church leadership. Another consequence is that liturgical leadership has become more complex for many leaders, who are expected to make use of a broad variety of liturgical resources in order to suit eucharistic worship to the seasons of the liturgical year, the biblical readings for a specific celebration, the church's priorities (war, peace, justice, mourning. . .), and the congregation's capacities. The priority of eucharistic celebration remains an important part of church leadership, and the complexity and labor involved have grown.

Returning to our models, we see the next presbyteral model that was introduced by Martin Luther and the Reformation. Luther's focus was on the Word, Christ as both accomplisher and message of salvation, as described in Holy Scripture.[11] The Eucharist continued to be an important presbyteral activity, but (for Protestants) the meaning shifted to emphasize the gospel as Luther expressed it: through Christ's death and resurrection, sinful humanity is justified before the holy God and brought into right relationship. The eucharistic elements continue to be holy but come to be understood as proclamation of divine forgiveness and invitation. The presbyter, therefore, continued to preside at Eucharist, but with a greater expectation of participants partaking instead of viewing.

More decisively, the Eucharist became an aspect of the proclaiming work of the pastor (note the shift in language from "priest"), which became the true center of presbyteral work. The core of the pastor's job came to be preaching and teaching the Word, communicating the gospel of God's justifying work and the resulting freedom given to the Christian. Luther did not intend that this role of proclamation should belong to the pastor alone. His intention was quite the opposite, anticipating that everyone would communicate the good news, starting in the family context. Luther even provided suitable materials, including the *Small Catechism* that continues to be used by Lutherans for Christian education.

Parenthetically, I note that this shift to a focus on proclamation and a desire for formation in the home did not remove the emphasis upon buildings. In Protestant areas, especially where Reformed and Anabaptist Christianity were dominant, there was often significant transformation in the buildings. Rood screens were taken down, statues removed or shattered, stained glass windows broken and replaced. However, while religious houses might be closed, cathedrals and parish churches largely remained, though with changed symbolism and function. Indeed, more churches were built to accommodate the growing variety of denominational identity. Creating and caring for church buildings remained central to the work of presbyters and even more necessary as competing denominations established structures cheek by jowl with existing ones.

Returning to our story, I note that the role of proclaiming the gospel rapidly became more complicated than Luther could have anticipated. Not only did presbyters, in preaching and teaching, need to clarify their differences from various Roman Catholic positions, including those established in the Counter-Reformation, but presbyters also needed to distinguish among a variety of Protestant understandings emerging in the sixteenth century and following. The differences between Lutheran, Zwinglian, Calvinist, Arminian, and other theological positions could be subtle but were often strongly held. Woe betide the person who got the answer wrong for their context! In other words, Luther might have intended that proclamation be shared by everyone in the congregation, but the complexities of theological difference rapidly ensured that this work would belong to trained professionals. In parallel, the Counter-Reformation meant that Roman Catholic priests needed more complex theological training, so they could distinguish their own positions from the variety of Protestant stances; this is the impetus that gave rise to modern seminaries. Moreover, theological developments also caused changes in worship style, so that proclamation demanded concomitant liturgical awareness.

This emphasis on preaching and teaching as the complex work of educated professionals who are capable of dedicating significant amounts of time to thought and preparation received two powerful boosts in the period of the seventeenth to twentieth centuries. The first was a series of important philosophical developments rooted in the work of Enlightenment thinkers. Transformations in Western philosophy did not leave Christianity untouched. Many philosophers of the time were also theologians, and while both presbyters and laypeople might leave the texts of Thomas Hobbes, René Descartes, John Locke, and Immanuel Kant untouched, the arguments they and others advanced have had a real impact on street-level thinking. The conversations have become more complicated and the necessary thinking more sophisticated.

Theological reflection is not the only part of presbyteral intellectual activity to have become more complex. Preceding Luther, in the fifteenth and early sixteenth centuries, new ways of reading texts—often with a skeptical eye—began to emerge. Critiques of the "Donation of Constantine" by Lorenzo Valla[12] and others, combined with work on the biblical text by Erasmus of Rotterdam and others[13] heralded more complex approaches to interpretation. The philosophical developments of the eighteenth through the twentieth centuries, however, supercharged the creation of modern critical methods of reading in both historical and narrative modes.[14] To understand the text more accurately, students of the Bible are expected to have significant familiarity with these tools of interpretation and be able to employ them. Before preaching or teaching, the presbyter is now expected to use multiple commentaries and other resources to understand, as much as possible, the intended meaning of the text. Communicating the gospel, therefore, in most Christian contexts in the Western world, is now a highly sophisticated activity dependent upon extensive learning and, more to our point, substantial work in the course of a presbyter's week.

In the twentieth century, transformations in presbyteral leadership continued, even accelerated. The next approach to consider is the professional model, with two aspects: therapeutic care and management. One of the effects of the intellectual growth that we have been tracing from the fifteenth century onward, and especially beginning in the seventeenth century, has been a strengthening of the so-called "hard sciences" (e.g., physics, chemistry, biology), with their emphasis upon measurability and repeatability, and the emergence of social sciences that attempt to develop their own methods consistent with the expectations of the hard sciences. The social sciences have had significant effects on the education and work of presbyters, most notably in what I call the professionalization of presbyters. The term "professional" previously meant simply membership in one of the professions: clergy, medicine, law. In my usage here, reasonably consistent with contemporary usage, it means something more like "possessed of formal qualifications, as defined by the relevant discipline, and prepared by an institute of advanced education (preferably one teaching at the graduate level)." In this sense, presbyters have become professionals.[15]

We will first consider the therapeutic aspect of professionalization. Pastoral care has been a responsibility of presbyters since before the period beginning in the eleventh century, the time that we are considering. However, prior to the twentieth century, pastoral care tended to be defined by specifically theological priorities. These might be sacramental or proclamatory or disciplinary, or might simply be about caring for people. The invention and progressive refinement of psychology, sociology, and related disciplines changed this.

In the twentieth century, pastoral care ceased to be either a theological or a human skill; instead, it became a highly trained scientific skill, a discipline that often receives far more time and attention in seminary education (for many seminaries) than any other field. Most seminary students receive three kinds of training in the discipline: classes, clinical pastoral education (now a formal program arrangement, designated as CPE), and congregational experience. All of these are either innovations or so transformed as to be effectively brand new in the twentieth century. Insofar as trainees had formal classwork in prior periods, it tended to focus on theology, liturgy, and, especially in Protestant circles, biblical studies (with a substantial dose of Hebrew and Greek). The move to CPE, specifically identified as professional and modeled in part on medical training, represented a significant shift in the preparation of clergy.[16] The purpose was to introduce social scientific theory in a practical setting, enabling clergy to take advantage of the latest developments at a high formal level, in a movement linked to the development of presbyteral training as a graduate-school activity and the appearance of the Master of Divinity degree.

Today, students ordinarily begin with at least one class in spiritual care, introducing them to relevant theory and often incorporating casework. This is followed by 480 hours of Clinical Pastoral Education (CPE), now a specific program with its own formalized approaches and trained supervisors, usually located in a hospital. CPE follows an "Action-Reflection" model, in which students engage in pastoral work on hospital wards, then meet with other students and a supervisor in order to reflect on some experience from their work in light of the theories to which they've been introduced. Those training to be chaplains often require two or three of these CPE "units." In addition, students will also undertake some sort of internship or fieldwork experience, usually with a clergy supervisor who will often have some training in supervision and a responsibility to submit formal reports to the seminary and/or judicatory. The skills developed in CPE are intended to be transferable to all pastoral situations, including home visits and street-level interactions. When the minister/pastor/priest visits, a parishioner is in highly trained hands.

The twentieth century was also the moment when we were introduced to management and administration as a field of formal study. The Master of Business Administration became a degree, and a very popular one. Although presbyters are not expected to have extensive training in this area, they are required to function in a world designed for it. Building management, human resources, and financial management are now complex tasks. Lay people may take leadership roles in relation to some of these matters, but presbyters are also expected to have skills in all of them. Presbyters are often personnel managers, with paid staff and volunteers. On a daily basis, presbyters make decisions about buildings that their organizations occupy and often rent to others. Presbyters are involved with writing and administering budgets as part of their ordinary tasks. All these pieces require significant practical, legal, and mission-related judgments, affecting multiple stakeholders and potentially creating substantial liability.

On top of all this, and without losing any of these considerations, many church members have become aware that their numbers are declining. This collides with a basic aspect of their church expectations: numerical growth. Therefore, presbyters are expected to take leadership around mission efforts that are oriented toward enlarging congregations. The emphasis upon raising numbers is partly oriented toward supporting buildings. In the 1960s, parts of the Anglosphere went through an enormous church construction spree, especially in the new suburbs that surrounded growing cities.[17] Plus, many of those medieval church buildings are still around; one estimate suggests that close to half of the nearly 19,000 ecclesiastical buildings in England and Wales date to the Middle Ages.[18] Presbyters are expected to increase the numbers of people in congregations partly so that the large numbers of small church communities can sustain buildings that are either aging and expensive or very old and very expensive.

We have accumulated, in the lives of most presbyters, the following priorities: eucharistic leadership, building construction and maintenance, preaching and teaching, therapeutic level pastoral care, trained management, and numbers-oriented mission. All of these continue to develop. The biggest transformation has been the introduction of the digital world, which includes every model and dramatically changes all of them. Presbyters, therefore, are expected to be capable in all these areas in the traditional (pre-2019 or, as I measure the world's time, Before COVID-19 Era) sense and in the contemporary/digital (2019 onward or COVID-19 Era) sense. This adds a whole new layer of expertise that presbyters are expected to demonstrate. We have placed very high expectations on the shoulders of presbyters. At the same time, we commonly offer small salaries and an assumption of mobility that tests personal relationships and family ties. This would be a tough gig even in a growing church.

However, our churches are not growing. As we have seen, they are shrinking, with all the concomitant effects of fewer participants and lay leaders, declining financial and other resources, and accelerating building issues. I have deliberately treated developments in presbyteral expectations at some length in order to encourage a feeling response.

Parishioners: This is why your minister/pastor/priest has considered quitting.
Presbyters: This is why you feel the way that you do.
The question before us is, "What can we do about it?"

Leadership in the Church: Today and Tomorrow

Our definition of leadership helps us to understand the models that we have seen, both from the perspective of how the models are helpful and how they are unhelpful. In an important sense, our discussion of models has slipped into a different way of thinking about leadership. We have been addressing presbyteral leadership—which is an important, often defining, part of overall church leadership—as if it were merely an accumulation of tasks. Unfortunately, the church very often does exactly that, and the task view is part of the problem with church leadership in a moment of profound change.

The challenge goes like this: Leading change is very difficult if the job is defined in terms of tasks, and the tasks are overwhelming. There are some things that can be done about this situation. The first is to clarify what church leadership is about today, and for that we will return to some of the things that we have already discussed. The second is to foster a team that can pick up necessary work that clergy need to drop in order to do their primary work. The third is to let go of tasks that do not contribute sufficiently to the work that needs to be done.

All the suggestions that have been named must be structured around a sense of purpose. In a later chapter, we will discuss the Gospel Vision Statement (GVS), which is an instrument designed to enable a church organization to develop, express, and follow a sense of purpose that serves the life of ambassadorship, of expressing what God means in us. The GVS will make concrete the overall sense of direction that leaders need if they are to lead in a shrinking church.

Before we reach that point, however, we can clarify some things about the work of presbyteral and other church leaders. Be aware that nearly everyone in the church thinks about leadership in terms of tasks. Church leaders must expect to feel pressure to be task-focused, both from others and from themselves. Tasks can keep you busy and make you look like you are doing your job and doing it well. Unfortunately, while you fill your calendar with work, your organization will keep shrinking.

Your real work, as distinct from anything that might show up in a job description, is (as Heifetz says) to mobilize people to solve tough problems. Your tough problem is very likely to revolve around finding gospel purpose and direction for your organization, even if that purpose is a healthy closure. This means that you need to keep your eyes on the bigger picture. The tasks that you keep to yourself must be tasks that you can shape so that they fit with what the organization is trying to accomplish. If and when you preside, if and when you preach, if and when you visit, if and when you engage with new ministries, you must always be considering how these activities serve the real work. If necessary, take time during your week to journal or otherwise reflect on your effectiveness in doing this.

The above means that you very likely will not be able to carry the whole load that people assign to you. One of the key characteristics of today's church leadership is that we need to work in teams. Many denominations are working hard to provide training for lay leaders, to strengthen their capacities to fulfill their roles as participants in the life of the church. Theologically and practically, this is a good thing because it identifies a significant flaw in the leadership-as-task approach: Most of the tasks that seem to be important and constitutive of being church have become focused on presbyters. There is reason to be disappointed that the pressure of a shrinking church has been needed to make us begin to change, but the change is real. Working in teams helps to share the load. Perhaps more powerfully, it helps to share the insights, making possible a whole kind of learning and growth that might not otherwise happen. A healthy team can also provide emotional and spiritual support, with shared prayer and concern.

A big part of the task of all church leaders, including presbyteral leaders, is to find volunteers and train them. Pastoral care teams are one example of what can be done; there are many others, because much of the church's life consists of activities that laypeople are able to do—and laypeople may have more relevant skills and training for some of them. The other aspect of teamwork is that congregations can be—and often are—served by teams of leaders. In this context, deacons play a growing role. Deacons do different things in different denominations. Historically, however, their priority has been *diakonia*, both undertaking its tasks and mobilizing others to them, as the name "deacon" suggests. An ambassadorial church is strengthened by the inclusion in leadership of people who emphasize *diakonia*, whether or not they wear the title of deacon.

Awkwardly, the team approach may be more necessary than it has been for much of recent memory, but often we need to do it when we are working with fewer people and resources. Fine. If you cannot do a task and there are no volunteers to do it, then that task cannot be done. If the church cannot function without that task being completed, then the church is ready for closure. When a congregation I was serving opted to close, this was exactly the process. We reached a point at which necessary volunteer roles could not be filled, so congregation members looked at one another and said, "I guess this is it. Time to close."

Many of the tasks that we do, however, are not truly necessary. I have commented before that when I arrived at the seminary where I serve, our convocation week was crammed full of activities. It was, in one way, fun and exciting, but it was also a crushing load. And, sometimes, it did not work very well because we simply did not have the staff needed to do everything properly. The solution was simple: We cut down on the convocation week schedule. There was some disappointment, and we lost some benefits. However, we are now all much saner at graduation events.

Look around your organization. If you and your leaders are overstressed, consider the question of what you can do without. Cutting may be painful, but so is overfunctioning and, of course, closing. One way or another, you are likely to face deep emotions in the group.

Exercises: How Church Leadership Became Too Big and Lost Focus

A. Your Life

1. Think about your leadership role(s) in the church. Does what you do lighten the load on a presbyter, taking some of the work we have identified in our models off the presbyter's shoulders?
2. Do you prefer a presbyter-centered church structure? Why or why not?
3. If your church is presbyter-centered, and if it were to move to a team approach, would you be willing and able to train and serve in a leadership role? If so, what sort of role would fit your gifts and calling?

B. Your Organization

1. Is your church presbyter-centered? How many of the models that we have discussed apply to presbyters in your congregations? Do you know whether your presbyters prefer it that way?
2. If your organization is not a congregation, is it centered on presbyteral or episcopal leadership? If so, what are the benefits to that? What are the limitations?
3. What limitations can you identify for a team approach to leadership in congregations and other church organizations? How do those limitations affect your understanding of the best way forward?
4. In earlier chapters, we have discussed the idea of shifting the church's focus to four kinds of transformation in the world (intellectual, psychic, moral, religious) and some of the exercise questions have emphasized thinking about ways that your church could do this better. What are some ways that your current church structure supports these changes? What are some ways that your current church structure limits or prevents these changes?

C. The World

1. This passage was rather internally focused, addressing the church's way of organizing itself. If you look closely at the changes that happened, however, you will notice that new models of presbyteral ministry appeared in response to changes in all of society. In addition to declining membership, what other changes in the world affect the church's future?
2. Are there ways that presbyters following these models have contributed to good changes in the world? What are some of the benefits of these developments for the church's relationships to other people?

CHAPTER 6

UNDER PRESSURE

I was with a large group of clergy, assembling to put on all our official garments—we call it "vesting," in case you have missed out on the opportunity to pile on the layers before a clergy occasion—when an archdeacon (a senior clergyperson who has a supervisory role in relationship to multiple parishes in a geographic area) came in looking very frustrated. I was friendly with him, and I had a leadership role, so naturally I asked what was up. "There's this parish where things keep blowing up and the situation makes no sense at all. I don't know why there's this explosion over here and that explosion over there." A few minutes of conversation easily clarified the situation. The parish was shrinking, had been for years, and parishioners were starting to notice.

The difficulty with all that we have discussed so far is that it can be very challenging to live transformatively when your organization is shrinking. Indeed, the larger themes can come to seem distant and irrelevant, even Pollyannaish, when everything is blowing up, and blowing up is exactly what tends to happen as numerical decline takes hold.

The purpose of this chapter is to draw our attention to important characteristics of numerical decline situations. The aspects that I name are common in systems that are growing in awareness of their challenge, in my experience, even if the gravity of the situation has not fully surfaced.

Before we jump into these pieces, though, I think that there might be some value in pointing out a shift in tone and approach that you have probably noticed. Chapters 1–5 focused on the groundwork—sociological, historical, philosophical, and theological—that we have needed to get us into the explicitly organization-oriented transformational work. Chapters 6–10 move into ways to put our principles to use in the organizations where we live.

High Anxiety

The first thing that emerges in a church feeling decline is a high level of anxiety. Everyone starts to feel the stress. Remember my opening story about arriving at the seminary where I am in leadership? Remember my reflections on the basic misunderstandings about the size and function of the organization? At that time in my life, I was doing some work with the Enneagram (a personality-typing tool that distinguishes among nine different emphases), asking about its usefulness. I do think that it has some value, but I am not interested in that debate right now. I can say that it gave me no help then. Why? Because pretty much everyone in the internal system was functioning as a phobic six. According to the Enneagram, people who function as phobic sixes tend to be loyal, hardworking, and reliable, but also subject to anxiety, stress, and insecurity; foreseeing trouble, they tend to worry and become unpredictable.[1] The system had generated so much stress and uncertainty that anxiety was the overriding characteristic of everyone in the system, in part because the people who worked there were genuinely loyal, hardworking, and committed, regardless of how one might assess their personalities. Of course, further experience gave me deeper insight into everyone. More to the point, though, we could not really change the system until we admitted that we had become small and were still shrinking, and decided that we were prepared to change, so high levels of anxiety remained for quite a while.

The archdeacon was encountering these sorts of anxieties. He was also noticing something else that occurs in highly stressed systems: unpredictability. The kinds of eruptions that he was seeing were irrational; they were not directly or logically connected to the source stresses, nor could they be evidently helpful toward resolution of the stresses. They were not obviously a consequence of declining membership, nor could they be understood as steps toward resolving the pressures of decline. Troubles were popping up all over the place and were, if anything, accelerating decline rather than mitigating it.

The pressure of decline adds new energy to old fissures and fault lines in the community, including ones that had never been named or even noticed. These need not be directly associated with the real problem, and they are unlikely to disappear until real work is done on the challenge of decline. Leaders need to see beyond the immediate stresses and prevent anxiety from controlling the story.

Warriors Emerge

Decades ago, a friend and I were both making a change, moving from the Christian heritages in which we grew up into a different denomination. This proved to be a healthy move for us. Our new religious home turned out to meet my basic criterion: Every denomination has challenges, so make sure that the church you join has challenges that you can endure along with elements that you can celebrate. Initially, our new congregation was a great place to be. It was a small community, but very engaged, with lively worship, friendly people, and plenty of opportunity for lay involvement. My friend and I became very active participants and were confirmed and married there (to each other!). I was elected to the church's council, even though I was a recent arrival. Perhaps I should have recognized this as a warning signal in addition to being an honor.

Warning of what? Well, unfortunately, the congregation was near the edge on the viability scale, depending upon the services of an older clergyperson—due for retirement—who donated a large portion of their salary back to congregational coffers. The congregation needed to keep the same clergy for financial reasons, even as age and other considerations meant retirement would be a good thing. In this context, the congregation really needed to sit down and come to terms with its challenge. That is not what happened. Instead, the newly recognized stresses of aging leadership and potential financial difficulty were subsumed into longstanding differences.

That is when the warriors emerged. The stress associated with questions of viability means that important things can become even more emotionally loaded, while unimportant things appear to be crucial. Disagreements that should have been minor, such as the process for choosing music or how the collection would be received, became major flash points in a substantial battle. The strong personalities that might have ordinarily been great assets in rebuilding became leaders in war.

I had seen these patterns develop before. I have watched it happen both at congregational and regional (synod, diocese, conference, etc.) levels. If an organization has not simply run out of energy, which also happens, then the strength that remains tends to be focused internally, in internecine squabbles. Sometimes, these concern major issues of mission and future. Often, they are focused at a much more mundane level, such as how much clergy time can be afforded and what parts of congregational life should receive clergy focus.

For many, the anxiety that accompanies declining numbers is rooted in the fear of loss of home. One refrain that I have heard too often from people is that their local church's doors must remain open until they die. After that, the place can close. The church is their home, and they will not give it up regardless of the implications for the congregation or larger church body. Home, in this case, designates the place where their grandparents and parents contributed mementos, may even have helped to create the building; home designates the place where they met their spouses; where they saw their children baptized, grow, and get married; where they have established friendships that have lasted a lifetime and seen them through hard days; where they built pews, fashioned hangings, cleaned windows and communion pieces. This sense of home is one reason that membership numbers decline far more rapidly than numbers of congregations. The local church is not merely a place to worship; it is also a lifetime or, more precisely, several lifetimes.

For other people, the church context is home because it is a place where they can speak their God-language, even if—perhaps, especially if—few people in the larger community where they live use that language. This sustains services in Latin, German, Dutch, or even sixteenth-century English, in neighborhoods where the primary language is twenty-first century English and the second language is Spanish, Punjabi, Cantonese, or Tagalog. There are also people for whom church is a continuation of a childhood's immigrant community. It welcomes the God-language; it also celebrates the occasions of a heritage, with the right foods and rituals, and all without difficult explanations. It is home.

The emergence of warriors should not cause surprise. Core issues of identity and life-meaning are often at stake.

Biases Gain Power

Our biases are a product of our human limitations. Biases prevent us from correctly understanding what is happening. In a healthy system, these can be balanced by other people and systems; at best, this situation helps us to recognize our biases and be transformed so that we are more and more able to overcome them. In a system under stress, biases can dominate. They can take over our thinking processes in our roles as leaders, and they can take over the thinking processes of everyone else in the system. The effect of accumulated and interacting biases can be that the whole system gets caught in a cycle of decline, not just in numbers (the starting point) but in every measurement that we can imagine. We need, therefore, to be aware of some of the important biases that tend to play an important role in conflict situations.

The first, potentially worst, kind of bias to address is the one caused by lack of awareness of considerations buried in our psyches. These things create a kind of mental block, a kind of psychic bias. There are questions that we will not consider, possible answers that we will not even imagine, because of issues that we issues that do not reveal themselves to us without serious reflection; in some cases, therapy is helpful. This can be a deeply buried bias, perhaps rooted in significant trauma or fear-based formation.

Childhood displacement might, for instance, cause connection to stable home to develop an outsize importance, thereby preventing consideration of options for church change that seem to threaten the church's identity as home (e.g., moving from the building, closing the congregation, eliminating use of the childhood language). Modern psychotherapy is built around the work of identifying and confronting these issues, so that they can become integrated into a healthy psyche rather than remaining oppressive by their obscurity from our understanding. This kind of bias differs from the other biases that we will consider because we may not know that we have it. Psychic transformation is the answer to it.

In a shrinking church, this kind of bias is part of the reason for the challenges that the archdeacon encountered, and which I also confronted in my new congregational home. When we are under pressure, especially from stresses that affect our life anchors—often, our sense of home and identity—our responses are not always purely reasoned considerations of the issues at hand. Instead, our reactions are emotionally affected by other aspects of our life histories. The result can be complex and disproportionate. We, ourselves, may not be fully aware of the role that a familiar church home, with familiar systems of operation, plays in our psyche. We always need to consider the possibility that we are not acting responsibly, that our decisions are not truly consistent with what we know—or what we would know if we asked and answered all the relevant questions. Similarly, we need to be aware of the operations of emotion in our organizations. For just this reason, some thinkers (such as Brené Brown[2]) encourage a focus on empathy, with its strong commitment to emotional awareness, as an important leadership characteristic. Church leaders tend to be strong on empathy, living it or, at least, honoring it. The point about bias, though, is that destructive emotions destroy, so we cannot allow them to dominate the organization's decisions.

Individual bias is selfish thinking; it gives priority to self-serving outcomes over options that might better serve the larger world.[3] Thus, I do not want to ask all the relevant questions and answer them correctly because I recognize, perhaps in a way that I will not fully express to myself and will commonly not reveal to others, that the outcome may not serve my personal interests as I understand them. This can be the self-interest of the intelligent person—at least, the person who is aware—who knows that there may be further questions to ask and answer and refuses to follow the path of reason. Individual bias chooses individual interest over the common good of the larger community.

I have seen a shrinking congregation die (and others compromised) because there was a need to revitalize a congregation's leadership, a change that involved moving a dominant person out of the authority structure where they had held significant control for many years; that person resisted because they did not wish to see their power compromised. In one specific case that I have in mind, the person insisted that the congregation depended upon their direction, which was probably accurate but certainly unhealthy. They used their power to undermine the clergy leadership, ultimately destroying the congregation itself and the larger multicongregation configuration of which it was a part. Where growth might have been possible, decline dominated, denominational discipline became necessary, and closure became unavoidable. This was a particularly strong case of individual bias. Not only did self-interest dominate the thinking process of the individual, but the good of the whole came to be defined in terms of that person's self-interest, at the risk of causing significant decline. That person simply would not accept an account of the congregation's life that did not suit their understanding of their own interests. In the longer term, as often happens, selfish shortsightedness contributed to the loss of the whole configuration, so that even the person's own interests were not served. Individual bias has destructive tendencies.

The same phenomenon occurs at the communal level, where it becomes a kind of group bias. A group chooses to place its own collective self-interest above the common good.[4] Obvious examples include the exclusion of Black people and women from church and societal leadership. The extent to which theology has been twisted to insist upon White supremacy and male rule has been nothing less than astounding. Less obvious examples occur around us—and implicate us—all the time. Industries and countries place profit over concern for workers, creating class resentment. Christians put the success of their own religion above the well-being of non-Christian peoples. The list goes on. Too easily, we fail to distinguish between serving our group and serving the common good of God's world. This captures us in precisely the cycle of decline that we hope to avoid; opposition grows between White and Black or Indigenous or Hispanic; between male and female. Workers who are mistreated become resentful. Christians and non-Christians find themselves at odds.

In a shrinking church, group bias is not always as enormous as these examples, though it certainly can be. There is a real possibility that declining church participation has exacerbated arguments over sex and gender issues in recent years, something that is worth remembering in the midst of intense conversation. There is a different risk that we face as leaders in denominations. We, as leaders, can stand in the way of transformation because we do not want our leadership group to lose power or—perhaps more immediately worrisome—employment. Alternatively, both leaders and members can stand in the way of transformation because our denominational identity has come to mean more to us than our gospel commitments.

A small-town congregation with which I worked was shrinking and, indeed, had shrunk to the point of nonviability. The remaining members were aware that they needed to make decisions about the future. One obvious answer was to join the stronger congregation in a partner denomination, housed in a building a few blocks away. That was the one option that the congregation was not prepared to discuss. There was a sense that joining the partner from another denomination would represent a kind of takeover by the partner denomination. Denominational loyalty triumphed over ministry considerations. Today, the congregation is closed; I do not know where the members are.

Both individual and group bias imply some awareness, which we may ignore or suppress, that we are responding on the strength of our own benefits, priorities, interests, or limited worldviews, rather than submitting to the challenge of knowing the truth and facing the implications of acting on it.

There is a further way that we resist the truth. We resist facing the long-term, complex problems and reject the kind of thinking that would make us aware of them; Lonergan calls this the "general bias of common sense."[5] We are willing to make numerous adjustments to avoid engaging with the intellectual and other sorts of challenging work that would result from listening to thinkers and researchers who call our attention to warning signs of difficult problems. The classic example of our time is global climate change; at least one political jurisdiction has resorted to forbidding use of the language of "climate change" in official documents to prevent these considerations from impinging on decision-making.[6] In some churches, notions of climate change are rejected as instances of culture war.[7] Instead of asking and answering the questions posed by climate science, some evangelical Christians use stories from the Bible to argue either that climate change is not happening or that action is not needed. For most Christians, this is an easy example, allowing us to feel comfortable about our attentiveness to the bigger issues. Most

Anglosphere Christians are aware of climate change and willing to do something about it (though I am probably not doing enough, and I may not be alone in that). There are other cases where we are insufficiently attentive and active.

We have not given appropriate attention, as the church, to the challenge that this book raises: decline in church participation. The difference that we have seen between declining attendance, which is quite large, and a decrease in numbers of congregations, which is proportionally much smaller, suggests that we have not taken this seriously enough. In the denominations with which I am most familiar, the effect has been successive waves of cutbacks at regional and national levels. Large challenges that touch every aspect of an organization often require a different kind of response from this sort of incremental adjustment.

Although congregations and other church organizations, including shared social justice efforts, publishing houses, and other kinds of ministries, are finding ways to work together so that common mission can be made sustainable, we have not made the challenge of shrinking numbers into a central focus of ecumenical discussion. Perhaps we do not want to name it for ourselves, or maybe we do not wish to speak it aloud to others. In any case, existing models of church seem to have run their course. One implication of being a people called to serve as ambassadors of reconciliation is that a permanent commitment to existing denominations cannot be sustained. If we do not stand together, at least among denominations with common core beliefs, we will fall apart. Existing denominations require quantities of resources that are less and less available to maintain organizational structures that are less and less sustainable. We cannot resolve these challenges without admitting them to ourselves and to others. We need to chart a course together, and a refusal to admit the scale and nature of the challenge interferes with our ability to do so.

Stress and Social Media

One part of my life history is political involvement. In my youth, politics was what I did. My first degree is in political science. It could as easily be described as a degree in practical politics, though I did read plenty of political theory. When not in class, I engaged in electoral politics at the local, provincial (equivalent of state in the United States), and federal levels. I even worked part-time in a very minor role in a federal cabinet minister's office for a while. A big part of political training is media preparation, because we needed to connect with the media and to be aware that media can become involved on its own volition, with its own priorities, and in ways that would not seem to us to be helpful. These were the olden days, the horse and buggy of communications compared to today's instant acceleration electric car. The world of media has changed.

When we have something to say publicly, the media can be very helpful getting the message out. That is worth remembering. However, when an organization is coming apart under the stresses of decline, then media will emphasize the pressures. Anxiety will be expressed and magnified. Warriors will dominate the story. This has been true since the birth of news media. It is even more true now. When I was involved in politics, we defined a problem as something to be faced and solved; a crisis, however, was a problem with the media engaged. In a social media world, the media are always engaged, and this world does not come with journalistic training or a code of ethics. The media is on all the time, and its measurement of success is number of clicks.

Social media, though it has benefits as a means of connecting with people (and we will see notable advantages as part of electronic church strategies in some of our Gospel Vision Statement examples), is also a comfortable home for propagating every one of the biases that we have discussed.

Social media rewards brief comments expressed in strong language. If complex, thoughtful commentary that requires subtlety of expression and needs space to discuss gets attention, it is only in drastically simplified form. Social media is designed to approach difficult issues by:

1) catering to the oversimplifications that risk feeding the inclination to ignore major issues and the theoretical approaches that frame them; or
2) inviting responses to such challenges with minimal, short-term, solutions that seem familiar or obvious; or
3) fostering conspiracy theories and other forms of misinformation based in ideas that appeal to simple prejudices.

Our "common sense" consists precisely of what seems normal or obvious to us: "Don't play in traffic. Don't try to live on junk food. . ." The tendency of media communication to play to our common sense is one reason that disinformation succeeds so powerfully. The data that people need to understand correctly is often obscured by brief, strong, even inflammatory presentation that is either wholly false or only partially true, while seeming somehow obvious or consistent with what our community has prepared us to believe.

Social media sources tend to feed the groups that share their viewpoints. Social media users contribute to this phenomenon by selecting friends, which tends to create groups of people with similar mindsets. Computer algorithms recognize these group selections and cater to them, serving them with suggestions of like-minded people and similar information sources, all in service of fostering time with the social media and increasing the number of advertisements viewed—advertisements which have, of course, been selected to match the likely interests of the group. In other words, social media is oriented toward sustaining group bias, in the ways that we think and act, in what we wear and the words that we use. We all know these things. There is, however, a further step that is more insidious and less obvious but is specifically designed to foster group bias: the interference of bots. A research group at the University of California, Berkeley, has discovered that using bots to make ideas more popular by pumping the numbers causes them to be chosen by more people, swaying the whole population.[8] Accomplished on a social media scale, this reinforces group bias.

Social media posts are immediately and constantly measured. Old news is truly old news, so the media themselves encourage a swift response, which can easily short-circuit efforts at critical thought. The social media cycle can be quite ugly. A church organization makes a decision that displeases someone. That person goes away and lets loose on social media, often without taking time to ask and answer the relevant questions. Indeed, sometimes those questions depend upon confidential information that is not accessible to the poster. The process of critical investigation and knowing requires a commitment to finding the truth, an exercise that requires time and energy, along with the humility inherent in a recognition that we might be wrong. Critical thinking also means overcoming our individual and unconscious biases, which is exactly the opposite of the rapid posting impulse.

In other words, social media can encourage people to take their limited and biased understanding, blow it up to beyond life size and fire it out rapidly. There, it will feed into the biases of an in-group that will circulate it swiftly; if it is exciting and outrageous enough, the story will go viral, shared and shared again. By virtue of being oversimplified and swiftly distributed, it will contribute to the general bias; it helps to form people's belief that this is simply common sense. The much more complicated truth tends to get left far behind.

I encourage people to get social media training as part of leadership in today's church. One of the consequences of the extent to which social media is democratic—everyone can post—is that it has effects that we cannot ignore even if we choose not to participate. We do not need to be active on social media if we prefer otherwise. However, we cannot successfully avoid the consequences of other people's engagement with social media, especially when we are in high stress situations.

Responding Helpfully

The reality of life is that a shrinking organization is often a high stress context for leaders who believe in the purpose of the organization and its value as a contributor to that purpose. There is no benefit in pretending otherwise or in suggesting that the church, with its emphasis on love, will be different. Here, I make some suggestions that are especially oriented toward individual leaders. The following chapters are more focused on shifts in the larger systems that create destructive pressures.

Leadership self-care is a high priority. I encourage leaders to take seriously the suggestions that we have discussed. The first of these, recognizing the larger cultural situation—and understanding that it is not your fault, and you cannot fix it—lowers the psychological pressure. A leader may be able to help one organization, such as a congregation, but will not be able to change the social dynamic. Interestingly, this acknowledgment of our limitations can establish a mindset that creates room for success because it lowers the pressure to save everything and everyone. Today's leaders are free to experiment simply because they cannot sustain the past.

Working with support can be helpful. A leadership coach lowers the stress level by providing a safe place to discuss challenges. Coaches help active leaders to think about the issues that arise, and to find solutions that match the purposes and values of our organizations. Part of intellectual transformation is ensuring that we ask and answer all the relevant questions. Coaches help us to ensure that we are identifying those questions and answering them as correctly and fully as possible. Coaches also help us to think about the consequences of our conclusions, so that we can make the wisest decisions, and follow them through responsibly. At best, a leadership coach will help in the work of self-appropriation, making us aware of the ways that we can grow in transformation.

Therapists provide assistance in identifying and responding to issues in leaders' psyches and lives. Therapists help us to recognize when we are responding out of our own psychological issues, in ways that are unhelpful or even irrelevant to the circumstances. Conversely, therapists assist us in noticing issues that we are suppressing when that suppression deprives us of important clues for understanding the situations to which we are responding. By doing these things, therapists support our development in psychic transformation.

Spiritual directors help leaders to recognize God at work in our lives. Spiritual directors encourage us to ask questions about God's presence and leading in our contexts, reminding us that we are not alone in crises. Not only might there be other resources in the community, but, more powerfully, God is at work in the transformation of the world. The outcomes are in God's purview. As they help us to reflect on God's work in the world, in our world, spiritual directors enrich our development in religious transformation.

All of these are (or ought to be) trained people, outside the specific situations in which leaders are engaged, enabling concentrated and purposeful reflection. Working with such people enables leaders to process challenging issues and situations with complete confidentiality and without the kinds of risks that talking with parishioners or people at judicatory levels inevitably brings. The remarkable and most important consequence of engaging with these kinds of support people is that it raises the likelihood of good outcomes for our organizations and for us.

Support people will also help us to sustain other components of self-care. There's a certain triteness in recommending appropriate rest, exercise, nutrition, and forms of security—including financial security. Whole industries are dedicated to reminding us of these things. They are correct to do so, even if they are trying to make a profit out of their emphases. Clergy and other church leaders sometimes need special encouragement, nonetheless. Our language of sacrifice and laying down our lives, combined with all sorts of insecurities about living up to the gospel call, can set us up to ignore good advice. In certain theologies, and in some ecclesiologies (understandings of the church), clergy and other church leaders are expected to dispense with basic aspects of life to serve the organization. Some people—including leaders who should know better—expect that church leaders can live so much at the higher levels on Maslow's hierarchy of needs (intellectual and spiritual satisfaction) that we should be able to overlook deficits, even substantial or crippling deficits, at lower levels (basic survival requirements). Transformation in the lives of leaders and organizations depends upon leaders who are enabled to be as healthy as they can possibly be.

Enabling leaders to be reasonably healthy and well cared-for, physically, emotionally, mentally, spiritually, and financially, can be a serious challenge for a shrinking church, especially as tight financial circumstances in the larger community and in governments can reinforce the organization's challenges. One helpful response is to admit that a shrinking church will have fewer paid leaders. At best, these people will be specially trained for the shrinking church context, with strong, relevant leadership and management skills. They must be prepared to work with teams of clergy who are paid for part time work and unpaid volunteers who also support the ministry. The reality of shrinking church is that a smaller coterie of highly trained and appropriately supported and remunerated leaders will need to function in a rather different structure from those that we inherited out of the 1960s and 1970s.

One of the most helpful responses to the stress of leadership in a shrinking organization is focus on organizational purpose. If people can come together to clarify what they are about, with a sustainable aim that is genuinely consistent with their identity, then falling numbers need not be so destructive. If people cannot do this, then the organization is failing; its situation must be recognized. In the next chapter, we will consider something that I call a Gospel Vision Statement, which is a very specific kind of tool for defining the direction of a Christian organization.

Exercises: Under Pressure

A. Your Life

1. We have briefly discussed a variety of the stresses that can emerge in church organizations (anxiety, warriors emerging, biases increasing, social media being destructive). Have you encountered any of these behaviors in church? If so, how have they affected the ways that you feel about church and think about church?
2. If you have not encountered any of these behaviors in church, why do you think that is? What does that say about your church? What does it say about you?

B. Your Organization

1. If you have encountered some of these unhealthy behaviors in church, do you think that they are connected to declining numbers, either in your organization or in your denomination? Why or why not?
2. What are the stress points in your organization—the differences that either do or could turn into battle locations under pressure?
3. Do you think that a church commitment to the transformations we have identified would enable a healthier organization? If so, suggest some ways.

C. The World

1. Have you encountered some of these unhealthy behaviors in the world around you? If so, what do you think has caused them? Is there a sense of fear of loss of home where you live?
2. Do you think that a church commitment to the transformations we have identified would enable a healthier world? If so, suggest some ways.

CHAPTER 7

FINDING NEW VISION FOR A CHURCH ORGANIZATION

Church organizations often have a difficult time finding new vision. This can be a result of a failure of imagination, but I doubt that is often the cause. In my experience, the opposite is more likely. Ask a church group for ideas and you will soon have a wall full of yellow sticky notes. More than once, I have encountered strategic plans created out of sticky notes. They consist of many ideas, pointing in multiple directions, trying to serve everybody. As Shakespeare's Hamlet says, "there's the rub": trying to serve everybody.

Churches are deeply aware of the universality of the divine call. We are specifically enjoined to invite everyone, especially those who are not welcomed elsewhere, into our life and, more profoundly, into the life of God's transformation. This means that our goals get larger as our numbers get smaller. The result is likely to be failure—we cannot reach everyone—and burnout.

The desire to serve everyone is especially problematic in a shrinking church. We simply cannot do all that we once did, let alone all that we can imagine doing. We do not have the resources. This book talks about finding vision in unlikely places. In an important sense, all places are unlikely; all of us are limited, troubled, and affected by destructive tendencies, and the places around us face the same challenges. However, there is something especially unlikely about our places and times. We are getting smaller. Less and less are we the dominant leaders or the most powerful support systems in our communities, even as needs mount in the places where we live and move and have our being. As we shrink and begin to wonder about survival of our congregations, our seminaries, our shared bodies and support systems, and even our denominations, we look around skeptically. Can these dry bones live? Can there be vision in these unlikely places?

This chapter proposes a way to find vision for shrinking churches, including those in shrinking places: a Gospel Vision Statement (GVS) that narrows the focus and specifies the task.

Gospel Vision Statement

Everybody knows that they need a mission statement; everyone knows that they are supposed to follow it. Most church organizations have one and it goes roughly like this: "Love Church of Localville welcomes all people, serving God through worship, hospitality, and service." Every time the congregation plans an event, someone refers to the mission statement and points out that the event provides hospitality or service for someone. Every time the congregation proposes a change to worship, someone refers to the mission statement and notes that the shift will add to the welcome for someone.

The mission statement is posted on a sign in a prominent location, perhaps out on the side of the street. That is where a mission statement like this belongs. Why? Because these statements are mostly written to communicate to the larger world. The job of a mission statement is to make a congregation look welcoming and, at best, to be welcoming. That is a good thing, as far as it goes. It is, however, a limited thing in a very important way. Mission statements are not really meant to guide a congregation. Commonly, they are far too broad. Indeed, they are so broad that they are not true.

An actual congregation knows perfectly well that it does not welcome all people. If it glories in a choir that specializes in Bach cantatas, accompanied by a fine organ with a highly trained professional working four manuals and a thirty-two-note pedalboard, the congregation is not especially welcoming people whose musical tastes run more to Drake or Taylor Swift or Charlie Parker. Likewise, a praise band playing contemporary Christian songs will not be attractive to the dyed-in-the-wool organ lover for whom the prior example is perfect. There is nothing wrong with either of the above options or the accompanying limitations. No congregation can be all things to all people; no organization of any kind can be all things to all people. An inclusive mission statement is a helpful reminder to a congregation that it should be friendly when people appear. After that point, it mostly ceases to be useful.

So much for mission statements. Have one. Post it outside. Then get down to the real work.

Every church congregation or other organization needs a Gospel Vision Statement. This is an internal statement, not meant to be shared with the public. A GVS is a specific statement about whom your community/congregation/parish/organization intends to reach with the good news of Christ Jesus and how you intend to reach them. A GVS identifies, explicitly, how your organization will foster transformation—intellectual, psychic, moral, and religious—in the world. A GVS is an explicit, internal guide that focuses all the organization's actions, especially those that are externally oriented.

A GVS is fundamentally different from the standard-issue mission statement because a GVS is purposefully exclusionary. I know—and you know that I know—that talking about a gospel vision as exclusionary feels wrong. The language of "gospel" does not belong in the same sentence as "exclusion" (unless by negation). This is the basic reason that most Christian organizations do not have a GVS or anything that resembles one, in any formal sense.

We do have limitations built into our systems and positions, though. I serve in a seminary supported by the Evangelical Lutheran Church in Canada. We welcome everyone. On the other hand, if an Anglican Church of Canada member applies to the Master of Divinity (MDiv) program, the basic ordination program, then I am bound by shared expectations to refer them to the Anglican seminary down the hall. If a United Church of Canada member applies to the MDiv program, then I am bound to refer them to the United Church seminary in another wing of the building. If a Lutheran Church Canada member applies to the MDiv program, then I am honor-bound to inform them that their church may not accept our degree and they may be uncomfortable with some of our expectations. Our seminary is very inclusive; it is also exclusionary. Exclusionary is not necessarily bad; sometimes, it is just focused.

A GVS is honest about these limitations. Indeed, part of the purpose of a GVS is to clarify limitations. A GVS defines the parameters of your reach: mission and location (Whom are you trying to reach? What are you God-called to accomplish?), identity (Who are you? Whom do you feel God-called to become?), and resources (To what do you have access? Do your resources match your mission, location, and identity?).

Mission: This is a *Gospel* Vision Statement. It is about communicating the good news of Christ Jesus. It is not about surviving as a congregation, maintaining the power of an individual or an in-group, keeping the building going, getting an infusion of new blood, or any of the other ideas that biases cause to circulate. Similarly, it is only incidentally (if at all) about providing a service to the community or sustaining things that people like about your area. It is about the good news, a way of identifying the organization's commitment to being an educational structure with room for explosions.

In my experience, this usually means that a church group needs to have some conversation about the meaning of the gospel before constructing a vision statement. For an organization to foster interiority (which we have also called "self-appropriation"), the kinds of transformations that we have discussed, the organization's members must have some initial understanding of transformation. Clarifying this first speeds up the process considerably. It also tends to excite the people who had a sense that there was something there but could not quite put their finger on it, as much as the people for whom it is new news.

The next thing to remember is that communicating the good news is about Show & Tell. Remember kindergarten? Your teacher was right. Showing does not really accomplish much without telling. If you brought your pet hamster and the rest of the kids could not distinguish your pet from a mouse or a rat, then the exercise failed in an important part of its purpose. The point was to bring your pet and tell people about it, so that everyone came out with a deeper understanding.

There is a line going around that people attribute to St. Francis of Assisi: "Preach the gospel at all times. If necessary, use words" (or some variation on this). This framing of communication has at least three problems: 1) It probably is not St. Francis; 2) It works only for an outstanding medieval saint who is also popular in the modern world; and 3) It is meaningless for the rest of us. Nobody has presented evidence that Francis said this, which makes the attribution highly unlikely. Moreover, Francis did use words, most famously—and perhaps most powerfully—in the Rule of St. Francis that guides multiple religious orders to this day. He was a traveling preacher, who went beyond the bounds of Christendom and into the Middle East to proclaim the gospel. To claim Francis as a voice against the need to verbalize (whether in written or oral form) the good news is to turn the Francis of history into little more than a popular garden ornament.

The only logic in claiming that Francis made such a statement is that he is one of very few people for whom we can imagine the idea working. The holiness of St. Francis stood out in medieval society, and in that context notable religious behavior was generally assumed to be in the Christian tradition. The only real question was about his orthodoxy, on the grounds that he might have been a Waldensian and deemed a heretic (a heretic from Christianity, of course) which was settled on the side of orthodoxy by declarations of papal approval of Francis's movement and rule. His commitment was to the church; indeed, some of his most visible actions were in the restoration of church buildings. He founded multiple Christian religious orders—again, with papal approval. Nobody considered that Francis might be a religious "none" because they did not exist. Atheists were most unlikely. A few Muslims and Jews could be found, but Francis's activities were utterly inconsistent with those options. Most people had never heard of Buddhists; Sikhism did not exist yet; Hinduism was not yet Hinduism, simply a collection of beliefs and commitments in a part of the world that had little reality for the medieval European. In short, of course Francis could be assumed to be a holy Christian without necessarily saying much; his world would make that assumption without his words.

That was then. This is now. Today, the average person seeing St. Francis on the street would likely assume that he is something odd and probably inspired by an Eastern religion, maybe Hare Krishna. At our point in history, words are even less optional than they were for Francis.

In a shrinking church, the silent approach that people attribute to St. Francis (even as it is entirely at odds with his very verbal life) makes less sense than ever. With declining numbers of Christians in our society and deep confusion about what Christianity means, our automatic assumption must be that Christian behavior will not be understood as Christian witness. Actions cannot stand alone. Being an ambassador means being prepared to speak. After all, who ever heard of an ambassador who did not use words?

There is, however, an important point behind the inclination to repeat the words attributed to St. Francis. The Christian gospel is appropriately unwelcome when Christianity is announced in words and failed in actions. This is one of the reasons that Christians find communicating about faith difficult. Our narrative can sound unconvincing even to ourselves when we feel shadowed by all the evil that is done in the name of the Christ. If our lives are not consistent with being ambassadors of reconciliation, then our words will not be either. The organization's mission, therefore, must incorporate elements of both showing and telling the gospel.

The core of the mission is to enable both participation in, and communication about, God's transformation of the world, in a way that invites others to participate. Your GVS, therefore, must name, clearly and bluntly, how your organization will focus on religious transformation, along with the necessary intellectual, psychic, and moral transformations, in the lives of the people whom you plan to reach. Because it simply is not true that "All you need is love," the GVS must also, either explicitly or implicitly, reflect how your organization intends to foster intellectual, psychic, moral, and religious transformations, internally. To move this conversation into standard church language, your organization must commit itself to discipleship—not merely to being disciples, but also to supporting the growth of discipleship in others. Through your life, as expressed in and guided by your GVS, people must be given the opportunity to know God and the world through God's vision of love. Through your life, as expressed in and guided by your GVS, people must be given the opportunity to place care for the other (human and not human) above self-interest. Through your life, as expressed in and guided by your GVS, people must be given the opportunity to recognize the biases built into their lives and psyches. Through your life, as expressed in and guided by your GVS, people must be given the opportunity to recognize the systems in society that bind and enslave. Your organization must truly be about God's transformation of the world; you must be ambassadors of reconciliation.

This brings us to the precise question that an organization needs to answer in a GVS. What is your organization trying to accomplish in communicating the good news? What, specifically? How does what you are doing differ from what other organizations within your denomination are doing? How does it differ from what other organizations from other denominations are doing or what similar organizations down the block are doing? If there is no difference—no truly *important to the world*, rather than just important to you, difference—then there is no reason for multiple organizations. If your congregation is doing the same thing as a congregation in the next block or within easy driving distance, then the two of you exist only for reasons of historical divergence that cannot be either justified or sustained in a shrinking church environment. The church simply does not have the resources to maintain endless duplication of functions.

A challenge for many church organizations is that they do not tend to think in mission terms at all, even when using the language. That is why broad mission statements of the sort that are posted on billboards everywhere are of limited value in directing action. Churches have a difficult time refining a statement of what they are called to accomplish. Church organizations have a sense of having come into existence, often in a completely different era, and now they are here. Once upon a time, this might have been enough to sustain an organization, though it cannot ever have been healthy because it leaves leaders to decide, almost entirely by themselves, what shape their work will take. In any case, in a shrinking church, "We're here because we're here because we're here because. . ." simply will not work. Five years from now, we will not be here.

Mission is all about clarity and focus. Brevity can be helpful, but it can also be overrated. If you need a paragraph to say it, then use a paragraph; if you need a page to say it, use a page. A GVS does not need to fit on a sign. The important thing is that the organization needs to be clear about what it is trying to do.

Location: Location, in this case, refers to the geographical parameters of your area of service. Put more bluntly: This is the area that you are trying to reach.

Your location may mean where your physical footprint is situated but, just as easily, it may not. Even in the years before the COVID-19 era, many church organizations—including congregations—served populations far beyond, or even distinct from, the place where their offices were situated. I have often used the distinction between neighborhood churches and destination churches to help congregations clarify their focus. One congregation where I raised this question was (and probably still is) a purely neighborhood church; the neighborhood name is in the church's name, and nearly every active member either lives in that neighborhood or previously lived there and is connected to the place by history/family/friends/employment or some other clear tie. Another church in the same city and same denomination, where I had similar conversations, drew people from all over the metropolitan area and beyond because of its formal worship and impressive music. Location meant something different in each of these cases.

The expansion of online activity, including worship and education, means that location can take on a significantly different character. In a visit to Colombia, I had the wonderful opportunity of visiting with a congregation whose core meeting place was an apartment in a neighborhood. The onsite attendees were from across a sizable urban area. However, they were numerically balanced with the online attendees, who were in isolated places across a large geographical region. All were engaged, both online and onsite, and all had a voice in worship. Geographical location has become a broader category for some church organizations.

Thus far, we have discussed the location of the people whom you currently serve. That may suffice for you. Maybe you and your organization simply want to focus on serving that area more richly and purposefully.

However, you may also want to move beyond, or even away from, your current area of service. In a GVS, you will clarify this, identifying the areas that you intend to reach. Be as precise as possible. Where this is defined by traditional geographic boundaries, be clear about them. If you intend to work online and have a fairly broad sense of where you are going, still be clear about the boundaries. In either case, lay them out on a map. Everyone in your organization (including members of the congregation, if that is where you lead) needs to know them.

Why is this so important? Because you are serving a community, and everyone needs to share in the task of understanding what that community is all about. Consider the neighborhood church that I mentioned above. When I began the work of helping them to understand their purpose, they were chasing the popular congregational hope: we need more young people. They were following what I think of as the "Vampire Theory" of evangelism: we need new blood (best expressed in Vincent Price's voice and followed by a maniacal laugh). In fact, the congregation had plenty of opportunity for growth, but it was most unlikely to be with young people. Younger people had either stayed in the area and grown old or had left the neighborhood; the demographic skewed older. However, the neighborhood was not stagnant. A couple of new housing developments were transforming the area and significantly increasing its population. Those housing developments were specifically aimed at retirees. A congregation mostly made up of older people now had the opportunity to invite many other older people to transformation. Bonuses included the greater likelihood that older people would welcome such an invitation (attendance in most churches trends older) and older people tend to be more generous with their time, energy, and money. The congregation needed only to recognize that their natural capacity matched neatly with their natural mission and set to work.

The world contains numerous resources to aid in the task of understanding the communities that you are trying to reach, whether they are in a local neighborhood or continent-wide, or in disparate portions of a country or continent. Replacing those resources is not the purpose here. My concern is only to encourage you to be careful and honest in identifying the geographical parameters of your service area and seek to understand them clearly and thoroughly.

Identity: Identity means: Know what you are about. Know what makes you you. Know what you feel called by God to be, what you hope to define as making you you.

Identity stands alongside geography as the other principle that defines a particular organization. It includes such elements as denomination, worship style, theological priorities, ministry priorities, and so on, the characteristics that either draw people to your organization or that you hope will draw people.

Recognizing an organization's identity can be a difficult and contentious process. There are numerous issues at stake. Some members will be engaged with the history of the organization, recent or very old. There may be debates that are driven by people who are especially attached to the original reasons for the founding or with the reasons that the organization was successful in the 1960s and 1970s. Others may be especially drawn to recent shifts in the life of the organization and the possibilities those suggest. Some may be dedicated to the denominational affiliation, while others see the denomination as a problem. Some may be in the organization because of its theological position, while others may see the very idea of doctrinal commitment as stultifying. In congregations and similar church bodies, some may be attached to the worship style even as others are focused on social justice ministry. Some people may want to focus on a particular neighborhood, while others want to reach out to a broad area. Some may prefer a small organization, while others want to be large. Up to a point, disagreement is a good thing in this conversation. Disagreement implies both some energy and some variety, both of which are encouraging.

Moreover, identity is not static. Conversation, including disagreement, can yield new formulations. Be open to the possibility that last year's identity may not be this year's or, perhaps more important, next year's. Priorities shift, as do membership and participation. The traditional identity may no longer serve.

Ultimately, in a shrinking church, stakeholders will need to agree. A diversity of ministries is fine, if they focus toward the same gospel-oriented goal and the organization has the resources necessary to sustain that diversity. The key, however, is focus. Definitionally, a shrinking church has fewer members this year than it had last year and is likely to have fewer members next year. Remember that this is not an indictment; it is demographic reality. An unfocused church organization risks dissipating its remaining energies by trying to do too many things and, therefore accomplishes little or nothing. A church organization must have a clear sense of its own identity, of what it is and what it feels God-called to be.

Resources: Inevitably, our conversation about identity flows into a discussion of resources. An organization's real identity, often distinct from its imagined identity, is deeply affected by the resources to which it has access. All the above considerations—mission, location, and identity—depend upon the ability of the organization to assemble resources to match its declarations.

Except in moments of unexpected crisis, no church organization has a mission for which it does not have access to sufficient resources. This may seem like a shocking statement. In fact, it is entirely mundane, even tautological (a tautology is a statement that is true because it is merely repetitive or because it is constructed so that it cannot be false). The tautology here is that a mission is defined in part by accessible resources. If an organization cannot access sufficient resources, then its intentions are not its mission. In short, your mission must reflect the resources to which you have access. There must be enough resources in the system, somewhere, to enable you to complete the necessary work.

This point cannot be emphasized strongly enough. I vividly recall working with the leadership of a congregation that had been given several years of judicatory support to get itself into shape, after the point at which closure seemed to be an obvious and inevitable outcome. They were served by a clergyperson whose specific task was to help them bring together a strategic plan for their future. Instead of careful assessment and planning, the congregation promptly engaged in a whirl of mission activity. In an area of the city where there was deep need, they went to work and created substantial programs for needy people in their downtown area. The congregation also engaged with musical and artistic communities for concerts and presentations. Their worship had a particular and very rich character, with substantial musical contributions. This was a faithful, imaginative, active congregation.

Unfortunately, the congregation did not have the resources to sustain the ministries that had been started. The building had significant issues resulting from insufficient maintenance and complicated linkages with a neighboring apartment complex of uncertain ownership. The programs for people in need could work only with extensive volunteer support from elsewhere, support that simply was not available on the required scale. Worship depended on the kindness of retired clergy, willing to work for minimal pay, and retirees were ceasing to be able to do it. The tiny coterie of surviving members asked me, "Who would be willing to close their congregation and move in with us?" The answer was, of course, "Nobody."

The congregation had created programs that, while good in themselves, were not supported by available resources. Some aspects of their work survived after their closure. The space was given over for musical and arts use. However, other programs could not continue. Perhaps, some organization from elsewhere stepped in to fill the gap. Meanwhile, people who had come to depend upon this ministry were set adrift. Should the missions have come into existence? Possibly, but not as the work of a group that did not have the resources to maintain them.

The moral of this story is that an organization's mission must reflect resources that are accessible within the system. I have purposefully used the word "accessible" and done so repeatedly. Accessible carries multiple implications in this context. One meaning is that the resources in your organization must be available for use. Funds that make you look wealthy but cannot be reached are unhelpful; similarly, ownership of a church building on valuable land means big numbers on a bottom line somewhere but may not bolster ministry capability. In a more complex example, a large membership suggests the capacity for big ministry projects, but if the members are older, or overcommitted, or otherwise limited, the true capacity will be smaller than it seems.

Conversely, accessible resources may mean resources that do not belong to your organization but are available through potential partners. Partnership gets its own chapter later in this book. However, we should note that strong partnerships are built around shared, or at least complementary, GVSs. Complementarity may mean potential for large-scale sharing. On the other hand, sometimes it means only that a neighbor has what you need and is not currently putting it to use, or not using it when and how you need it. Your organization may need a meeting space that is available elsewhere. At a deeper level of engagement, they may have a refugee committee that is too small to manage bringing in a family but could contribute to refugee work that your organization hopes to do. Remember, also, that the neighbor may not be of your denomination, or even your religion, or of any religion at all. In this case, "neighbor" means "someone else who can contribute to the mission that you have set out in your GVS." Who knows, shared resources might lead to larger partnerships.

Resources must also be relevant to the mission that you name and the identity that you claim. Your organization may have tremendous resources but not ones that particularly match the organization's hopes, in which case your GVS is not really *your* GVS. It is somebody else's, masquerading as yours. The resources to which you have access reflect the organization that you really are, rather than some other one that you might remember being, or imagine being, or wish you were.

All the above may mean that you cannot undertake a mission that you identify in your location and consistent with your identity. This may be deeply disappointing. It is also reality.

People in the Anglosphere world tend to be more Pelagian, which is to say more inclined to rely on human power than divine power, than Pelagius ever could have been. I attended a convention where a church tried to convey to the people assembled that there was a deep need for volunteers, causing significant challenges for the organization (sound familiar?). Evidently, the organizers had decided that simply appealing or nagging was not going to resolve a problem that had been growing over the years, so they decided to go with a visual representation. They chose a powerful image, which played out vividly on the stage. A group walked on, sharing the weight of an enormous, inflated globe, so that the people were carrying the world together. They formed up in the middle of the stage, holding the world high in the air. Then one needed to leave for some perfectly good reason, then another, then another. At the end, the earth fell, no longer carried by the people.

I understand the reason for the brief play: if the church wanted the ministries to continue, then the time had come for people to step up and play their part. However, presenting the challenge in this way may not have been helpful. It seemed to focus on human effort as sustaining the world, rather than naming the moment as divine invitation to join the ministries or else rethink the mission. When we claim to uphold the world by our own efforts, we risk losing the awareness of God at work. Then, we too easily fall into efforts to force the world to follow our will or find ourselves in burnout and despair.

However, our world teaches us that all we need to do is raise productivity by working both harder and smarter. Every set of circumstances can be changed if only we have the will. So, we mouth the theology, preaching that God is transforming the world. At the same time, we resolve to work 24/7—and demand that everyone else work 24/7—to make sure that God's work gets done. Too often, we are power-driven and goal-driven, the creations of a competitive, production-oriented society. The Bangles have a point when they call the beginning of the standard work week, "manic Monday."[1]

All this inclination is intensified by the common management slogan, "Do more with less." The slogan, of course, is a way of justifying the sorts of cutbacks that have become common in the corporate world as means of increasing share value and short-term, though not always long-term, profitability. For a shrinking church, however, this becomes a way of thinking about ways that we can sustain existing organizations even as resources decline. There is a belief that we can keep most of our traditional ways of operating simply by increasing productivity with existing personnel. Technology will help, but the biggest adjustment is simply to expand every portfolio—as we have seen when discussing the ways that the role of the parish presbyter (priest/pastor/minister) has grown by accumulation.

The reality, however, is that there is not much extra space in the lives of church leaders. They were not taking it easy before the church started shrinking. Moreover, solutions such as technology have ways of creating increased workload in other ways at the same time as they trim the demands of traditional tasks. For example, computers may speed up bulletin production—though higher bulletin expectations limit the benefit—but they also increase communications expectations in a broad variety of ways.

I have chosen a countercultural slogan: "Do less with less." I promote it every time I have an opportunity, though my colleagues might tell you that I am not as good at living it as I am at preaching it. Many things are worth doing. Indeed, far more things are worth doing than we can do. However, a shrinking organization can do only a small subset. The point is to identify your mission, clarify your priorities, and be willing to make hard choices when questions emerge.

Do less with less. Admit that the job of fulfilling the purposes of your organization's life, of your life, belongs to God. Focus on what your organization reasonably can do. Step away from what it cannot do. Taking this approach changes the questions that people in the organization ask and answer, the meanings that they seek in their work. Instead of attempting to do everything and be everything, they can do the things that are necessary and be the people that they must be to fulfill the GVS. The result is that fewer things are done, and more is accomplished.

Review: I strongly encourage organizations to review their GVSs regularly. At the same time, I discourage large and complex review processes. Working with boards/councils (congregation, parish, organization) to do a basic review over a couple of meetings in the time leading up to the annual meeting will usually suffice. Too much review is a good way to let process overtake progress.

If the GVS appears to be invalid because it cannot be fulfilled for whatever reason, then a substantial process will be necessary. It will be time to create a new GVS or consider closure, if a GVS is not a reasonable possibility. An additional consideration in any review is the time horizon: How long do we anticipate being able to sustain the mission that we are undertaking? The organization may be able to assemble a GVS today that serves the next two or three years but may also be aware that the intended mission has a limited horizon or that the organization itself is unlikely to be able to continue. This can be a perfectly reasonable thing to do, if planning continues for what will happen afterward. A GVS for today is not a substitute for thinking about tomorrow. Instead, the GVS is a condition for being able to undertake longer-term planning.

Preparing to Create a GVS

A helpful way to begin preparing a GVS is to introduce people to some pieces of the conversation that we have named already.

1. Background

Emphasizing that people today are not joining any volunteer groups with long-term commitments and that the numerical growth narrative is unhelpful does much to clarify the nature of the work ahead. Recognition of this limits the amount of time dedicated to deploring secularization or focusing on the sins of the church, making them issues only when they are relevant to the specific work to be done, as when the group is committed to engaging with antiracism or decolonization initiatives. Pointing out that people are not joining today also helps to move away from the "bums in pews" focus. Numerical increase may be a byproduct of commitment to transformation; very likely, it will not. The focus on the numerical growth narrative is simply off point; it is not what the gospel is all about. Leaders are best to save themselves time and energy by laying out the social situation right at the beginning.

2. Ambassadors

One of the reasons that people are trapped by the numerical growth narrative is that they do not know how to talk about Christianity in any sense that goes beyond the warm, welcoming community narrative. The notion of a personal friendship with Jesus does not reflect the experience of God that many people have had, nor does it cohere with the theology that they encounter in their church. However, the complex history of Christian thinking, when connected to the complicated world around, does not always provide a clear account of the faith or the reasons that it might be desirable. Emphasizing that the richness of Christianity is in the invitation to know the world from the perspective of God's love and in the task of engaging with others in the life of love provides people with a clear and compelling understanding of our reasons for doing what we do.

3. Self-Appropriation and Transformation

Some work on self-appropriation and transformation may be useful in helping people to understand what gospel mission looks like today. My personal recommendation is viewing and discussing *Groundhog Day*. Following that with conversation about attending to their own asking and answering questions, with consideration for the feelings and other factors that affect their own accuracy, can help them to clarify what self-appropriation looks like. They may then be ready to engage in conversation about the conditions needed to help people around them engage in intellectual, psychic, moral, and religious transformation, knowing the power of God's love in their lives.

GVS Examples

The conversation may be easier with some examples of a GVS, so here are a few fictional examples along with some explanation of how they work. The samples are completely made up; they do not specifically resemble any congregations that I have seen. However, they draw from churches that I have observed and from knowledge developed over many years of church life, so they are akin to real situations. I have presented them in a variety of formats; people are welcome to use these or any other that helps them to become clear on the elements of a GVS.

1. First Reformed Church of Schooltown

First Reformed Church of Schooltown (FRC) serves the academic community of Schooltown (pop. 950,000), through lectures, conversations, book studies, and thoughtful worship and preaching. FRC is located in the immediate proximity of a major university, and within reasonable traveling distance (less than 15 minutes' drive) of another, smaller, university, and a large community college. The core membership, in our congregation of approximately 150 regular attendees, travels from across the city and its environs. Our members are predominantly faculty, students, and academically interested members of the larger community, drawn by the intellectual heritage of Reformed Christian faith, with liberal inclinations and room for freedom of thought and expression.

Our pastor brings a PhD in systematic theology and teaches a course in Reformed theology at a university-affiliated seminary. In addition, we have several theologically aware scholars in various disciplines, who lead and participate in conversations. We are able to host lectures from thinkers in local institutions of higher learning and visiting scholars, with events organized by a committee. Some of the scholarly presentations are nonreligious, but are focused toward the kinds of changes in the world that we believe are God's work. Our teaching work, therefore, is not pastor-centric, a development that we see as consistent with our heritage. This communal strength is a distinctive thing about our congregation that enables us to sustain a learning community.

We are developing an online presence, live-streaming worship, offering lectures and conversations in hybrid format, posting lectures on YouTube, and encouraging our members to engage with Christian faith in healthy ways online, including through social media. The conversations that we have with people of different viewpoints, in-person and online, are proving to be genuinely transformational; online is a new effort that is proving successful for us. We see an expanding opportunity here. A few of these connections result in people joining us, but many more show up as food for thought—even making their way into scholarly publications!

Our building is old but well kept, with a hall suitable for up to 120 people and a committee room suitable for up to 15. When necessary, we can rent facilities from the university. Financially, we are consistently able to meet our budget, supporting our ministries and building. Our numbers of attendees are fairly stable, though we are smaller in the summer as students leave for other places. Our members tend to fall into two categories: stable members, who tend to be older (60 and above) and students, who tend to be younger (25 and younger, with occasional graduate students who are slightly older) and are often temporarily with us. The temporary nature of our student community can be a challenge. Some of the students connect with us online after moving on, but not in great numbers. We are strengthening our presence on Facebook in an effort to foster continued engagement.

Our work with faculty seems to bring us enough members to keep our ministries strong and engaging. This may be a challenge as generations change, but for now, we are thriving and contributing with a kind of proclamation of the good news that few congregations seem able to accomplish.

2. Faith Lutheran Parish of Norway Corner and Farmville

Location: Faith Lutheran Parish (FLP) serves a large rural area, including two small towns, Norway Corner (pop. 2,500) and Farmville (pop. 1,500), located in Rural County, eight miles apart. Each town has a Lutheran church. Over the past 50 years, both towns have lost more than one-third of their people and the trend is even greater in the surrounding farms. Current townspeople are often retirees from farms that no longer support individual family operations, having been incorporated into larger agribusinesses.

Mission: Our work is with shrinking and aging rural populations, providing what feels like late-life care for disappearing communities. The people at FLP work in partnership with St. Martin's Roman Catholic Church and Norway Nazarene Church, together responding in three ways: 1) direct support for those in need, with a food bank, thrift shop, and cooking classes; 2) social and cultural activities with a faith dimension for the communities, including people from different religions talking about what they do; and 3) support of a parish nurse. Supporting talks from people other religions is an experiment, as is a parish nurse.

Identity: Both of our congregations have Norwegian origins, with a Pietist background. We continue to celebrate our Norwegian heritage. At the same time, we have grown to include people from a variety of backgrounds, so that all our services are in English, and our churches reflect a kind of middle-of-the-road liberal

Lutheranism. Our Sunday attendance, combining the two congregations, totals approximately 55 people—nearly all of whom are aged 65 or older. We are in the process of discussing whether going down to one congregation would enable us to serve our members and the larger community more effectively. We take joy in contributing to God's work in our communities and will be able to do so for some time to come. We are aware that our time will come to an end unless population trends shift, though we are not yet certain how long we will last. This awareness can be emotionally challenging, but we draw life from the contribution that we make to other people's lives and our witness to God's love.

Resources: Financially, we are okay for now because of our limited clergy expenses and our church partnership, but anticipated roofing expenses for one of our buildings will be challenging unless we choose to close it. Many of our congregation members are very active in volunteer capacities, providing leadership and organizational energy for our activities. Our congregations are extensively lay led, which is good but can be a heavy load. A pastor leads eucharistic services one Sunday per month in the two places, and one Sunday per month we participate in an online Eucharist led from another Lutheran church. The pastor also provides one third–time pastoral support to the congregations. Other services are conducted by trained lay ministers, who make up a parish worship committee of 4 people (2 from each congregation). Our parish nurse and community activities are supported by an outreach committee that includes 1 person from each of our congregations and 2 people from each of St. Martin's Roman Catholic and Norway Nazarene. With our 2 congregations, and with our Roman Catholic and Nazarene partners, we communicate God's love to our area.

3. Bethel African Methodist Episcopal Church of Southville

Serving: We at Bethel (BAME) work especially with the African American population of Southville, a majority-Black town. Southville is an agricultural community, historically dependent upon tobacco growing and processing but moving into a variety of crops with the decline of the tobacco industry. Southville's numbers have been shrinking for decades. Today's population of 26,000 is down from a peak of 41,000 in the early 1980s, and the community tends toward older and retired people.

Gospel Mission: We call all people to do justice, love mercy, and walk humbly with God (Micah 6:8), and we are a strong voice for racial justice in our town, state, and country.

Our ministries:
Walk Humbly in Worship: We provide times for praising God in worship on Tuesday evening, Wednesday morning, and Sunday morning, with words from

our pastor. We have a choir that continues the musical traditions of the African American worship heritage. For young people, we have a "Prayer in the Streets" program, which invites our young leaders to provide worship once a month in the high school parking lot and a local park, with music that fits their world (including the voices of local rappers).

Do Justice: We hold monthly meetings to discuss issues of justice in our community, in partnership with faculty and leaders from Southville Community College, which has active and engaged Black studies and political science departments. We are especially concerned about the future of our young people. Southville does not offer them much hope, and without hope they fall into destructive lives. Many of our conversations about justice touch upon these issues, and we are working closely with the college to encourage young people to attend. We sponsor a number of bursaries for Black people, and our "Prayer in the Streets" program includes invitations to enroll in college. We vocally support community leaders who work for justice. Our congregation includes a number of active politicians, and we have a strong tradition of Sunday voting as a congregation.

Love Mercy: Southville has a homeless population that is large for a city of its size. Every Tuesday, Bethel opens its doors to people in need, making available showers in our downstairs facilities (supervised by trained people) for use by the community, and providing supper. Tuesday evening worship is especially oriented to the needs of these people.

Identity: Founded in 1836, Bethel has a long history as a voice for justice and mercy in Southville. Our members have been active in the civil rights movement and continue to work with the NAACP. Our worship is joyful, and the preaching is powerful, in the African American tradition. Unfortunately, our membership of approximately 150 people is aging (average age of about 70, with some members in their 90s). We are working to reach young people, especially with our "Prayer in the Streets" program. Some appreciate the work that we do, but they are not inclined to join.

Bringing What We Have: We have a strong partnership with Southville Community College. Our building is well kept but old and will need significant renovations in the next five years. Our congregation is aging and shrinking. However, we are dedicated to the work of God in the world. We are in conversations about the future with a local majority-Black Baptist church and with other AME churches in our county. Some sort of merger is likely, though even that risks being more in the nature of staving off the inevitable than establishing a vigorous ministry. Bethel AME is determined to ensure that discussions focus on mission.

4. St. Stanislaus Roman Catholic Church of Metropolis

Whom do we serve?
St. Stanislaus Roman Catholic Church (SRC) is a neighborhood church in the Polishtown area of Metropolis (pop. 3 million). SRC continues to serve the Polish community, sharing a Polish-born and trained priest with another Roman Catholic parish across the city. Now, the neighborhood is predominantly Haitian, the result of substantial immigration over the past 15 years. Total weekly mass attendance is approximately 250 and growing, as the Haitian community grows. By working with the Haitian community, we also serve the whole city of Metropolis and people in Haiti.

Who are we?
As the name suggests, Polishtown is historically Polish and our parish was founded in 1893, with our current building completed in 1910. However, much of the traditional community has moved away. We retain the traditional Catholicism of our Polish roots, balanced with a lively culture brought by our newer Haitian members. Aside from our weekly Polish-language service, we function in a mixture of English and Creole.

What is our gospel-based mission?
Our major ministry is with and on behalf of the Haitian community. This is our main opportunity for mission. For the Haitian community, we offer masses and other spiritual services, provided by a part-time Haitian priest who is also a social worker in the community. We have created a Haitian services center with a full-time coordinator (a Roman Catholic deacon) and part-time staffers and volunteers, sponsoring and caring for immigrants, providing a social center, transition training, a jobs board, computer access, and other supports; the center is open six days a week. We also seek to work with the city of Metropolis, both its official bodies and the broader community, to help them understand Haitian people and their religion, culture, gifts, and practical needs, to overcome prejudices that can be destructive of the immigrant community.

What are our resources?
Our building has plenty of space, but it is aging and is undergoing significant renovation. Both Polish and Haitian services are live-streamed. We also sponsor hybrid events that connect the Haitian immigrant community with people in Haiti, although Haitian internet access can be limited and unreliable. Financially, we depend upon a combination of parish givings and government grants that support immigrant services. Grants require annual renewal, which causes some stress because of uncertainty about government budgets. The diocese has generously supported work on our building, in recognition of the value of our ministry.

5. Northern Lake United Church

We serve	the mostly Anishnaabeg population of Northern Lake Band area (pop. 715)
We are	• our native group and language is Ojibwe • we are all fluent in English, so our worship is mostly English with Ojibwe portions • we seek to bring together our two heritages: Ojibwe and European
We do	Supporting and caring for our community: • we work closely with the Northern Lake Band organization to care for all our relations • we are a spiritual centre for our community, providing baptisms, weddings, and funerals for everyone, and sharing with the elders in the ceremonies of our band • we are helping to revive awareness of the life of the spirit among our people • in partnership with the band, we deliver meals on a weekly basis to people in need • we have a store that sells used clothing and new things (clothing, household items, art) made by local Indigenous people—the store is very popular with visitors who cottage or hunt in the area Education for change: • in partnership with Kairos Canada, a social justice organization, we have created programs to help settler people in nearby communities understand our ways of caring for the land and honoring our animal partners—this has resulted in important changes to land use and forestry agreements • we have three people trained to mentor the Kairos blanket exercise, which helps people (especially settler people) to understand some of the impact of colonization
We have	• a small church building, with up-to-date kitchen and plumbing (thanks to a grant from the band) • close partnerships with the Northern Lake Band and Kairos Canada • a part-time worship leader and pastor, trained through Sandy-Saulteaux Spiritual Centre and supported by a grant from the band • a full-time manager for the store, paid from store income • an active congregation of 11 people of all ages, which is small but currently viable with band support

6. Praise Pentecostal Church of Smalltown

Question	Data	Present	Future
Location	• Smalltown (pop. 3,500), at the intersection of Routes 1000 and 9999 • regional church, with people from across a large area in two counties, several towns	regular Sunday attendance of approximately 300—down from 2011 peak of 400	• population and social engagement decline in the area means ongoing losses in attendance and aging overall membership, which are challenges • some discussion at the county level of finding ways to increase employment, which may mean growth possibilities
Identity	• preaching Jesus Christ as Savior and Lord • lively charismatic worship with praise band • largest church in the area • youngest church in the area and only one focusing on youth ministry, which is probably our greatest strength	mostly in-person with online ministry	mostly online, with in-person ministry

Question	Data	Present	Future
Mission	• reaching young people • major focus is ministry to young people • active groups for junior (elementary school age) and senior (high school age) participants • lively activities, Bible study, Christian education • each youth group serves once per month in the local lunch program • senior group does free tutoring for kids in need of school help	• in-person youth attendance numbers have declined in recent years and covid had an impact • online group, moderated by the youth pastor and a small group of volunteers (the senior pastor has admin privileges) that maintains a healthy environment and provides a forum for group discussion of questions that matter to young people, in addition to study and prayer • online a blessing in covid, including reaching beyond our location area • 20% of youth who move away continue to have some level of engagement with our online ministry	• more of an electronic commitment • monitoring our operational systems, aware that everything is shifting
Resources	• full-time youth pastor • full-time senior pastor • full-time secretary • strong internet facilities, including broadcast room with new computers, microphones, and cameras • large and flexible building complex, completed in 1983	• focused on in-person operations • meetings and activities usually occur in our complex, requiring people to drive	planning and assembling resources for renovations, probably to focus more on capacity for online work and for rental use of spaces

Finding New Vision for a Church Organization

7. Christ Church Episcopal Cathedral of Big City

Christ Church Episcopal Cathedral (CCEC) is the seat of the Bishop of Big Diocese and a parish church in the heart of Big City (pop 2.5 million).

Roles:
1. As Cathedral, has responsibilities to the whole diocese; draws members from whole urban area and environs
2. As parish church, serves downtown core with two distinct populations
   a. Office workers
   b. Vulnerable downtown residents

Focuses for Mission:
CCEC has two core focuses for mission, seeking to reach different populations in our area.

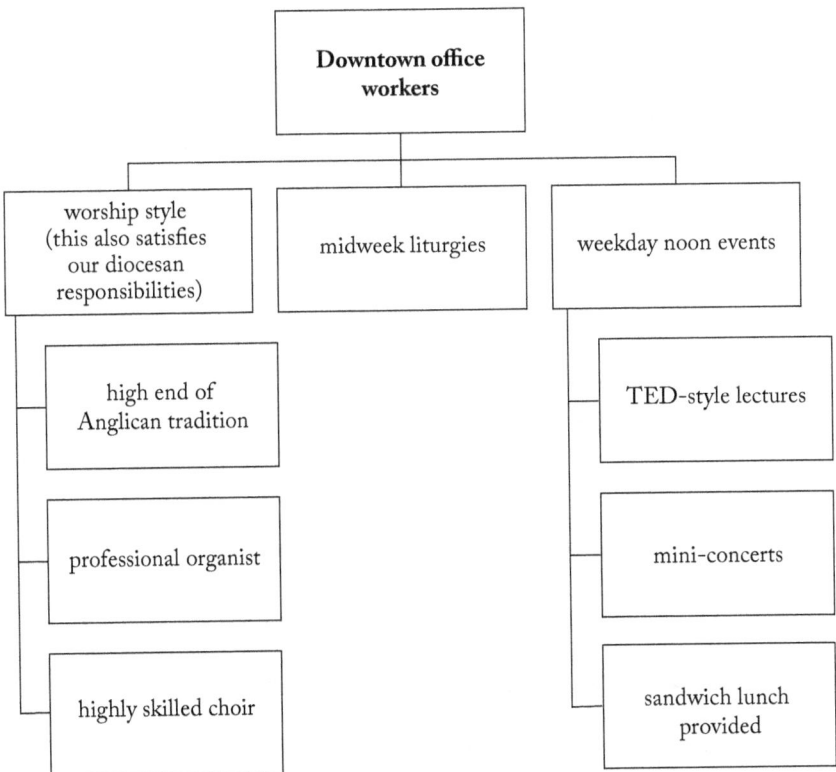

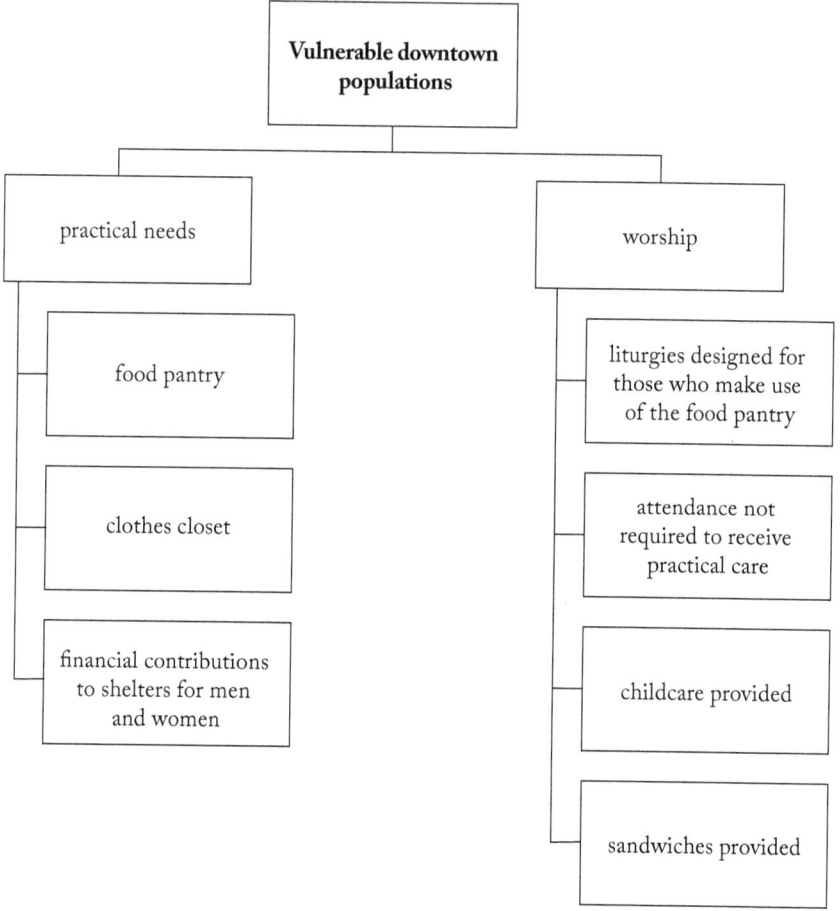

Possible Partnerships:
1. Conversations have begun about possible partnerships with other parishes, may lead to more parishioners at the Cathedral.

Strengths and Limitations to Monitor
1. Strengths
    a. Current finances
        i. Solid endowment
        ii. Generous congregational giving
    b. Capable paid staff
        i. Two priests who serve full-time
        ii. One full-time office administrator
        iii. Paid catering team
    c. Discussions of partnerships with other parishes

2. Limitations
    a. Sunday congregation aging and shrinking
    b. Fewer volunteers
3. Some Matters to Monitor Regularly
    a. How does the shrinking volunteer pool affect the paid staff?
    b. Will we need to hire more staff?
    c. How does shrinking Sunday attendance affect our overall finances?
    d. Will the endowment continue to provide the funds we need to sustain our ministries?
    e. How are partnerships with other parishes affecting our attendance, support for our ministry focuses, and our financial situation?

These GVSs share some important qualities, worthy of attention:

Unique: Each of these GVSs is different from all the others; they diversify the church (remember Heifetz's emphasis upon valuing diversity). Each of them expresses a gospel mission that is particular to its identity and context. All are somewhat inclusive, while also being exclusionary. If you are not fond of serious theological discourse and the Reformed tradition, then First Reformed Church will be an awkward home. If you simply want to slip in for worship, Faith Lutheran Parish might work for you, but the constant need for volunteers to sustain ministry in a challenging rural setting might make it uncomfortable. If you love the Black Methodist style of praise and preaching, then Bethel African Methodist Episcopal might well suit but Christ Church Episcopal Cathedral is likely to feel a bit slow. The point follows for every example. There are reasons to become part of them and reasons not to do so. Together, they enable the church to serve a broad variety of people.

Internal: I am sure that you can see why these are not appropriate for posting on your sign, out front, even if we were to imagine a sign large enough. The GVS is simply not the thing that one says to passersby who might be interested in visiting. These are also not strategic plans, though they make a great beginning for strategic planning. They speak to the priorities that a congregation wants in its plan but lack the level of detail and breadth of consideration that should appear in a strategic plan. Indeed, I encourage organizations to have such a plan and to build it directly from their GVS—but make GVS construction and strategic planning into separate, sequential processes. A GVS should remain a GVS.

Informative: Each GVS conveys information that all who are active in the congregation ought to have, so that they can be engaged with the ministry focus, the gospel focus, of the congregation. None of the information in any of them is the kind of thing that needs to be confidential. Much of it should be reasonably evident to attentive members of the congregation.

Gospel Focus: In every case, even as they recognize the risks to their own existence, these congregations are focusing on sharing God's good news. For First Reformed (FRC), that is obvious: the congregation emphasizes theology and ways that it relates to other disciplines and major questions in people's lives. FRC is all about transformation, starting with the intellect. This is great for a congregation with lots of academics in an academic town. For Faith Lutheran, the work is more indirect; however, bringing social and cultural activities with a faith dimension (communicating faith) and supporting a parish nurse (who does medical work and pastoral work, showing God's love) are ways to both show and tell. Bethel AME is explicitly focused on a commitment to educational work around justice (toward both understanding and communicating—leading to transformation of self and other), with a drive for moral transformation (including concrete care for the Black community), all continually rooted in religious transformation. St. Stanislaus's work with Haitian immigrants connects faith life with the concrete needs of a community starting out in a different country, while also speaking diaconally to the larger community out of Haitian faith and life. This engages Haitian immigrants in all kinds of transformation and enables them to touch the life of the city. Northern Lake United focuses upon changed relationships between (1) humanity and the world and (2) settler and Indigenous peoples, engaging in teaching and public engagement—especially in partnership with the band and its leadership. Praise Pentecostal provides ministry to young people, supporting them in their challenges—enabling them to grow by asking and answering questions—and engaging them with service in the community. Christ Church Episcopal works with two communities: the downtown business population, for whom they provide both entertainment and lectures (speaking the faith) and those who especially need support, for whom they provide both practical supports and specific worship opportunities. In every case, the gospel is being communicated in both word and action.

Build on the Past: The GVS examples reflect directions in which the congregations are already going and for which they are at least somewhat equipped. We have some great examples of this, such as St. Stanislaus's turning to its history of welcoming immigrants to serve Haitians, First Reformed turning its intellectual heritage into online conversations, Bethel AME building on both its justice orientation with new conversations incorporating the college and drawing upon its commitment to the African American musical heritage to foster praise-oriented rap music with young people, and Christ Church carrying its liturgical heritage into worship specially designed for the downtown population that uses the parish's social supports.

These congregations are, as Heifetz would say, building on the past. This is part of the point: God does not ordinarily call our organizations to missions for which we have no capacity. I will not say that never occurs; in moments of great crisis for neighborhoods and nations, it can happen, though such moments can also mean the discovery that we are capable of tasks that seem impossible. Moses felt ill-prepared for the task of leading the Hebrew people, but God's help enabled him. You may also find yourself and your congregation called by a great demand to respond to needs that seem to be beyond you. However, most of the time, we are invited to work for which we have some capacity.

Ultimate View and Taking Time: Saying that these examples work with existing capacities is not the same as saying that the GVS always speaks to a strong future for the organization. Instead, the emphasis is upon the ultimacy of God's transformative work. The majority of our examples indicate declining numbers, with Faith Lutheran anticipating its own closure, Bethel AME considering the possibility, Praise Pentecostal seeing fewer people and moving toward online engagement, and Christ Church Episcopal hinting that some diocesan consolidation may help to sustain them (cathedrals tend to have their own survival dynamic because dioceses ordinarily ensure continuance). The counterexamples are First Reformed, with a ministry that is currently producing stable numbers because it works with reasonably stable institutions, and St. Stanislaus, where an immigrant community is enabling growth.

All these examples involve projects that are unfolding over significant periods of time. More radical, though, is that many of the major outcomes will be clear only in the long term or very long term, if ever. Who knows what will come out of Faith Lutheran's engagement with public events where people talk about their lives from the perspectives of different faith traditions? Who knows what will come out of First Reformed's connections with scholars and others thinking about the world's questions? Who knows what will come out of Northern Lake United's cooperative work on environmental justice?

Experiments: All of them reflect experimentation, most at a level that substantially changes their identity (their DNA, as Heifetz puts it). Perhaps the most dramatic example is St. Stanislaus's shift from being a largely Polish parish to predominantly Haitian, with a whole new language, set of customs, and kind of ministry to undertake. Faith Lutheran is entering the interfaith conversation (!) and trying out the work of supporting a parish nurse. The shift to online ministry at First Reformed and Praise Pentecostal is an important, future-oriented experiment that affects their traditional onsite operations. Bethel AME is going beyond its building and outside its classic gospel music heritage to embrace contemporary Black street culture in their town. Northern Lake United is running a store with Indigenous products, while also engaging with settler communities to help them understand Indigenous life and ways. Christ Church Episcopal is leveraging its intellectual heritage to reach a noontime crowd with lectures, concerts, and lunch, and its liturgical heritage with special services. Experiments can be big or small. The important thing is to make them happen, as long as resources can support them and in ways that serve the congregation's GVS.

The last sentence about experiments indicates exactly why a GVS should be both helpful and nonthreatening. A GVS should not be a scary thing to talk about or to create. It builds on the gifts that are already in the congregation, on things that people are already doing. As Bradley Morrison points out, the vast majority of congregations are "already missional."[2] The purpose of a GVS is to focus the mission and ensure that people are both displaying and speaking the good news publicly. If the language of "Gospel Vision Statement" is off-putting, call it a "Ministry Vision Statement" or something similar. Do not lose the point, though. A GVS is about the communicating the good news, or it is about nothing at all.

Building the GVS

Of the GVS elements that we have named, geographical reach might be the easiest to clarify. A quick survey of the locations of existing participants will provide a good start. If people want to change their geographical focus, by shifting or broadening, then they are raising an identity question. Identity questions are, in principle, more difficult to resolve because they more directly refer to the reasons that people participate in the organization. Those reasons can collide, especially when there is a need to focus. Resource questions tend to follow along with identity questions. What we regard as resources tends to be defined by what we want to accomplish. An enormous facility, such as the one that I found when I arrived in my current role, is only a resource if it can be made to serve our identity; if it cannot be made to serve, perhaps by transformation, sale, or rent, then it is not a resource, but a challenge for the organization. For people seeking to clarify organizational identity, I recommend something that I call a SLOC analysis.

You may have heard of, and even used, SWOT analysis. The acronym SWOT stands for Strengths, Weaknesses, Opportunities, Threats. This is a quick and relatively easy way to analyze your organizational situation. "Strengths" and "weaknesses" describe your internal situation, while "opportunities" refers to possibilities that your organization could live out, and "threats" are forces (often external) that could be destructive to your organization and its capacity to fulfill its mission.

There are a variety of criticisms of this approach. I count myself among those who find it unhelpful. Your organization will, of course, want to identify strengths; only organizations that are very nearly dead are without some strengths. Your organization may also have weaknesses, but those are not especially relevant to imagining the future. Moreover, the term "weaknesses" can be deeply insulting and demoralizing to people in the organization who have been doing their best to respond to difficult situations; labeling your congregation's building care a "weakness" will hurt the feelings of people who have committed themselves to the work for many years, even if they have not been altogether successful in their labors. As for opportunities, the ones that you want to help people identify are those that are consistent with your mission. Those are where energies should be applied. In that case, your organization does not usually face threats, in the genuine sense of attacking forces.

I have created an alternative: SLOC analysis,[3] standing for Strengths, Limitations, Opportunities, Challenges. The most obvious difference is that SLOC analysis is more encouraging in its language. "Limitations" and "challenges" are less emotionally laden terms than "weaknesses" and "threats." More important, though, SLOC is more focused than SWOT tends to be. SLOC specifically asks the kinds of questions that you will need to answer when constructing a Gospel Vision Statement.

Strengths: The key is to start by identifying your organization's strengths. This is the core principle of Appreciative Inquiry (AI), an approach to understanding an organization that is built on the assumption that strengths are the most important thing. The kinds of questions that AI suggests are sympathetic, intended to help people to recognize that the work they have contributed is not meaningless; it makes a difference (which is not the same thing as saying that the organization can go on along the existing path). Strengths show what people care about, what participants in the life of your organization truly emphasize—rather than what everyone claims to see as a priority. Examine your organization fairly, honestly, kindly. What are its strengths? What does it do well?

Strengths include a variety of things, some obvious, some not so evident. The capacities of the people in the organization, including their levels of availability, are important considerations. Available resources, the elements that can be brought together to accomplish tasks, matter. Partnerships count. When listing strengths, the yellow sticky note approach can be helpful because different people will recognize different strengths—even different kinds of strengths—in the organization.

The important challenge is to be honest about strengths. They can be easily inflated, especially by people who look at the organization and see it as it was twenty-five or fifty years ago. This is where we get into the problem of believing that we are larger and/or stronger than we really are, only temporarily inconvenienced. We think that we still have capacities that are no longer available. We may be right in saying that Jennifer is a fine organizer and Bob has great management skills, but if Jennifer and Bob are now eighty, they may not have the same energy and availability that they once had. We look at our buildings and imagine all the activities that they could sustain, forgetting that the building is now suffering from years of insufficient care, that we do not have the money or volunteers to update facilities or to prepare spaces and ensure support for users, and that management of a building with multiple and diverse users is a major commitment.

Naming our strengths is, therefore, both exciting and challenging. It can be a moment of great discovery, as we recognize capacities that we had not fully known before. It can also be a moment of disillusionment, as we recognize implications of the changes that have occurred in our lives. We are God's people, with great hope in the transformative work of God in our lives and the life of the world. We are also members of a shrinking church, a reality that imposes boundaries on who we are and what we can do.

Limitations: The notion that there are boundaries on our capacities reminds us that we need to name them for our organization. Every one of your organization's strengths will have associated limitations. Limitations are not best understood as weaknesses. The language of "weaknesses" implies some level of failure, with a need for corrective action, and can easily lead a group away from its focus. One of the limitations of the neighborhood church that we discussed earlier was a shortage of young people and ministry to young people; seen as a weakness, this might have implied a need to focus on developing this aspect of ministry, whereas, seen as a limitation, this simply suggested that pursuing a different goal—ministry to seniors—was a more helpful path. Limitations may, indeed, be a reason for action, perhaps for refocusing, training, or new action.

On the other hand, limitations often function simply as parameters for the strengths. A congregation that has a rock band for worship and includes intense sound and light elements has a kind of music and presentation as a strength. At the same time, this strength constructs a whole set of limitations, not the least of which is that people living with some physical conditions such as autism or epilepsy are unlikely to find that congregation to be a comfortable place to worship. They may feel more at home in the congregation down the street that is built around quiet, meditative, somewhat repetitive liturgy.

Limitations, therefore, are often best understood as parameters rather than weaknesses. Limitations are the aspects of our identities and capacities that define what we genuinely can and will do. Working with them is difficult because they tend to be the locations of serious conflict. Some limitations are exactly the sorts of things that we most wish to preserve about ourselves. If a change in worship style from formal with organ to informal with praise band would mean the departure of most of the congregation, then it is unlikely to be a worthwhile shift, even if it offers growth potential, though a second service (different time? different day?) could be an interesting option. Other limitations are the aspects of our organizations where challenges are most necessary. If your congregation is right around the corner from a shelter for women in need, perhaps the congregation needs to consider whether it might be able to adjust its way of being—pushing the boundaries of its existing limitations—to serve the neighbors whom God has provided.

The kinship between limitations and weaknesses emerges when an organization has not been honest with itself about its strengths. If the group claims strengths that it does not have, then the critique of those claims will tend to emerge in the conversation about limitations. This is a moment when people can begin to admit that they are not really able or do not truly want to live up to some of the capacities listed under strengths. In that sense, the conversation about limitations serves as something of a self-checking mechanism for assertions about the organization's capabilities.

At the end of the strengths and limitations conversations, the group should be able to say something about its identity and resources. These two categories are ways of getting at the issue of how an organization defines itself. In the process, the group will have gotten halfway to a GVS.

Opportunities: Identifying opportunities might be the most difficult portion of the work. It involves a balance of imagination and realism. You are seeking insights into possibilities that match the strengths and limitations of the organization and enable the group to respond helpfully to the challenges that the organization faces. This means that "opportunities" is not simply a random category of things that could be done.

Imagination is needed to propose a vision for life and purpose that will engage the organization and serve God's transformational work in the world. In order to get there, the group will need to combine a clear understanding of the good news with a deep awareness and understanding of the people and area that the organization serves. A truly diaconal church must always be dedicated to knowing the world and its needs; this is the meaning of being in God's service. Brainstorming can be a helpful place to start, especially with a group of capable and dedicated thinkers.

Ultimately, though, realism will need to rule, so the final list cannot be simply an assemblage of yellow sticky notes. As we have already seen, a GVS that does not reflect the organization and its context is not really that organization's GVS. Therefore, a true insight into the possibilities for an organization will reflect organizational realities as much as it shows true knowledge of the world. Genuine opportunities are not merely things that need to be done. The world contains a truly infinite number of these and many of them require very long-term commitment, significant knowledge, and substantial resources. Assembling a list of things that an organization might do is easy. Turning that into a list of opportunities for *your* organization is vastly more difficult. This requires a much more complex set of insights into who we are and what we can do.

Thinking about opportunities will help to clarify the mission and location aspects of a GVS. If the group is dedicated to missions that are largely focused on the local neighborhood, and has resources especially suited to fulfilling those missions, then the neighborhood is where their mission is located. Conversely, if there is enthusiasm for—and commitment to—missions that are citywide or even national or international, and the group has access to the necessary resources, then the larger world is where their mission is located.

There is something systematic about the process that we are working through here. Clarity about strengths illuminates limitations. A solid, honest, grasp of strengths and limitations helps to bring definition to opportunities. The systematic aspect of thinking must go beyond the process of discernment, however. As people consider opportunities, they need to remember—and the leaders may be called upon to remind them—that the organization will be called upon to structure itself according to the opportunities to which they commit themselves. If the group is not ready to commit itself to a design suited to the mission(s) that they finally select, then that is not really their mission; it may be nothing more than something that they would like to think of as their mission.

In other words, every organization comes with its own set of challenges, as does every selection of opportunities.

Challenges: Challenges are not usually threats. They are not ordinarily purposeful attacks designed to undermine us. Even the issues that might cause difficulties for our organizations are not often genuine threats. Moreover, thinking of our challenges as threats can be counterproductive; that approach has an unfortunate potential to create a battle mindset, concealing complex realities and driving away from the gospel priorities associated with being ambassadors of reconciliation.

Instead, challenges are conditions that call for action, while also limiting our options. Declining attendance, diminishing resources, and lack of clarity about mission are all examples of challenges. Faced with any or all of the above, as we commonly are in a shrinking church, we need to do something. The greater and more immediate the challenges, the fewer options we are likely to have.

However, we may still be able to identify possibilities for moving forward. A tightly focused mission, carefully designed to match our identity and resources, may be both possible and a source of new vigor. Either alternatively or simultaneously, there may be options for partnerships. Then again, as we have seen and will discuss again, closure, the death of an organization, is not a threat to Christians. It is a moment for us to look for God's work of transformation, of resurrection.

We need to approach naming challenges in a spirit of honesty, with as little fear as possible. Commonly, identifying the challenges that we face is not intellectually difficult. Most of them will have come up in parking lot conversations or posed themselves as irresolvable in the dreams of leaders. The difficulty naming the challenges tends to be more psychological than intellectual. Resistance tends to come from emotional factors. If the budget is a problem, people generally know it but are not very happy about admitting it and needing to deal with it. If the building is a problem, people can avert their eyes from developing issues and sound quite threatened when the issue is named; the building is often home to committed members. The difficulty is in the need to address our emotional responses, so that we can begin to consider possibilities that may not look like the present.

The challenges are often connected to identity and resources. If attendance is shrinking, then we become aware that our identity, including aspects of the church that matter deeply to us, is not attracting people. This may mean that we will need to let go of pieces of us that we regard as nonnegotiable, parts of organizational life that we do not feel ready to change. We may find that we lack the resources to sustain aspects of church that we have treated as indispensable. Again, limited resources may mean letting go of parts of church life that we have traditionally held tightly. In a shrinking church, we tend to live with declining resources of all kinds—including financial—and that causes anxiety and doubt. When the church overall is shrinking and membership is likely to decline for some time to come, hope can be difficult to find.

Simply engaging in the work of producing a GVS can bring both hopes and fears to the surface, enabling the group to give thoughtful consideration to the validity and implications of both. The process can be beneficial. Ultimately, the result should be focus that will enable the group to move forward on a common trajectory.

Lead With Focus

The core point of the argument in this chapter is that, in a shrinking church, leaders must lead with focus. Know your mission. Play within it.[4]

In 1960, we could plant a congregation with the expectation that it could do everything for everybody, that is, everything that we wanted it to do wherever we wanted it done. In fact, even then, as we have seen, a congregation would still be limited by the choices that members made. However, there was plenty of room to accommodate a wide variety of demands, even ones that were inconsistent or contradictory. If the arrangement did not work out, then we could plant another congregation nearby, and the two could balance each other. Besides, many denominations worked on the principle of a congregation in every neighborhood, so cities, and even large towns, provided multiple options within the same denomination.

Today, those sorts of accommodations are not options. A congregation, like a seminary and even a denomination, must make choices and live by them. A GVS is designed to focus the purpose of the organization. Having one is absolutely necessary. Moreover, the GVS must be followed consistently or, if it ceases to serve the congregation well for some reason, reconceived to meet the new situation.

Working With a GVS

The big challenge of working with a GVS takes us right back to where we started: Christians do not want to leave anyone out. No, let me rephrase that: Christians fundamentally believe that everyone should be included; everyone should be able to participate as fully as they wish; and everyone should receive the care that they request. The church should be inclusive.

When First Reformed (FRC) chooses to focus on the academic community, they are pitching themselves above the heads of some people and outside the interests of others. When St. Stanislaus (SRC) commits to work with the Haitian community, they make theological, pastoral, linguistic, stylistic, and other choices that may override the preferences of other people in the area. Sticking to these decisions can be a challenge. Criticizing FRC for being too intellectual and, therefore, too exclusive or elitist would be very easy. Attacking SRC for ignoring the Anglo community in their neighborhood would be simple. However, both communities have found a specific mission purpose, people to whom they are speaking the good news, serving as ambassadors of reconciliation. Other people can either choose to join the ministry or find another congregation. These ministries should not be lost.

Often, however, the challenge is more complicated than that. People in the congregation will spot needs that are real and touch the congregation. A member of Christ Church Episcopal (CCEC) will recognize that older members of the congregation are starting to be resident in seniors' facilities and press the parish council to expand the ministry to seniors significantly. These are CCEC people and should receive greater attention; plus, they know people who might be interested in the church. What then? Ministry to seniors is not in the CCEC GVS. A colleague of mine tells of being in a meeting where someone proposed a new ministry idea and received a brilliant response: "Yes, that's a great idea, but it's not in our mandate." If it is not in the GVS, then it is not in the mandate. If there is general belief that it should be in the GVS, then the GVS needs revision. In the case of CCEC, ministry to seniors in facilities around the city and suburbs is not part of the mission, or even closely associated with the mission. It is beyond the horizon of the congregation's mission. CCEC carries specific diocesan responsibilities and serves the downtown core. Clergy and lay ministers may participate in some sort of roster for hospitals and care homes, as a parish in the city; this comes with the territory. Beyond that, ministry to seniors' facilities is a space for someone else's gospel vision.

If the voices raising the idea of expanded ministry to seniors are influential and the proposal excites some people, it may be proposed as an addition to the GVS. This sets up the next problem: mission creep. We start out with clarity and then add pieces. Very soon, we have lost clarity about our purpose. Commonly, we have also stretched our resources beyond what we can reasonably accomplish. GVSs are meant to be integrated documents. They identify the people whom a ministry is trying to serve. They also name the resources available to support that work. Continually adding to a GVS—or, worse, departing from it—soon creates a mess. In the case of CCEC, the addition of a focus on ministry to seniors' facilities will move away from an emphasis on the downtown core to engagement with people across the city. This will be a problem fairly immediately because CCEC has a shrinking, aging congregation and a declining volunteer base. The congregation is only able to sustain existing ministries with the support of substantial paid staff. Probably, the expectation built into the idea is that clergy will simply add to their existing workload, but they are already using all their capacity for existing ministries. This is a long way of reminding us of the importance of doing less with less. This means just saying "No." Simple addition is not a beneficial way to change a GVS.

A GVS develops healthily in one of two ways. One way is that a mission shifts character by changing size or by finding new methods. Praise Pentecostal, in our examples, is changing in both ways. Fewer people are attending in person, but the online work is developing momentum. Their GVS shows a real shift toward online work, which is having an impact on every aspect of their ministry, including their use of physical facilities. The other way is a significant change in the community that a congregation is trying to reach. This happened for St. Stanislaus, which started as a predominantly Polish ministry and is now in the advanced stages of becoming a Haitian ministry. Some aspects of the Polish ministry remain because resources are available to sustain those pieces, but they are clearly legacy activities.

Faith Lutheran (FLP) gives us an interesting example of working with a GVS. The congregations have committed to a mission that has a time horizon. They cannot be specific about the date, but they envision that their ministry will end within a reasonably imaginable time frame. This is a GVS which admits the very real possibility that no new GVS will follow. If their communities continue to die, then they will also die. The power of the GVS is that FLP is recognizing this and living it purposefully, rather than fatalistically. This is a cross-oriented gospel vision. It reminds us that when no GVS is possible, the time for closure has come—a point that we will consider in a later chapter on closure of ministries.

Further Steps in Transformation

All the sample GVSs that we have seen are ways of focusing current capacities toward transformation. Our thinking about intellectual, psychic, moral, and religious transformation encourages us to consider next steps, ways of taking the work deeper into fostering self-appropriation in congregations and the world beyond. A GVS is purposefully brief and will always miss something of the message content that we want to convey. In this case, we are unable to express the importance of inviting people into the world-changing vision of self-engagement to which God calls us.

Within the organization (including congregations), and eventually beyond, we can strengthen our ministry by offering programs that help people to understand the importance of self-appropriation. If the organization is oriented toward transformation in its members, its partners, and those whom it seeks to serve, then it must always be seeking to grow in its own self-appropriation. The members must be engaged in developing skills in understanding and fostering their own availability to God's work of intellectual, psychic, moral, and religious transformation in their own selves. Only then can members participate in enabling others to know these transformations in their lives.

We need to learn to ask ourselves questions about the ways that we think, feel, and act. Sargent Shriver is a helpful example of what can be accomplished because he was able to identify the questions that he needed to ask, while also recognizing God at work in his life. If we train ourselves to ask questions about our own acts of understanding and deciding, then we can recognize places where we have not been sufficiently open to the movement of the power that we know as the Holy Spirit. If, for instance, we find ourselves reacting harshly to recent immigrants, such as the Haitians from our St. Stanislaus example, we can ask ourselves what is happening when we interact with them. How do we imagine ourselves in those interactions? What interferes? Is there a prejudicial gut feeling, indicating a need for psychic transformation? Is there insufficient understanding, to be answered with asking and answering further questions about who the Haitians are, what they have left, and ways they contribute upon arrival? Is there a resistance that is based in selfishness, a desire to withhold what has become mine? What is causing the inappropriate response?

Ultimately, the purpose of engaging in this ongoing work of self-understanding, of self-engagement, is to be available to God. We do not accomplish our own transformation. In technical theological terms, the process that we are discussing is called "sanctification." This language speaks to our being made holy; 2 Corinthians 5:21 names it as being made "the righteousness of God." This is the divine inbreaking that we have called "explosions." This is not our job, but the work of the power that we call the Holy Spirit. However, resolutely marching more deeply into our own misunderstandings, our own moral failings, and our own psychological limitations causes destruction in our lives and the life of the world. This way of life functions as a resistance to God. God can and will overcome it, but the pain that we create for ourselves and others in the process can be immense. There is far greater joy in choosing to participate in God's transformative work in us and the world. Thus, the church's organizations need to sustain training in self-appropriation for all as the core of the church's mission.

Communicate

A central role of a leader is always to communicate. The importance of this role increases as an organization faces greater stress. A shrinking church is a rising stress situation.

There are some points that a leader needs to emphasize in the context of declining membership.

Urgency: An organization may not have grasped the urgency of the situation. People who watch budgets and congregational reports carefully, while observing the overall health of the organization, are few. Often, only one or two people meet this description, even when anxiety is common. In a congregation, these people tend to be clergy and council chairs/wardens or other senior-level lay leaders, along with treasurers who can see rising costs and declining giving. In other organizations, they tend to be CEOs, CFOs, and board chairs. In any case, most members, employees, and other stakeholders have little sense of the larger challenges that the organization faces.

As a leader, you may be the person who holds the role of sharing the challenging news. My first piece of advice comes from *The Hitchhiker's Guide to the Galaxy*: "Don't Panic."[5] When a new leader arrives and discovers that the situation is much worse than anyone admitted, one likely first inclination is to respond out of insufficiently processed emotion. When a leader begins to delve into the life of the organization and meets all the stress-induced warfare or other destructive behavior, one possible first inclination (and I have seen it emerge) is to respond out of strong and unreflective emotion. This is unlikely to help, partly because it evokes many of the least healthy responses to the situation.

Instead, this is the moment to take time and clarify the situation. Heifetz encourages us to begin by diagnosing the system, the nature of the challenge, and the political landscape.[6] We need to understand the circumstances, asking and answering the relevant questions (and Heifetz offers a useful framework for identifying questions to be considered). Expressing the urgency of the situation certainly involves emotion. However, at these sorts of moments, an organization is much more in need of two things: reasonably detailed assessment and a process for discernment. Conviction and calm are important, as is having some answers prepared. The SLOC process is intended to help the group get to both the information and the approach to decision-making. Whether you use this or another method, your organization will need to take seriously being attentive, intelligent, reasonable, responsible, and—most of all—loving.

Being ambassadors of reconciliation does not mean engaging in avoidance of conflict. A GVS reached by a process that avoids conflict is at significant risk of failing either because it is simply an inaccurate representation of the congregation and its possibilities, or because it fails to respond to pressures within the congregation. If the conflict simmers beneath the surface, it will emerge eventually. In the case where serious conflict derails or is likely to derail a GVS process, then leaders are wise to participate in conflict management training or engage a leader from outside. Heifetz has reminded us to value diversity of viewpoints.[7] He also encourages us to invite differences, using thoughtfully designed and led processes that enable people to take different positions and to work productively after debate is concluded.[8] With diversity comes conflict. Leaders, therefore, are called to expect conflict, prepare themselves for it, and make opportunities for it, setting the expectation that the group will hear a variety of opinions, understandings, and ideas that appear to go in different directions. This means including people who may be troublesome or whose vision disagrees with yours, requiring you to stretch your capacity for bearing conflict.[9]

The purpose of the SLOC process is to help the group to discern a healthy way forward. When the views are on the table, your task as a leader is to enable the group to make decisions and some of these may be difficult. If the group is reasonably cohesive and has a more or less shared understanding of its situation, then a variety of viewpoints may be brought together into common ground for a GVS. If an organization is viable, then you can reach this point. If there is not enough agreement for a GVS, whether because of diverging views or as a result of interpersonal conflict, then the group will need to consider an intervention by a professional in conflict resolution or, in some cases, closure.

Theological Purpose and Organizational Direction: The point of working with a GVS is that it enables leaders to focus on the point. The challenges that your organization faces must be named with theological purpose. The focus must be on the good news of Christ Jesus, which must be communicated constantly.

This may seem obvious. However, in the midst of crisis, it is not always clear. We can easily become sidetracked with emphasis on attendance, or buildings, or the financial picture. That makes sense. These tend to be the presenting issues and the priorities of people around us. Your auditors and bankers probably do not really care whether the organization is serving as an ambassador of reconciliation, fostering intellectual, psychic, moral, and religious transformation. They do care whether you can meet the bills that are coming due in the next twelve months.

A GVS stands as a ready reminder that we engage with church because of the importance of God's transformative work in the life of the world and in our lives. This is what provides organizational direction. Survival of the organization is not the reason for our participation. The gospel is the reason. Leaders, therefore, must continually communicate about the links between the good news, with its call to be ambassadors of reconciliation, and the mission named in the GVS. If this is lost, then the congregation is at risk of floundering.

Hope: Leaders convey hope. Heifetz says, "inspire people"[10]; as a Christian theologian, I would say, "remind people that God inspires them." In a shrinking church, that feels like a strange thing to say because there is a real risk that hope rings false in the situation. It need not, however. Instead, hope can be the voice that changes the narrative.

Hope is both theological and practical. Theologically, hope asserts that God is with us, that God is performing God's transformative work in us and the world, and that we can recognize it and participate in it. However much we tend to center ourselves, our organizations, our narratives, we are but a small part of the universe and of history. God is present in and to all of it, pointing out and fostering the kinds of transformations that are needed.

This is not a simple or simplistic kind of hope. Modernity stripped religion from the picture, imagining that humanity could bring about a kind of perfect world without religious transformation—as in Kant's argument that economic progress would eliminate war.[11] Progress seemed inevitable. Christian hope is not the assumption that progress will simply happen. This runs directly counter to our critique of destructiveness (sin), rooted in the lack of transformation in people's lives. Assumptions of inevitable progress are also completely inconsistent with the data of the world as we encounter it. Interestingly, the failure of that vision often contributes to our own lack of hope. We do things like remember the optimism of the 1960s and notice that the Age of Aquarius has not arrived. We face a whole range of challenges that were only beginning to be imagined then. Christian hope does not promise anything as easy as generational change—or any of the anticipated shifts that were expected to come with it—for a solution to the world's problems.

Instead, hope is the assertion that our engagement in the life of transformation is meaningful and worthwhile, that the power that we call the Holy Spirit is present in us and in the world, literally inspiring. Precisely because God continues to be with us and all of creation, enriching us and drawing us into life through the power of love, our moments of growth are participations in God's remaking of all things. Our smallest acts of love attain cosmic value and importance. We do not need to have 2,000 people attending our churches every Sunday to contribute, to be part of God's great work. Nor are we responsible for reaching everyone, in every way. We are called to be whom we are called to be.

If the message of this book could be distilled into a single phrase, that might be it: "We are called to be whom we are called to be." Every organization needs to find out whom it is called to be and live that role, transformatively. To do that, we often work with partners, because transformation is a communal activity.

Exercises: Finding New Vision for Church Organizations

A. Your Life

1. Take all the thinking that you have done about yourself. Assemble a brief GVS for your life, based on the core commitments to which you are called.

B. Your Organization

1. Take all the thinking that you have done about your organization. Assemble a brief and hypothetical GVS for your organization. If you are reading this book with others in your organization, work together with them. Remember that constructing a real GVS involves everyone in the organization, so this GVS will only be hypothetical unless everyone is engaged in the process. The purpose of the exercise is to help you to: 1) get some practice with the mechanics of a GVS, and 2) think about organization's direction and future.

C. The World

1. How does your personal GVS enable you to be an ambassador of reconciliation, supporting the four transformations in the world?
2. How does your organization's GVS enable your organization to be an ambassador of reconciliation, supporting the four transformations in the world?

CHAPTER 8

PARTNER, THOUGHTFULLY

The good news, as we have discussed it, is about being ambassadors of reconciliation. Reconciliation is precisely about partnering. If we are not prepared to be partners with others, then we are, at most, tolerating others. We are not engaging with God's transformative work in us or in the world. Truly understanding others through the vision of God's love, truly being reconciled with them, means recognizing the gifts that they bring to the world, even when they disagree with us about significant issues.

In fact, churches are partnering today. We ought to do so, and we must do so. As we say in a seminary partnership where I am, "Mission drawn. Necessity driven." The disagreements and style differences that have driven churches apart over the last millennium are real and significant, but they cannot be allowed to define our identities forever. Only the deepest issues that genuinely affect our understanding of the gospel can stand between us. In the language of the Lund Principle, we should "act together in all matters except those in which deep differences of conviction compel [us] to act separately."[1] This is true for substantial theological reasons: the gospel calls us to live in love with other followers of Jesus, so living in competition or, worse yet, enmity is a betrayal of our core purpose. Also, the commitment to act together is pressing for strong practical reasons: declining numbers and resources often give us little choice.

Moreover, if our account of transformation is correct, if the church is invited to participate in the intellectual, psychic, moral, and spiritual transformation of people's lives, then the church's sense of partnership must go beyond our Christian siblings. We must be prepared to work with people with different formal religious commitments and with none at all, insofar as they share our understandings of transformation.

Most people see the need to act in partnership today, so we will not dwell on the point at greater length. However, we also recognize that some partnerships will not work well at all, while other partnerships have a particular and strictly defined value. A commitment to reconciliation carries us to the point of willingness to live in reconciliation. It does not help us where reconciliation can happen only in a limited way or not at all. Destructive partnerships do not contribute to transformation in the ways that we would hope. Instead, they can be part of the recipe for a cycle of decline. Consequently, our focus will be on the knotty problem of discerning when and how to enter into partnerships.

Good Partnerships

Partnerships are, in principle, a good thing. However, not all partnerships are good ones. I was among the senior staff in a judicatory, sitting down for our weekly meeting. A staff member raised a very interesting question. "Why do we go to all the effort to bring all these congregations together when so many of the new arrangements fail soon afterward? It doesn't seem worth it." That got me thinking. Even the simplest partnerships take a significant amount of work to construct; more complex ones can take years and every ounce of energy that the organizations involved are able to muster. If an organization, such as a congregation, is facing real challenges, then the work of building the partnership may, itself, be sufficient to kill the organization. At the same time, there are shining examples of successes in partnerships.

I spent time reviewing the successes and failures and came to a simple but revealing conclusion: The purpose of the partnership defines potential outcomes. Often, congregations were joined together in new configurations so that they could survive. If survival is the goal, then the ceiling that is established is survival. Fulfillment of the goal is the best possible outcome. Cases that lead to a less-than-optimal result abound, which means that closure is common. All they aimed for was survival and many did not make it. We could join three or four congregations into a shared configuration, and they would find themselves with a mutual commitment that extended only as far as sharing the bills, an activity often accompanied by complaints about how much of the presbyter's time is given to each and where the presbyter lives, and so on. We could add a congregation of thirty people to a congregation of thirty people and end up with a congregation of thirty to forty people, with few willing to go to a different building and people from both congregations unhappy about having to share pews. In other words, survival is not an adequate reason for a partnership; it does not engage people enough to promise a future, even as it drains the energy that might have been used in finding an alternative possibility.

In contrast, the partnerships that survived and thrived were defined by a sense of common mission, reaching either the same or related locations, with similar or complementary identities, and with resources that provided mutual support. One of my favorite examples is of a congregation (call it Church A) that needed to close because their beautiful historic building, with notable artwork, faced structural problems that would have required millions of dollars in renovation and repair, a commitment far beyond the capacity of the small but active membership. They were considering the possibility of moving in with, and becoming part of, another congregation in their denomination (call it Church B), located in a nearby neighborhood in the same city. As the small congregation of Church A discussed the idea with the other group, the main questions for Church B were about the active urban ministries that had been central to the life of Church A. Would there be space for the food, clothing, and social ministries? Would the new congregation

(Church A + B) embrace them and participate in them? The answers were very encouraging, and the move occurred on the strength of shared commitment to a range of ministries in the city. The outcome was excellent, with a large percentage of the congregation of Church A making the move and the ministries being sustained.

The information that goes into a Gospel Vision Statement (GVS) is the same basic information that guides the partnership question. Partnerships that are simply about survival, about maintaining basic operations, have a low ceiling: if successful, they will enable survival. Partnerships that enable your mission focus (or help you to find a new mission focus), are consistent with your location and identity considerations, and provide shared resources, are the kinds of partnerships that can succeed for you.

The first questions to be considered, therefore, are about your mission focus. What is your mission? Having a clear sense of mission is a strong way to enter into a partnership. It enables your organization to know that its meaning is not being jettisoned. Remember that being church is predominantly about meaning, about how the world is to be understood correctly in light of God's love, and about how we are called to act in response. Church is fundamentally about being outward looking, participating in God's work of transformation. This is theologically correct. It is also organizationally sound. Any consideration of a partnership will cause some uncertainty in all the communities that are affected. If everyone is clear that your organization has a mission and knows it and is committed to sustaining that mission in any partnership arrangement, then your organization will move forward with greater confidence, with a sense that the communities that you serve will continue to be served as God has called you to serve them.

We can see this with the example of churches A and B, in our case of a successful partnership. Church A brings a range of new and exciting ministries to the life of Church B. This means an expansion of Church B's mission, enriching Church B. At the same time, Church B's life carries on, so that Church A, in joining Church B, inherits a new set of commitments. Their missions were not the same but were sufficiently compatible and complementary that a partnership had solid potential. The shared denominational commitment linked to the ministry priorities in such a way that both churches could see their identities sustained and even expanded.

The possibility of changed mission in a partnership is important, may even be vital in every sense of the word. New life can come from a partnership that brings a new sense of possibility, new opportunities for being ambassadors of reconciliation. If all partners in a new configuration bring strengths that can be complementary and are open to a new sense of mission, the outcome can be powerful. At best, the new configuration will be one that can imagine together the components of a GVS that will represent a common vision.

Church A and Church B served adjacent and overlapping geographical areas, with largely similar demographics, within the same city. In both cases, they related to a predominantly urban population, in a community with significant needs for support—a postindustrial city that had declined from its powerful position in the continental economy, which had never really needed its large number of churches and needed few but active congregations by the time of the merger. Few were needed because of a relatively small number of Christians. Active were needed because of the broad range of people with specific needs to which a diaconal church could respond. The combination of mission, location, and identity was a strong indicator that the relationship could work.

The resource relationship between Church A and Church B was simple, clear, and mutually beneficial. Church B had more room than it could use, including flexible use spaces that were ideal for the mission work that Church A sought to continue. Members of both churches were interested in sustaining the activities, so that the human resources were available. Because the location continued to be suitable, no added resources were needed to ensure that common work could occur. There were no additional costs for either congregation, while some obvious savings could be focused on ministry. This was easy.

We need to recognize that the process is not always this straightforward. There are often major issues of denomination involved. Working across denominations can be very difficult; even when we use the same words, we do not always mean the same thing. Denominations, and the theological/ecclesiological heritages they carry, often bring very different expectations. Whether or not denominational differences affect a partnership, numerous other considerations intrude: buildings, financial resources (and lack thereof), human resources (including employee futures), formal and informal authority structures, worship expectations, and so on. The list can seem endless.

Too easily, we can assume that agreement and general support will be enough. This seems to be especially true in cases where a partnership seems likely, such as neighboring congregations in the same denomination. Perhaps surprisingly, this is a risky situation, in spite of examples like Church A and Church B, above. Too often, this—apparently simple and logical—act is unwise. If Church Y and Church Z are both in danger of closure, the obvious answer is to join them together; this makes even greater sense when there is goodwill on both sides.

Unfortunately, the mere act of connecting one dying organization to another dying organization does not ensure life for either one. Indeed, the effort involved may accelerate the process of death for both. The work of coming together takes time and energy that shrinking organizations may not have to give. Partnership development requires a lot of meetings, plenty of deep thinking, serious consideration of financial situations—both records of the past and implications for the future—a massive amount of communication, and more. Often, the process simply takes time. This is real, hard, work, and not for the faint of heart or the tired and disenchanted. It is, indeed, best done while organizations have excess capacity to manage the transition. The effort needed to continue with the organization's original ministry while also sustaining conversations about partnership and possibilities is substantial. If organizations lack the capacity for this, they stand at risk of burning out leaders—who may then be unavailable for action after the partnership is consummated—or poorly done work because insufficient resources were assigned to the task. The work of creating and growing into a partnership is easy to underestimate.

Unless Church Y and Church Z have, or can develop, a strong vision for integrated or complementary ministry beyond the moment of partnership, there may be very little point in the work. That is why building a shared GVS, whether it bears that name or not, is tremendously important. The pieces that go into a GVS are basic conditions for partnership success. A church partnership, like any other church organization, needs to know the answers to three questions. Who are we? Whom we trying to reach? With what are we trying to reach them? Without solid answers to these questions, a partnership is unlikely to be stronger than the partners and may be weaker.

This means that we need to choose our partners carefully, based in our answers to the GVS questions. At least as important, partnerships need to build together purposefully, ensuring that they serve gospel purposes together.

The Meaning of Partnerships in a Shrinking Church

Partnerships take on new meaning in a shrinking church. Our openness to partnerships today signals some important shifts. By definition, partnering means choosing to work with others rather than relying on our own capacities. This is a choice that we make because we are shifting away from a sense that the gospel has called us to separation from people with whom we could work together. We are moving into a sense that the gospel call places reconciliation above competition. This belief has always been part of the church's life and thought. However, separation between the churches of East and West (finalized in 1054 CE), followed by the Protestant Reformation of the sixteenth century and successive splits, has tended to harden differences. Moreover, one of the impulses of modernity has been the desire to create clear and bounded categories, an effort that we see most obviously in the work of Carl Linnaeus, the inventor of the system that we use to name biological organisms. Unfortunately, we also see the emphasis of categorization less helpfully in the invention of races and racism. The effect of church separation and society's desire for defined categories is that the church has lived in an environment where difference has stood out above similarity. Thus, churches, whether denominational or independent, have tended to focus on the things that distinguish us, rather than the things that bind us together.

This is not altogether inappropriate. Some of the differences are only in style, which may seem pointless, but is not necessarily. Stylistic distinctions can serve different personalities. I have visited a variety of church congregations which would not be my first choice for a church home because they worship in a less-structured way than I prefer or their services have a different balance among elements (readings, preaching, Eucharist, prayers) than suits me best. As long as there have been plenty of Christians to fill plenty of pews, we have had room for many denominations in villages, towns, and cities everywhere. That is less true as time passes, which means that we may need to make some compromises in our selections, submitting to other people's preferences in various ways.

There are differences that go deeper and are not so easily overcome, though. Over the past half-century, a number of issues, predominantly related to sex and gender (ordination of women, sexual identity, gender identity, abortion) and race (immigration, acceptance of racialized minorities), have opened fault lines that often run through denominations. The 2024 split in the United Methodist Church in the United States is only one of the more recent examples of an experience that has been common to churches throughout the Anglosphere. These differences limit partnerships.

In a shrinking church where the numbers narrative is not helpful, we are forced to get past an emphasis on difference, where and when that is possible. If religious transformation is the encounter with transforming love, and if meeting God has the effect of enabling us to know the world as God knows it—in transforming love—then we are called to participate in God's transformative work with people who disagree with us in other ways. Where we can participate together in some aspect of intellectual, psychic, moral, or religious transformation, shared action is valuable, even across lines of deep disagreement.

One of my favorite examples of ecumenism in mission is the Association of Theological Schools (ATS), the main seminary professional body in North America. In ATS, we work with Christian seminaries of all kinds. The selection includes a broad variety of Protestant, Roman Catholic, and Orthodox schools; big and small, liberal and conservative; with different ethnic heritages and predominant languages, all sharing insights into ways that we can serve God. We meet and discuss our common challenges—including the difficulties of working in a shrinking church—and pass along the wisdom that we have gained through hard work, often of a painful sort. Being a seminary today is not easy; ATS is one of our main supports. The Association is also our accrediting body. Volunteering on an accrediting team means learning about other denominations, their priorities and systems, because we accredit schools on the basis of their sense of call rather than ours. An accrediting investigation team will ordinarily include people from a whole variety of denominations, so that the seminary must communicate its meanings to others, while others seek to understand. We do a lot of work to support each other, even when our theologies and politics are different, sometimes opposed. We also hold each other accountable to common institutional goals, with a view to stronger theological education that meets shared standards. There are limits to the ways in which we can work together because of our disagreements; however, within the bounds of the specific set of priorities that ATS brings, we can accomplish important goals. Partnering in this way is not always easy but it has proved to be worthwhile for us, because it contributes to our life of transformation.

The key to discerning whether a shared venture is possible is always defined by our Gospel Vision Statement (GVS), itself crafted in relation to our commitment to transformation. If a partnership serves some aspect of the GVS, then it is worthy of consideration. If a partnership undermines our GVS, preventing significant kinds of transformation to which we are committed, then it must be avoided—even if it seems desirable for financial or other reasons. We need to be prepared to make choices.

There is not always a bright and obvious line between partnerships that serve our GVS and ones that undermine our GVS. Some partnerships are broadly destructive; these must be avoided and, indeed, opposed. On the other hand, some partnerships bring evident benefits but are not ones that serve our GVS; these are good missions—for someone else. We will always need to return to the task of asking and answering all the relevant questions and making the best judgments that we can in the face of complex decisions for our organizations. The argument of this book is that there are no "drop in the data, pop out the decision" systems that can help us to resolve our challenges. Instead, we are called to the life of self-appropriation, of growing in God's transformation, so that we can make good decisions and live them well as questions emerge in our own lives and the lives of our organizations.

Ambassadors Beyond a Shrinking Church

This positioning takes us precisely to the location where we started in discussing the good news. In the letter to the Corinthians from which we quoted, Paul was encouraging the Christians in Corinth to be generous to people in need, rather than focusing on their own sectarianism. That is one of the reasons why he emphasized the priority of being ambassadors of reconciliation. In the world that we know as Christians, the new creation made and lit by divine love, transformation calls for a kind of generosity of spirit, an openness to the ways that God works through others in the world and through the world itself.

If religious transformation is not about making people into Christians, but is about inviting them to encounter God's love, and if religious transformation is deeply linked with intellectual, psychic, and moral transformation, then the world is full of potential partners. There are many people everywhere who are engaged with all these aspects of human development. An ambassadorial church, a diaconal church, will find these people and work with them.

We can return to our examples of GVS statements for samples of ways that this can be done. First Reformed Church undertakes a rather cerebral kind of ministry, one oriented toward asking and answering questions about the world. Some of those questions are explicitly about the relationship between Christianity and particular issues. Some of them are about issues that Christians should consider but are raised and discussed by scholars who are not Christian. This work fosters intellectual and moral transformation, while opposing bias, within the congregation. It is a means of discipling. The process also engages participants from the congregation with scholars, who may or may not be Christian, in ways that feed their scholarly work. It is a means of evangelism. Everybody grows. That is gospel vision.

With their food pantry and clothes closet, Faith Lutheran Parish (FLP) undertakes some of the most familiar kinds of church outreach activities. Their financial contribution to a local shelter for women is innovative, and a great idea, but it does fit with a traditional model of supporting local social services. To see where they shift the model, I want to focus on some of their less standard commitments. They work in partnership with a Roman Catholic church, which is an important starting place. Then, they go beyond explicit Christianity, supporting social and cultural activities with a faith dimension—including people from different religions talking about their lives and meanings. FLP is supporting interfaith conversation in a gentle, accessible way, enabling intellectual transformation: asking and answering questions permits people to understand others in ways that prejudice prevents. The same parish supports a parish nurse. Parish nurses are qualified nurses, often retired or late in their careers, who visit people and bring both healthcare attention and a spiritual presence. They work with people who are Christians and people who are not. Especially in places with limited or expensive healthcare options, these people foster religious transformation.

Northern Lake United (NLU) works closely with their Indigenous community, especially in partnership with the band. As a participant in band functions, NLU is part of an interweaving of traditional Anishnaabeg and Christian religious understanding and practice. This is a complex activity that can prove fruitful; for some Christians, the encounter with Indigenous views has transformed their relationship with the world, reminding them of God's eternal presence in and to all things. For NLU, the partnership enriches their religious life and enables unity and wholeness in their persons, so that Indigenous life can exist harmoniously with Christian life for them. The partnership also makes NLU financially viable when they might not otherwise be so, while enabling NLU to accomplish valuable work that serves the goals of the band community, so that the relationship is mutually beneficial.

St. Stanislaus Roman Catholic (SRC) is working with the Haitian community, which has a complex Roman Catholic identity. Catholicism in Haiti can be intermingled with aspects of folk religion to which the parish must be attentive. Beyond this is the much larger web of partnerships with political entities: the city and the state. As political entities, they may not be especially concerned with religious outcomes. Their priorities are with ensuring that new immigrants understand how the country functions, are mentally and physically well, and can adjust to the norms of the country's society. The church is in a position to support all these, while learning from those Haitians who bring significant levels of self-appropriation, and supporting ongoing intellectual, psychic, moral, and religious transformation in the lives of the people who turn to SRC. In addition, SRC is taking an educational role in the larger community, working with the city to ensure that people understand what the Haitian people bring, fostering transformation in the whole city.

Bethel AME (BAME) has developed a strong connection with Southville Community College. This enables BAME to reflect more deeply on the meaning of justice in the contemporary world, especially as it relates to the lives of Black people. The call to "Do justice" is central to the life and work of BAME, so richer academic resources permit the church community to do more to foster intellectual transformation in church and world. At the same time, BAME makes financial resources available to increase enrollment of Black people at the college and encourages young Black people to study there. This benefits the college (every school likes recruitment networks!), while helping to draw people toward intellectual, psychic, and moral transformation at school and away from destructive patterns of street life. Because all this is surrounded by an atmosphere of worship in an African American tradition and by a commitment to love people facing life challenges, it serves religious transformation.

Praise Pentecostal Church (PPC) enables young people, the congregation's core mission focus, to get an experience of working with people of different or no faith background. The younger youth group participates in the community's lunch program, and the older youth group provides tutoring for students. These experiences can be transformational in a variety of ways, sparking new questions and encouraging different ways of being. Nonetheless, this is an instance where we could easily imagine a stronger set of partnerships, if the congregation were willing. Expanding community connections could enrich the youth experience. In addition, the information about decreasing in-person attendance hints at potential for ecumenical engagement, while efforts to work in a world of growing diversity may also suggest that at least some interfaith activities could be beneficial.

Christ Church Episcopal (CCEC) is a cathedral, so it carries the duality that comes with serving a diocese (a multiparish administrative area under the supervision of a bishop) as the seat of the bishop, in addition to their work as a downtown parish. This complexity makes for a significant administrative load that, in a situation of declining membership, limits their capacity to manage partnerships. They are in conversation with other local Episcopalian parishes, presumably with the assumption that some closures will be necessary, and this may add parishioners. If they can expand their own volunteer capacity, there may be room to expand ecumenical and/or interfaith engagement, perhaps around some of their existing kinds of downtown engagements.

Benefiting From Partnerships

We can understand partnerships as narrowly task oriented. This can be a helpful way to avoid mission creep. If we consistently remember the specific reasons that we entered into a partnership, then we will be less tempted to multiply meetings, events, and longer-term plans that do not reflect our GVS decisions. Keeping relationships defined is a good thing.

Our commitment to self-appropriation, though, invites us to reflect on the meanings of what we are doing, so that we are in an ongoing process of transformation. Without adding to our tasks, so that we are not departing from our GVS, we can helpfully commit to routinely considering what we are learning from our activities in partnerships. We can do this in small groups. This follows a model that is common in Clinical Pastoral Education (CPE) and other contexts, called "Action-Reflection" (AR). The AR model is built around purposeful reflection on our interactions with others, so that we garner lessons as we go. This approach has the straightforward benefit that today's mistakes can help us to prevent tomorrow's blunders. AR also has the more complex advantage that it enables us to engage with different ways of understanding the world in ways that prove transformative for us. A lifelong Lutheran at FLP might take the opportunity to learn from their Roman Catholic partners about religious orders and some ways that their presence enriches a sense of God's presence.

The AR model can be adapted to context. In CPE, it depends upon highly trained and skilled directors, who work to maintain a safe space while asking and inviting deep and challenging questions. This may work in some church contexts, especially where there are already strong small groups. Most contexts, such as church councils, will need a lighter touch, but the point remains. I tend to find that helping people to think about evangelism in the sense in which we have discussed it—beginning with others helping us to understand faith more deeply, then sharing our own, then seeking ways that we can serve loving justice together—can be a helpful way to prepare for partnership and to live in to partnered relationships. Partnerships are good places for us to practice being attentive and seeking to understand new things in new ways. God uses them to transform us.

Exercises: Partner, Thoughtfully

  A. Your Life
  1. Do you like working with partners? Are there specific ways that you do like partnering and ways that you don't, or particular kinds of tasks that you find work better with partners and kinds that work better without?
  2. Does your personal GVS reflect your thinking about partnering?
  3. Do your missions sometimes require you to work with partners when you might not prefer to do so?

  B. Your Organization
  1. Is "mission drawn, necessity driven" relevant to your organization? If so, what does it mean in your context?
  2. Does your organization partner with another organization within your denomination? If so, for what?
  3. Does your organization partner with another organization within another Christian denomination? If so, for what?
  4. Does your organization partner with another organization within another religion? If so, for what?
  5. Does your GVS envisage partnerships? Existing? New?

  C. The World
  1. Do you have personal partnerships that help you to participate in any or all of the four transformations in the world beyond the church? If so, in what ways?
  2. Does your organization have partnerships that help the organization to participate in any or all of the four transformations in the world beyond the church? If so, in what ways?

CHAPTER 9

CONSIDERING CLOSURE

One of the characteristics of the shrinking church is an increasingly large differential between the percentage of decline in membership and the percentage of decline in church organizations, most notably congregations. We do not close nearly enough congregations. Consider some examples. Between 1965 and 2017, membership in the Anglican Church of Canada dropped by 74 percent, while the number of congregations fell by only 39 percent.[1] Between 1960 and 2023, membership in the United Church of Christ (in the USA) declined by 68 percent, but the number of congregations decreased by only 44 percent.[2] The Church of England saw a 69 percent decrease in the number of Christmas communicants between 1962 and 2022, but only a 13 percent decrease in the number of places of worship; even recognizing that some of those buildings will be places of occasional worship (sometimes called "chapels of ease" or similar), the difference is astounding and unsustainable.[3] The Lutheran Church Missouri Synod (in the USA) is an unusual case: Its membership declined by 39 percent between 1970 and 2023, while its number of congregations actually increased slightly.[4] The decline in numbers of attendees is out of proportion to the closure of congregations—sometimes, by a very large margin.

Up to a point, some divergence is to be expected. There will always be a lag between membership decline and congregational closures. Congregations can often continue productively with fewer people than they saw in their peak days. Focused ministry, with clearly defined purpose, can work well in congregations that have previously sustained a broad variety of activities going in different directions. Uses can be found for parts of church buildings, such as gymnasiums, that no longer see routine use by the church itself. In addition, decisions about closure are not straightforward. A simple process that automatically mandates closure of congregations when they fall below a certain number would likely accelerate decline by cutting off faithful members, some of whom are reliable givers of time, skills, energy, and money. Worse yet, such a process would overlook the valuable roles of small congregations in worship and community action, especially in areas where depopulation and the departure of major employers creates a painful vacuum of public life and support.

There is a "however," though. There is a point where the effort to sustain organizations overtakes the capacity of the system. Mission, whether external or internal, suffers. The people working to maintain the organizations suffer. In many congregations, this means that older faithful people who have served the church for many years are burdened with the tasks of keeping the organizations operating. Clergy are overwhelmed and facing burnout, combining unsustainable workloads with shrinking budgets and rising legal and governmental demands. Maintaining numbers of congregations far greater than justified by the number of congregants is not a way to enable the sorts of transformations that we have been considering. Instead, it is a recipe for unhealthy institutionalism and general hopelessness.

Should an Organization Close?

Closure is not failure. There is a time to call it a day and close a ministry, whether it is a congregation, a seminary, or a judicatory body. True leaders can recognize this and enable healthy endings. There are numerous ways to craft a formal assessment of the state of an organization; congregations, especially, can be measured by many tools. A simple one (useful for both congregations and other organizations) is a vitality/viability graph, with quadrants. Organizations rating high on both vitality and viability are worthwhile and capable of surviving. Organizations rating low on both are due for closure. High vitality with low viability raises the question of whether other resources might be available to support the organization or whether it might be viable if reorganized. High viability with low vitality raises the question of whether expanded organizational support or changed leadership might create new possibilities. Either of these borderline cases might be due for closure if the questions raised cannot be answered satisfactorily. The advantages of this approach are its simplicity and clarity, especially in obvious cases. Extreme cases as the low end of the spectrum immediately fall into the category of closure, focusing attention on the more complex situations. An organization with clear gospel purpose and plenty of resources can and should continue. An organization with neither a gospel-based sense of direction nor the capacity to operate is simply awaiting a suitable process. One substantial difficulty is in determining what to do with organizations that appear to be somewhere between the extremes.

This is one of the moments when a Gospel Vision Statement (GVS) is helpful. The first question is whether the organization can create a GVS, given appropriate leadership and facilitation support. If not, then we have our answer. A church organization that cannot construct an internally consistent statement that clarifies the organization's mission, the area it plans to serve, the core pieces of its identity that it intends to retain, and the resources to which it has access, is not going to thrive. At best, it will continue to totter until the day that it falls through resource failure, whether human, financial, or physical. In contrast, an organization that can produce or has produced a GVS that is both visionary and realistic, displaying both a gospel commitment and the capacity to fulfill it, has a future even if it might take a different form.

If the organization produces a GVS and cannot live it out, the organization must either develop a new one or begin to consider closure. The GVS functions like a very simplified and focused strategic plan. It specifies the strategic goal for the organization and identifies the resources to fulfill it. There are, of course, multiple reasons for a GVS to become unhelpful. It may become out of date because of changing circumstances. If the goal is to work with students at a local postsecondary campus and the campus is closed, then a new GVS is needed. The people whom the organization sought to reach are simply not there. The research underlying the GVS may prove to have been faulty. If the goal is to reach people from the downtown core with a quiet, meditative lunchtime service, and the original indicators are that this is a viable mission, then discovering that people do not really have the freedom to attend, even online, suggests that a new GVS is needed. Neither of these needs to be a fatal situation. Trying an experiment and recognizing that a new route is needed shows creativity and a willingness to take risks. If, however, the organization repeatedly tries to construct a GVS and cannot create one that is successful, then closure is likely the best outcome.

The key benefit of making decisions based on a GVS is that the organization effectively sets its own criteria for closure, criteria which may be local but purposefully serve the larger vision generated by the good news of Christ Jesus. A successful GVS is one where the mission, identity, location, and resources continue to be aligned, and the gospel is communicated. The mission continues to be fulfilled in the location by people who have a sense of call to the mission, and the necessary resources are still available and will likely be available into a reasonable future. In a sense, this way of thinking is not very different from the question of vitality and viability, but more unified and specified. The GVS approach brings together vitality and viability with a mission focus. The criteria for closure are established by the organization's own GVS. If an organization cannot fulfill its GVS, then it must face the question of whether closure is the logical outcome.

The whole process of creating a GVS is, therefore, an assessment tool of its own, useful to leaders. Whether an organization can get there is a useful question. So is how it gets there. This is all important data for leaders seeking to understand their organizations and find a way forward. Inability to assemble a GVS is an obvious indicator, as is failing to live up to commitments made in one. However, there are many other delicate judgments to make, so leaders must be attentive, gathering data on the organization's capacity all the way through the process. Reaching a GVS easily, simply, and clearly is likely to be a very good sign if people are genuinely engaged with it and prepared to support it. If the process is easy because all but a few have essentially opted out, then quick and easy may be another way of saying nonviable. Alternatively, a somewhat contentious process can be a good sign of broad involvement and commitment if, in the end, everyone (or nearly everyone) is prepared to support the final product.

Remember that a GVS that is created must also be supported and must have organizational follow-through. Remember, also, that the whole point of a GVS is that a church organization is about God's transformation of the world, rather than survival of the organization itself. Therefore, closure should always remain an option.

The Larger View

One big advantage of a GVS is that, if done properly, it takes the larger view. We have discussed the general bias toward common sense, which really is nothing more than the assertion that we tend to prefer choices that serve our own more or less immediate concerns and current attitudes, rather than attending to the bigger picture—a more general understanding of the world and the consequences of our decisions. I have noticed that organizations, perhaps especially congregations, tend to focus narrowly on their own particular circumstances when the question of closure arises. The question tends to be whether they can survive and, if so, what steps will be needed to make that possible.

In contrast, a GVS begins theologically, with the question of gospel mission. The issues of location and identity bring an internal focus to the challenge. However, they are not the starting point. The starting point is God's transformative work in the world. In this, it differs from most strategic plans, which tend to begin with some combination of market conditions and the organization itself, with its own dynamics of being and acting. The point of the church is that we are given a capacity to understand the meaning of history, to recognize the larger picture of what God is doing. We are truly being church when this conditions our planning.

Beginning with the gospel means that the leaders charged with attending to the GVS and the ways that an organization is succeeding with its GVS are in a position to ask the question, "Are we serving God, living out the gospel, in the best way that we can by continuing?" Put differently, a GVS allows the community within, and perhaps the communities affected by, the organization to consider whether closing might serve the gospel better.

The organization can also begin to think about ways that closing might enable them to fulfill a new mission. For example, many longstanding congregations have facilities that are located in close proximity to other congregations of their own and close partner denominations, often in older neighborhoods. Cities grow, and they do not necessarily have churches in new subdivisions. Selling a facility and relocating to a growing part of town is one option. However, today's circumstances mean that many congregations do not have the capacity to move themselves and create something new. A dying congregation, though, can sometimes close its facilities and sell them to start a fund with a view to beginning a new congregation elsewhere. Some judicatories have funds for this very purpose, making the process relatively easy.

I have also seen instances where closures could have enabled new beginnings, but funds were dissipated to little purpose. These kinds of endings suggest that some GVS-style thinking is also beneficial when the organization has decided that its life cycle is complete. At the very least, if an organization has some voice in the future of any remaining assets, there is virtue in giving thought to ways that they can be used for a purpose that serves the work of the church in a substantial way.

Preparing the Community

The challenge in all this work is to see closure as a creative act that participates in God's mission of transformation in the world. Closure does not escape the gospel imperative. Closure is a contribution to the mission. Death is a precursor to resurrection. Trying heroic measures to keep alive an organization that does not have the capacity to fulfill a gospel mission is not a gift to the world. If we allow some organizations to die, we can find new ways to be ambassadors of reconciliation. Death can make contributions to new life.

Closing in a way that makes a helpful impact does not happen without careful thinking and planning. Simply leaving the last person standing to turn out the lights and walk away does not tend to be constructive. It is, however, what tends to happen when we leave big decisions about the future until too late to be able to choose direction. Recognizing the challenges and engaging with real questions about the future while we still have energy and resources to reach decisions make for more productive and satisfying outcomes.

The first key to preparation is communication, gentle but clear, and provided over as long a period of time as possible. When closing a church congregation, I preached sermons that I think of as the "death cycle" for the better part of two years. The congregation was clear about where things were going even before we reached an annual meeting at which they proposed that the time for closing had come. Those sermons focused on the good news. The first ones tended to emphasize themes of death and the pain that accompanies it, while recognizing that it is not the end. Later ones tended to focus on ways in which new life can come about. I tried not to be heavy-handed about the themes. I felt the need to name our direction but not to make Sundays a constant downer. Too much heaviness would simply have been. . . heavy. On the other hand, averting my gaze and leaning on sweetness and light would have misled everyone. People needed to hear, multiple times, that I understood their reality and that it would be okay.

The "okayness" was connected to many conversations about what would happen afterward. We needed to plan for outcomes, helping people to address their individual needs and the needs of the community. Would people still go to church and, if so, where? Who would provide pastoral support, whether people felt able to attend or not? Could there still be a thrift store in the community if our building was no longer a church home? How would we manage liturgical closure? Thinking these things through over time prepared us for the moment when closure would occur.

Decision and Aftermath

Closure is a difficult decision. Most of the ones with which I have been connected have all happened when other options vanish. There is no way forward except closure, so the time has arrived. The main advantage that I see in this approach is that inevitability often, but not always, eases the process. Recognizing that they cannot manage anything else, people approach closure with grief, but also with a sense that it must be done. From the perspective of leading the process, this is probably the easiest way to lead into closure. If everyone feels that they have done everything that they could and now it is simply time to let go, some aspects of the grieving process have already shown themselves. At least some members—and probably the leading ones—of the organization have already worked through denial, for instance.

This approach has an important weakness, though, and it is one that I hope we have highlighted in earlier parts of this book: Waiting until we have no other options takes away much of our agency in decision-making around closure and its implications. Part of the point of focusing on mission and working with a GVS is to ensure that we see existential challenges coming and can make mission-focused decisions about them. This enables us to engage with closure, with organizational death, as a prelude to resurrection rather than simply as a final endpoint. Recognizing that the day when we will not be able to fulfill our mission is coming means that we can give thought to the future of our mission and the people whom we serve, to the destination of whatever resources we have, and to the future of the organization's people (members, employees, etc.). We can consider these issues while we still have functioning leadership, with the capacity to manage a substantial process for shutdown. The result will still be closure, but it is closure with a sense of future.

However closure occurs, there is likely to be a sense of grief among people who have deep connections to the organization. Pastoral support may be needed, especially if the organization is a congregation. That is one time (of many times) when partners can be helpful. Perhaps more deeply, the closure of an organization can be a moment when our commitment to transformation is both revealed and tested. If an organization has been engaged in self-appropriation, that will become evident in the stress that the group faces when deciding to close down and carrying out the tasks. We will see understanding of the organization's situation, responsiveness to the feelings that emerge, determination to serve the larger good, and, most of all, love toward what has been, what is, and what will be. Transformation serves closure when that is the gospel mission.

Exercises: Considering Closure

A. Your Life
1. What are your feelings about the closure of congregations and other church organizations?
2. Have you had an experience of the closure of a church organization? If so, how do you feel about it? Did you feel involved in the process? Did you want to be involved? Do you think that it was necessary? Was it a good thing?
3. If you were a longtime member of a congregation considering closure because there are too few people to sustain it, how do you think you would respond? Would you be willing to provide leadership through the closing process? If so, why? If not, why not?

B. Your Organization
1. Is there a reasonable chance that your organization might need to close in the foreseeable future? If so, is decline in attendance/membership/participation in the church part of the reason?
2. A GVS can envisage the possibility of closure, as we have seen in the example of First Lutheran Parish. Does your hypothetical GVS do that? Do you think it would be helpful for closure to appear in your organization's GVS as a possibility?
3. Many denominations are shrinking rapidly. Could you imagine your denomination merging with another denomination or closing altogether? What would be the likely implications for your organization?

C. The World
1. What implications do you see for the world if your organization were to close? Can you identify ways to mitigate any destructive consequences?

CHAPTER 10

VISION IN UNLIKELY PLACES

This book has been an effort to engage with the life of a shrinking church. The cover photo poses us a challenge, with an old church building set in the middle of a wheat field and the light creating an angled glow on the wheat. The building carries the beauty of its past; people worshiped here, so the structure carries the meanings of love and sorrow and joy and transformation that have been a part of its life. The building is now retired, no longer the center of a Christian community. The building is, however, at the center of a golden field of wheat.

The wheat surrounds the building. The wheat may even be seen as preventing access to the worship space. The field is an unlikely place, the wheat an unlikely ally. However, the light has a different idea. To the light, the wheat is gold. To the light, the wheat is what happens when seed falls on good soil and is well nurtured. To the light, the field of wheat is God-love, when the building no longer houses Christian love.

This suggests two lessons to me. The first is that God raises up a world that responds to God's love, even when the church is present only as memory. God is the sower; God invites the loving response. The second, related, lesson is that all places seem unlikely to a shrinking church because our focus tends to be on the church itself, no matter what we claim. As an employee of the church structure, married to an employee of the church structure, I am very aware of the limitation.

Of course, the light is not God. Light does not understand. It does not love, as we know love. Wheat is not human. It is not attentive, intelligent, reasonable, or responsible. However, the image invites us to see life and love where we might easily locate only death. Where there is no visible church presence, there is still God's love. God is still at work and we are still invited to cooperate with God's action, to accept the invitation that spirit offers us. There are potential partners in the life of transformation. All places that seem unlikely become possible when the vision is one that reaches everyone where they are.

For us as church people, we make a significant transition when we realize that the church is not the only volunteer institution that is shrinking. Our numbers are declining alongside numerous other organizations. This is not a situation that we can fix. It is the direction that society in general is taking. I have discovered that people are surprised to realize this, because we have been so attached to the assumption that the issue is the church and its meanings, whether we are being undermined by a world-historical process like secularization or more immediate pressure caused by the church's own failures. The recognition of the situation is a release of stress.

The larger shift, though, comes from the change in direction that the realization inspires. Knowing that we are affected by a shift in society that is bigger than us, bigger than the church, bigger even the conversation about religion in our world, helps us to realize that we need to relate differently to the community outside the church. This is where turning again to our biblical and theological resources changes us.

Relinquishing the idea that Christianity is about a ticket to the Kingdom (however that is imagined), a ticket that we possess while others do not, moves us into a different mindset about what salvation means to us. Similarly, letting go of the priority of bringing other people into our organization changes our sense of what we are trying to accomplish. The idea that we are ambassadors is not new. The notion that ambassadorship is specifically about reconciliation, as we are reimagining ambassadorship, is different for many people. This is the core of the shift to a diaconally focused church from a presbyterally focused church. Now ambassadorship, understood in a specific way, is the meaning of our organizations.

As I have discussed it, ambassadorship is primarily the activity of supporting others in intellectual, psychic, moral, and religious transformation, and in self-appropriation. We are supporting people in learning to ask and answer questions; engage with their emotionality, even at the deepest levels; move beyond concern for self to care for the greater good; and to live with love as the fundamental motive and directive force in life. We are inviting people to attend to themselves as people who ask and answer questions, respond to the world with emotions, make moral judgments, and receive and give love, and we are encouraging people to consider ways that they can do all these things more truly and richly. We are assisting people to learn and grow in ways to which God calls all of us, with the hope and prayer that one day they will come to know the God whose spirit conveys the love that upholds them and enables them through this process of transformation. When we live purposefully as ambassadorial church, we are participating in these sorts of transformations in people's lives every time we undertake loving action.

The intention of a Gospel Vision Statement (GVS) is to focus our energies on purposeful ambassadorial activity.[1] When we respond to every suggestion that comes along, we cannot easily focus on anything. The result tends to be limited results with maximum resource expenditure. Especially in a world where we have limited and declining resources, the result of trying to do everything is likely to be a combination of faster decline (as people drop out) and burnout (for the remaining participants). A GVS helps us to decide whom we can engage effectively in the process of transformation in the area that we serve, how we can do that in a manner consistent with our current and desired identity, and the quantity and kind of resources that we can bring to bear on the challenge. Thus, our priorities can be set by our gospel focus, rather than by the pressures of daily requests and "somebody should do this."

A GVS also helps us to recognize when we can work best with partners and assists us to identify suitable partners. Others who can contribute to our purposeful ambassadorial engagement and/or who have an ambassadorial engagement in which we can live out our purpose are possible partners. A GVS for the partnership helps to ensure that it is a viable relationship. Importantly, our partners may be people with Christian commitments, other faith commitments, or no religious commitment at all. One consequence of recognizing the elements of transformation as processes, rather than necessarily single moments, and as activities in which many people are and can be engaged, rather than requiring specifically Christian identity and membership, is that we can discover partners where we had not expected. We can find partners in unlikely places, just as we find vision.

I hope that following the suggestions made here may ease the church's present situation. Naming challenging realities and responding to them directly can be less practically and psychologically painful than making piecemeal adjustments. The levels of pressure that emerge in shrinking churches can be immense. Today, they are often public, making the results especially harsh. Finding transformation and focus in the ways that I suggest may calm organizational situations or, at least, clarify outcomes. Moreover, limiting and focusing our commitments can make life much easier—and notably so when we cannot reasonably expect a significant increase in resources. This book may call readers to new tasks. I hope it also provides new energy and—perhaps, more important—new focus.

However, nothing said in this book will insulate church organizations from the consequences of dramatic social change. That is why a chapter on closure is so important. The church is overdue for closures of numerous congregations. One effect of the decline in membership that compromises congregations is that other church organizations, including seminaries, regional and national support systems, and judicatories, are shrinking or closing. Put more strongly, a number of national churches are in significant danger of disappearing entirely, based on ages of members and current numerical trajectories. My suggestions are not intended to prevent these outcomes. If there is a change in church participation situations, that will be because of a shift in societal direction. The church might be a part of that, but today's church is not in the politically and socially dominant position needed to redesign the community structure of the countries in the Anglosphere.

We cannot change the world situation by ourselves. I believe, however, that committing ourselves to a life of self-appropriation and transformation, and inviting others to that same life, positions us to participate in God's creation of a new and more constructive world. I believe that the life of transformation can provide us and others with glimpses of God's Kingdom. With this (theological) hope in mind, I wish to draw attention to some specific elements of this book that I think offer particular value.

Theology: Our account of transformation is theologically helpful in a world where we need to connect with people who are not interested in making the commitment to church life that many of us have done all our lives. The church comes to be about its meanings, rather than about others' willingness to attend. The vision engages people who are simply trying to accomplish good things in the world. It connects to people who bring different religious backgrounds or no religious background. Everyone can participate in intellectual, psychic, and moral transformation, and everyone has either known the touch of love (religious transformation) or needs it. Supporting people in these processes and helping them to see meaning in the world works for many people.

Sense of purpose: The theological approach invites the church to a renewed sense of purpose. This vision engages us in a way of being that enables us to participate in our own transformation. That transformation serves God and does so in immediately practical ways. Understanding more accurately, making better decisions, and engaging the world around us more deeply are activities that are meaningful for people on a daily basis—both in church and beyond. We can invite our members to undertake transformative activities in the world, carrying and speaking to Christian priorities, without having to start at the "Come to church" or "Turn to Christ" places where many members are uncomfortable and much of society is unprepared to listen. We can offer this invitation because the sense of purpose that I describe is not based in disappointment or frustration. Rather than assuming that people are leaving church because of church, whether that is a product of secularization or of church failures, we are recognizing that people do not join organizations. Our activities are, therefore, oriented toward the assumption that our numbers will not grow, but God will transform us and the whole world, and we can participate in this transformation.

Training for decisions: The emphasis on self-appropriation serves as a reminder that choices about ways forward for church organizations depend upon the decisions of people within and related to the organizations themselves. We can learn from each other, but we do not have universal models to follow in the way that the parish/congregation models of the late twentieth century provided. At the same time, we are all aware that not all decisions are good ones. The priority of self-appropriation is partly about helping us to learn what makes a decision better and enabling us to improve. As we make better decisions, we—members of the church—improve as leaders and participants in organizations, yielding a better, more faithful, organization.

Resources: I have made a serious effort to engage with concrete situations in the life of the church. One way of doing this has been to focus on providing resources that touch the actual life situations of congregations and other church organizations. Reflections on accessible materials, such as the movie *Groundhog Day* and books about Sargent Shriver, are intended to provide useful starting places for discussions about transformation and self-appropriation. The discussion about the

GVS provides an account of reasons for creating one, processes to enable the work, samples of what a GVS can look like, and suggestions for working with a GVS. The sections on partnerships and closure are intended to serve as practical advice for organizations considering these options. Perhaps most important, the sequence of exercises is designed to help integrate the book's contents with the trajectory of your life, your organization's life, and the life of the world. The intention is that the whole book should connect God's good news of Christ Jesus with the specific challenges of life in a shrinking church.

This book has been an effort to engage with the challenge of a shrinking church. I believe that God is calling us to shift our vision, moving away from the priority of numerical growth and embracing the possibility of deep transformation in our lives and the life of the world. I have suggested that God invites us to commit to intellectual, psychic, moral, and religious transformations. Engagement with transformation begins with committing to change in us, often through the agency of other people, who may or may not be Christians. The process continues with a willingness to share our stories of transformation, so that others may be changed with us, then gains power to cause change in the world through connection to others who are open to living a transformed life.

This book is intended to serve as both guidebook and workbook. It is a guidebook in that it addresses some hard questions about life in challenging times and proposes some steps that may help us to find paths forward. It is a workbook in that it seeks to enable readers, through asking and answering questions, to engage directly with the transformations that I describe. This is an invitation for us as individuals and organizations to be attentive, intelligent, reasonable, responsible, and loving. It is an invitation for us all to be more deeply God's church.

My prayer for all (and, perhaps, especially those who read this book) is that finding a way into the life of ambassadorial church, of self-appropriation and transformation, will be the discovery of new meaning. I pray that this life will enable you to know God at work in this, God's new creation, and that you—individual, congregation, seminary, task force, working group, denomination, church organization of any kind—will be a means by which others can experience the explosions of God's love in their lives, in their worlds. This I know for certain: there is life in Christ, and through him I have found the love of the Holy Spirit that enables me to respond to this, God's glorious world, with true joy.

Peace be with you.

Exercises: Vision in Unlikely Places

A. Your Life
1. Has reading this book enriched your life? If so, in what ways?
2. Do you feel better equipped to respond to the challenges of life in the church today? If so, in what ways?
3. Do you have a deeper sense of the meaning of Christianity in your life? What have you learned that has been helpful? Will the four transformations play a role in your life?
4. Look back to your exercise responses after the introduction. You were invited to identify some goals for your reading, some things that you wanted to learn. Have your hopes been fulfilled? Are there portions of the book that you want to read again? Are there other resources that you now want to engage with, to continue your development?

B. Your Organization
1. Has work with this book suggested some next steps for your organization? If so, take some time to chart them out.
2. Has your organization created a GVS? Will it do so?
3. What other resources in the book are likely to prove helpful for your organization?

C. The World
1. Do you think that the directions suggested in this book can make a difference in the world? If your answer is no, then indicate why not. If your answer is yes, name some possible ways.

ACKNOWLEDGMENTS

Deepest thanks to Carl Bromley, Mark Powers, Anne Zaccardelli, Katherine Lim, Anita Manbodh, and everyone else at Seabury, who have been endlessly helpful and supportive in getting this book into your hands (or onto your screen). Replaces first sentence. Heartfelt thanks also to Jamie Price and Laureen Wray, who reviewed my draft and made excellent suggestions for improvement. To Rita Harrison, who had no idea that marrying me would also mean reading and rereading manuscripts, patiently catching errors, infelicitous phrasings, and awkward oversights (and showing all these to an impatient husband and protective author), I owe more appreciation than I can express. Where this book is strong, all of you deserve much credit; where this book is weak, the failure is mine alone.

Thank you to Lutheran Theological Seminary, Saskatoon, for the opportunity to participate in the work of God's love with you. My appreciation also for the sabbatical time needed to write this book.

To my family, Rita, Richard, and Charles, thank you for walking with me. The important things that I know have been taught by you, even when the words came from elsewhere.

NOTES

Introduction: What this book does and why

1. Susan Beaumont, *How To Lead When You Don't Know Where You're Going: Leading in a Liminal Season* (Rowman & Littlefield, 2019).

2. Beaumont, *How to Lead*, 59.

3. See, for example, Andrew Root's series of books on ministry in a secular age: *Faith Formation in a Secular Age: Responding to the Church's Obsession with Youthfulness* (Grand Rapids, MI: Baker Academic, 2017); *The Pastor in a Secular Age: Ministry to People Who No Longer Need a God* (Grand Rapids, MI: Baker Academic, 2019); *The Congregation in a Secular Age: Keeping Sacred Time Against the Speed of Modern Life* (Grand Rapids, MI: Baker Academic, 2021).

4. Robert D. Putnam, *Bowling Alone: The Collapse and Revival of American Community*, revised and updated (Simon & Schuster, 2020).

Chapter 1 The First Step

1. Pam Wasserman, "World Population Growth by Faith," Population Education, January 12, 2024, accessed July 21, 2024, https://populationeducation.org/world-population-by-religion-a-global-tapestry-of-faith/.

2. Wasserman, "World Population Growth by Faith."

3. John Locke, "A Letter Concerning Toleration," in *A Letter Concerning Toleration and Other Writings*, ed. Mark Goldie (Liberty Fund, 2010), https://oll.libertyfund.org/titles/goldie-a-letter-concerning-toleration-and-other-writings.

4. Friedrich Nietzsche, *The Gay Science*, trans. Walter Kaufmann (Vintage Books, 1964), 167–182.

5. Putnam, *Bowling Alone*, 18–19. The nineteenth century had already seen growth in church membership, at least in the USA where revivalism had taken hold. However, while we do not have direct measurements for U.S. church membership before the twentieth century, estimates suggest that the peak occurred before 1860, followed by decline. In any case, all evidence indicates that membership levels were significantly lower (compared to total population) than the twentieth century peak. Roger Finke and Rodney Stark, "Turning Pews into People: Estimating 19th Century Church Membership," *Journal for the Scientific Study of Religion*

25, no. 2 (1986): 180–92. https://doi.org/10.2307/1385475. Accessed March 16, 2025. Lyman Stone, "Yes, Early America Was Unchurched: There's Not Actually Much Historical Debate on This," *Medium*, April 25, 2017. https://medium.com/migration-issues/yes-early-america-was-unchurched-82c3b6c9a914. Accessed March 16, 2025.

6. Putnam, *Bowling Alone*, 367–401.

7. In a trenchant review, William A. Galston draws together a range of critiques of Putnam's work: William A. Galston, review of *Bowling Alone: The Collapse and Revival of American Community*, in *Journal of Policy Analysis and Management* 20, no. 4 (2001): 788–790, https://doi.org/10.1002/pam.1035.

8. This is consistent with Galston's suggestion that Putnam underemphasizes the impact of the decline of institutions, such as political parties, that once affirmatively recruited individuals at the grassroots into wider networks" (Galston, 790). The military and war-oriented government systems functioned as those kinds of institutions.

9. Kristin DiMaggio, "All Eyes on the North American Membership Initiative: How Lions Clubs International is Boosting Membership in North America," *Lion Magazine*, July 10, 2020, accessed October 8, 2024, https://lionmagazine.org/articles/all-eyes-on-nami/.

10. Tony Thomas, "Rotary Membership Trends," Rotary Central Melbourne, accessed October 8, 2024, https://rotaryclubcentralmelbourne.org.au/stories/rotary-membership-trends.

11. William Cross and Lisa Young, "Are Canadian Political Parties Empty Vessels? Membership, Engagement, and Policy Capacity," *IRPP Choices* 12, no. 4 (June 2006): 16–17, accessed October 8, 2024, https://irpp.org/wp-content/uploads/assets/research/strengthening-canadian-democracy/the-shifting-place-of-political-parties-in-canadian-public-life/vol12no4.pdf.

12. Liam Morland, "The Problem: Membership Decline," in *Membership Retention in Scout Troops* (Waterloo, 2002), accessed October 7, 2024, https://scoutdocs.ca/Membership_Retention/node5.html.

13. Danny Dorling, Dan Vickers, Bethan Thomas, John Pritchard, and Dimitris Ballas, *Changing UK: The Way We Live Now* (British Broadcasting Corporation, December 2008), 23–25, accessed November 18, 2024, https://www.dannydorling.org/books/changinguk/Changing_UK_report_sheffield_webv1.pdf.

14. Dorling et al., 26–28.

15. Gavin Thompson, Oliver Hawkins, Aliyah Dar, and Mark Taylor, *Olympic Britain: Social and Economic Change Since the 1908 and 1948 London Games* (UK House of Commons Library, 2012), 141–142, accessed

October 8, 2024, https://www.parliament.uk/contentassets/3c816b8b 41994f35bfb9b7e912d8699e/olympicbritain.pdf#page=147.

16. United Grand Lodge of England, "Forging a Thriving Future: The Strategy for Freemasonry 2022 and Beyond," March 30, 2023, accessed October 8, 2024, https://www.ugle.org.uk/discover-freemasonry/blog/forging-thriving-future-strategy-freemasonry-2022-and-beyond.

17. Josh Nicholas, "Australians Aren't Joining In Any More—and It Appears to Be Having Big Political Consequences," *Guardian*, November 11, 2023, https://www.theguardian.com/australia-news/2023/nov/12/australians-arent-joining-in-any-more-and-it-appears-to-be-having-big-political-consequences (accessed October 8, 2024).

18. Thomas, "Rotary Membership Trends."

19. Richard Num, "Freemasonry in Australia," *Pietre-Stones: Review of Freemasonry*, December 2003, accessed October 8, 2024, http://www.freemasons-freemasonry.com/freemasonry_australia.html.

20. Michael Head, "Declining Memberships and Australia's Political Party Registration Test: Legal Doubts and Democratic Principles," *Alternative Law Journal* 47, no. 2 (June 2022): 130–136, https://search.informit.org/doi/10.3316/informit.20220705069988.

21. Charles Mann, *The Wizard and the Prophet: Two Remarkable Scientists and Their Dueling Visions to Shape Tomorrow's World* (Knopf, 2018).

22. Byung-Chul Han, *The Burnout Society* (Stanford University Press, 2015), 8–9.

23. Han, *Burnout Society*, 10.

24. Jim Davis, Michael Graham, and Ryan P. Burge, *The Great Dechurching: Who's Leaving, Why Are They Going, and What Will It Take to Bring Them Back?* (Zondervan, 2023).

25. Davis, Graham, and Burge, *Dechurching*, 120.

26. Dialogue Institute and Journal of Ecumenical Studies, Leonard Swidler, "The Dialogue Decalogue: Ground Rules for Interreligious, Interideological Dialogue," accessed July 12, 2024, https://dialogueinstitute.org/s/DIALOGUE-DECALOGUEEDITEDWITHSKITAIR5-5-18.pdf.

27. R. H. Pratt, "The Advantages of Mingling Indians With Whites," in *Proceedings of the National Conference of Charities and Correction at the Nineteenth Annual Session Held In Denver, Col., June 23–29, 1892*, ed. Isabel C. Barrows (Geo. H. Ellis: 1892), 46, https://carlisleindian.dickinson.edu/sites/default/files/docs-resources/CIS-Resources_1892-PrattSpeech.pdf.

28. Campus Ministry Today, Bill Bright, "Four Spiritual Laws: The Basics Series" (Campus Crusade for Christ, 2007), accessed November 28, 2024, https://campusministry.org/docs/tools/FourSpiritualLaws.pdf.

29. General Synod of the Anglican Church of Canada, "Statistics 1959-2017," accessed July 12, 2024, https://www.anglican.ca/ask/faq/number-of-anglicans/statistical-archive/.

30. Matthew Puddister, "Membership Decline Steepens," *Anglican Journal*, May 1, 2024, https://anglicanjournal.com/membership-decline-steepens/ (accessed July 12, 2024).

31. Brian Clarke and Stuart Macdonald, "Working Paper—United Church of Canada Statistics," January 6, 2011, accessed July 12, 2024, http://individual.utoronto.ca/clarkemacdonald/clarkemacdonald/Welcome_files/unitedchurch.pdf.

32. Evangelical Lutheran Church in Canada, "Rejoicing in Hope, Registration Package, 2025 National Convention," chrome-extension://efaidnbmnnnibpcajpcglclefindmkaj/https://elcic.ca/wp-content/uploads/2025/03/2025-Convention-Registration-Package.pdf. Accessed April 1, 2025. p. 2.

33. Kevin J. Jones, "Canada Census Shows 2 Million Fewer Catholics as Disaffiliation Grows," *Catholic News Agency*, October 27, 2022, https://www.catholicnewsagency.com/news/252672/canada-census-shows-2-million-fewer-catholics-as-disaffiliation-grows (accessed October 2, 2024).

34. Michael Swan, "Canadians Rank Low in Mass Attendance," *Catholic Register*, February 2, 2023, https://www.catholicregister.org/item/35218-canadians-rank-low-in-mass-attendance (accessed October 2, 2024).

35. The Association of Religion Data Archive, "Evangelical Lutheran Church in America (1988–Present)," https://thearda.com/us-religion/group-profiles/groups?D=314 (accessed July 13, 2024).

36. Evangelical Lutheran Church in America, "ELCA Facts," accessed July 13, 2024, https://www.elca.org/elca-facts.

37. Episcopal Church, C. Kirk Hadaway, "Is the Episcopal Church Growing (or Declining)?" accessed July 13, 2024, https://www.episcopalchurch.org/wp-content/uploads/2021/03/2004GrowthReport.pdf.

38. David Paulsen, "Episcopal Church's Latest Parochial Reports Point to Denominational Decline, Hope for Future," *Episcopal News Service*, September 21, 2023, https://episcopalnewsservice.org/2023/09/21/episcopal-churchs-latest-parochial-reports-highlight-denominational-decline-hope-for-future/ (accessed July 13, 2024).

39. United Church of Christ, "2014 Yearbook," accessed July 13, 2024, https://new.uccfiles.com/pdf/Summary-Stats-1955-2013.pdf.

40. United Church of Christ, *A Statistical Profile With Reflection/Discussion Questions for Church Leaders* (2023), accessed July 13, 2024, https://www.ucc.org/wp-content/uploads/2024/03/2023statisticalreport.v11webUPDATED.pdf.

41. Ryan Burge, "The Catholic Church Is in Trouble in Places Where It Used to Dominate: States like Pennsylvania and Massachusetts Are Losing Catholics by the Thousands," *Graphs About Religion* (blog), October 12, 2023, https://www.graphsaboutreligion.com/p/the-catholic-church-is-in-trouble.

42. Ryan Burge, "Catholic Mass Attendance Has Fallen by Half: Is Politics to Blame?" *Graphs About Religion* (blog), May 7, 2023, https://www.graphsaboutreligion.com/p/catholic-mass-attendance-has-fallen.

43. Ronald F. Neuss, ed., *Facts and Figures About the Church of England 3* (London: The Central Board of Finance of the Church of England, 1965), 60, https://www.churchofengland.org/sites/default/files/2019-09/church-statistics-1965.pdf.

44. Neuss, *Facts and Figures*, 16.

45. Ken Eames, *Statistics for Mission 2022* (London: Church of England, 2023), 19, https://www.churchofengland.org/sites/default/files/2023-11/statisticsformission2022.pdf.

46. Eames, *Statistics for Mission 2022*, 20.

47. John Hayward, "Methodist Church 2000–2020," *Church Growth Modelling* (blog), https://churchmodel.org.uk/church-growth-models/limited-enthusiasm/demographics-2/methodist-church-2000-2020/.

48. "Being a Member of the Methodist Church," Methodist Church in Great Britain, accessed July 24, 2024, https://www.methodist.org.uk/about/membership/.

49. Peter Brierley, "Christianity in the UK: Measuring the Christian Population in the UK," Faith Survey, accessed July 24, 2024, https://faithsurvey.co.uk/uk-christianity.html.

50. Uniting Church Assembly, "8 Key Takeaways from the Act2 Report," October 6, 2023, accessed October 7, 2023, https://uniting.church/8-key-takeaways/.

51. Uniting Church Assembly, "8 Key Takeaways."

52. Uniting Church Assembly, "8 Key Takeaways."

53. Kathy Jacka and Ruth Powell, "Changes in Church Attendance in Australia: Overall Church Decline Is Offset by Signs of Growth in Some Churches," NCLS Research, October

2021, accessed October 8, 2024, https://www.ncls.org.au/articles/changes-in-church-attendance-in-australia/.

54. Aaron Earls, "Southern Baptist Membership Decline Slows, Baptisms and Attendance Grow," Lifeway Research, May 7, 2024, accessed July 12, 2024, https://news.lifeway.com/2024/05/07/southern-baptist-membership-decline-slows-baptisms-and-attendance-grow/.

55. Yearbook of American and Canadian Churches, "The Lutheran Church—Missouri Synod (LCMS)," accessed July 13, 2024, https://www.yearbookofchurches.org/lutheran-church-missouri-synod-lcms.

56. Lutheran Church Missouri Synod, *2023 Annual Report*, 23, accessed July 13, 2024, https://files.lcms.org/file/preview/annual-report-2023.

57. Yearbook of American and Canadian Churches, "Lutheran Church–Canada," accessed July 13, 2024,

https://www.yearbookofchurches.org/lutheran-church-canada .

58. Lutheran Church Canada, "LCC Summarized Statistics 2019–2022," https://www.lutheranchurchcanada.ca/wp-content/uploads/sites/11/2024/02/2019-2022-summarized.pdf

59. Neil Carlson, "Membership Trends in the CRCNA, 1965 to 2022," May 6, 2022, accessed July 13, 2024, https://network.crcna.org/sites/default/files/DW603%20CRCNA%20membership%20trends%201965%20to%202022%20CoD%2020220525.pdf.

60. Walter J. Burghardt, "Contemplation: A Long, Loving Look at the Real," *Church* (1989), accessed November 17, 2024, https://www.alliesonthejourney.com/uploads/7/4/7/4/74742015/burghardt_-_contemplation_a_long_loving.pdf.

61. Apologies to all whose churches show significant progress, both in the kinds that have been named and in other ways, and those who are not named. This is an intentionally broad and general grouping that cannot go too deep for considerations of space. I am aware that much is omitted.

62. Eames, *Statistics for Mission 2022*.

Chapter 2 The Good News in a Shrinking Church

1. 2 Cor. 5:16–21.

2. Some readers will hear, in these words, an echo of a verse attributed to St. Teresa of Avila: "Christ has no body but yours, / No hands, no feet on earth but yours. . ." This is a troubling saying when used loosely. Because it is simply "attributed to" her rather than specifically located in Teresa's writings, it tends to float around without context. The saying may simply be understood as an invitation to participate in God's transformative work,

a reminder that God invites all of us to engage our whole beings in the life of divine love. Treated in this way, the text is a valuable and pointed reminder. However, the wording can (and, in my experience, sometimes does) lead to an important misunderstanding. The exclusiveness of the phrases, "no body but yours" and "no hands, no feet on earth but yours" is open to being interpreted as a claim that limits God's activity to humanity and risks asserting the ultimacy of human will. Teresa would certainly not have intended this, if she could even imagine such a position.

3. The predominant liberal account of economics, as in Adam Smith's *Wealth of Nations*, is built upon the priority of individual self-interest. Marx argues that capitalism is not really individualist in a Smithian sense but is an expression of class self-interest. Marx's answer is class struggle (as in the *Manifesto of the Communist Party*) in which the worker class overthrows the capitalist owner class. In both visions, the major decisions of society are defined by self-interest.

4. The word "idealist" is commonly used in two senses. Most often, it refers to a tendency to focus on a vision of what ought to be, to the exclusion of attention to what is. This is often called "moral idealism." In a more technical sense, "idealism" is a philosophical tradition that grounds reality in nonmaterial being, such as Plato's Ideas. Both senses are relevant to the point being made. An idealistic attitude too easily ignores or rejects the concrete circumstances of life, becoming destructively unrealistic. At its worst, this attitude can lead to violent efforts to enforce an imagined utopia. Philosophical idealism is always at risk of devaluing material existence because the really real is nonphysical; this shows up most evidently in Gnosticism. Hans Jonas is one of the twentieth century's most profound thinkers on Gnosticism. Moral and philosophical idealism can be linked; some have argued that this occurred in Germany up to and including the Nazi era. On the risks of moral idealism see Daniel Chirot, *You Say You Want a Revolution? Radical Idealism and Its Tragic Consequences* (Princeton University Press, 2020). On Gnosticism, including its relation to existentialism and nihilism (nihilism, especially, is a radical form of moral idealism) see Hans Jonas, *The Gnostic Religion: The Message of the Alien God and the Beginnings of Christianity*, 2nd ed. (Beacon Press, 1963). On linkages between moral idealism and philosophical idealism in Nazi Germany see V. J. McGill, "Notes on Philosophy in Nazi Germany," *Science & Society* 4, no. 1 (Winter 1940): 12–28, Hans Jonas, "Heidegger and Theology," *Review of Metaphysics* 18, no. 2 (December 1964): 207–33. A study that goes into the complexities between the German philosophical idealist tradition and Nazism is Lesley Chamberlain, *Street Life and Morals: German Philosophy in Hitler's Lifetime* (London: Reaktion Books, 2021).

5. A helpful account of Lonergan's understanding of grace, a viewpoint that informs this passage, appears in Mark T. Miller, *The Quest for God & the Good Life: Lonergan's Theological Anthropology* (Catholic University of America Press, 2013), 141–75.

6. Irenaeus, *Five Books of S. Irenaeus, Bishop of Lyons, Against Heresies*, trans. John Keble (London: J. Parker, 1872), https://archive.org/details/fivebooksofsiren42iren.

7. Stanley Hauerwas and William H. Willimon, *Resident Aliens: Life in the Christian Colony* (Abingdon Press, 2014).

8. For example: Richard Van Kirk, "The Barque of Peter Will Reach Its Destination," *Catholic Stand: A Little Vatican Apostolate*, November 11, 2018, accessed October 11, 2024, https://catholicstand.com/the-barque-of-peter-will-reach-its-destination/.

9. Anglican-Lutheran International Commission (ALIC III), *To Love and Serve the Lord:* Diakonia *in the Life of the Church: The Jerusalem Report of the Anglican–Lutheran International Commission (ALIC III)* (Lutheran World Federation, 2012), 10, https://www.anglicancommunion.org/media/102228/OEA-ALIC_report-EN.pdf.

10. Irenaeus, *Heresies*, I, 10, I; p. 33. Cf. also III, 16, 6–7; 267–269.

11. Augustine, *Confessions*, trans. Henry Chadwick (Oxford University Press, 1991), XI, vii, (9), 226.

12. Dorothy L. Sayers, "Why Work?" in *Creed or Chaos? Why Christians Must Choose Either Dogma or Disaster (Or, Why It Really Does Matter What You Believe)* (Sophia Institute Press, 1999), 109–111.

13. Dorothy L. Sayers, *The Zeal of Thy House* (Harcourt, Brace and Company, 1937), 69–75. For a more thorough discussion of Sayers on work and its relationship with good and evil, see William H. Harrison, "Loving the Creation, Loving the Creator: Dorothy L. Sayers's Theology of Work," in *Anglican Theological Review* 86, no. 2 (Summer 2004): 239–57.

Chapter 3 The Organized Church in a Post-Church Age

1. There has been extensive research on the "nones," in recent years. Key assessments include: James Emery White, *The Rise of the Nones: Understanding and Reaching the Religiously Unaffiliated* (Baker Books, 2014); Elizabeth Drescher, *Choosing Our Religion: The Spiritual Lives of America's Nones* (Oxford University Press, 2016); and Ryan P. Burge, *The Nones: Where They Came From, Who They Are, and Where They Are Going*, 2nd ed. (Fortress Press, 2023).

2. Ryan P. Burge, "Are Today's Nones Less Religious Than Nones From the Past?" *Graphs About Religion* (blog), November 28, 2024, accessed November 28, 2024, https://www.graphsaboutreligion.com/p/are-todays-nones-less-religious-than.

3. James Powell, "Sunday Shopping," *Today in Ottawa's History* (blog), April 13, 2019, https://todayinottawashistory.wordpress.com/tag/lords-day-act/.

4. Rosemary Haughton, *The Transformation of Man: A Study of Conversion and Community* (Geoffrey Chapman, 1967), 155, *cf.* 150. I was led to Haughton's work and this particular definition by Charles Hefling, *Why Doctrines?*, 2nd ed. (The Lonergan Institute, 2000), 55.

5. Immanuel Kant, *The Critique of Pure Reason* (Willey Books, 1899).

6. Freud's introduction of the notion of the "unconscious" into formal study created widespread awareness that there is much about ourselves that we do not know. What we do not know interferes with our capacity to know and decide. See, for example, Sigmund Freud, *Psychopathology of Everyday Life*, trans. A. A. Brill (Mentor/Macmillan, 1952). A helpful discussion of Freud on knowing, especially as it relates to God, appears in Alvin J. Reines, "Freud's Concepts of Reality and God: A Text Study," *Hebrew Union College Annual* 61 (1990): 219–70, https://www.jstor.org/stable/23508177.

7. Friedrich Nietzsche, *The Will to Power*, trans. Walter Kaufmann and R. J. Hollingdale (New York: Vintage Books, 1968).

8. Lonergan discusses self-appropriation extensively in Bernard Lonergan, *Collected Works of Bernard Lonergan*, vol. 5, *Understanding and Being: The Halifax Lectures on Insight*, ed. Mark D. Morelli and Elizabeth A. Morelli (University of Toronto Press, 1990).

9. Specifically as intellectual conversion, Lonergan addresses this topic in Bernard Lonergan, *Collected Works of Bernard Lonergan*, vol. 14, *Method in Theology*, 2nd ed., ed. Robert M. Doran and John D. Dadosky (University of Toronto Press, 2017), 223–25. The core discussion about knowing as asking and answering questions is the focus of Bernard Lonergan, *Collected Works of Bernard Lonergan*, vol. 3, *Insight: A Study of Human Understanding*, 5th ed., ed. Frederick E. Crowe and Robert M. Doran (University of Toronto Press, 1992). The first chapter assembles the basic materials of the account, 27–56.

10. Lonergan, *Method*, 22.

11. Lonergan, *Method*, 22.

12. Lonergan, *Method*, 23.

13. Benjamin Weiser, "Here's What Happens When Your Lawyer Uses ChatGPT," *New York Times*, May 27, 2023, https://www.nytimes.

com/2023/05/27/nyregion/avianca-airline-lawsuit-chatgpt.html. As readers will recognize, AI continues to develop. However, as Tshilidzi Marwala reminds us, even when AI seems accurate, it may not be conveying the truth. Tshilidzi Marwala, "Never Assume That the Accuracy of Artificial Intelligence Information Equals the Truth," United Nations University, July 18, 2024, accessed November 28, 2024, https://unu.edu/article/never-assume-accuracy-artificial-intelligence-information-equals-truth.

14. As, for example, in moral feelings (including those of conscience) that Freud treats as taboos or, similarly, compulsion prohibitions. Sigmund Freud, *Totem and Taboo*, in *The Basic Writings of Sigmund Freud*, trans. A. A. Brill (New York: Modern Library, 1938), 826–828.

15. The notion of a Freudian slip is based on Freud's account of parapraxis in *Psychopathology of Everyday Life*. Note that mere slips of the tongue, which can be the results of a variety of processes, do not count as Freudian. Freudian slips suggest the presence of subconscious elements that are repressed. Freud begins with cases of forgetfulness in quotations, recall of names, and similar cases. "What is common to all these cases is the fact that the forgotten or distorted material becomes connected through some associative road with an unconscious stream of thought, which gives rise to the influence that comes to light as forgetting" (22). Speech blunders of the sort that we most commonly think of as Freudian slips are addressed in 37–58; such blunders can betray complexes (57) or inner conflicts (58).

16. C. G. Jung and Marie-Louise von Franz, *Man and His Symbols* (Doubleday, 1964).

17. Robert M. Doran, *Theology and the Dialectics of History* (University of Toronto Press, 1990), 59–63.

18. Doran appears to reject this aspect of development as part of psychic conversion (Doran, 60). I disagree, because both the symbols/insights relationship and the feelings/values relationship are integrally linked aspects of a deeper understanding of our psyches and their effects on our knowing, judging, and deciding selves.

19. Stephen Happel and James J. Walter, *Conversion and Discipleship: A Christian Foundation for Ethics and Doctrine* (Fortress Press, 1986), 108.

20. "Moral conversion changes the criterion of one's decisions and choices from satisfactions to values." Lonergan, *Method*, 225–26.

21. Lonergan, *Method*, 23.

22. "From a causal viewpoint, one would say that first there is God's gift of his love. Next, the eye of this love reveals values in their splendor, while the strength of this love brings about their realization, and that is moral conversion. Finally, among the values discerned by the eye of

love is the value of believing the truths taught by the religious tradition, and in such tradition and belief are the seeds of intellectual conversion." Lonergan, *Method*, 228–29.

23. Lonergan, *Method*, 227.

24. *Groundhog Day*, directed by Harold Ramis (Columbia Pictures, 1993).

Chapter 4 Leadership in a Shrinking Church

1. This is a commonplace of Christian theology. However, I think that there is some benefit to thinking about it specifically in relation to leadership. I referenced Sayers's theology of creativity in our conversation about good and evil. In a chapter called "Problem Picture," in *The Mind of the Maker*, she points out that "the artist does not see life as a problem to be solved, but as a medium for creation," emphasizing that our contributions to the world are about God's long-term transformative work rather than our determination to "solve" a particular issue right now. Sayers, *The Mind of the Maker*, 188.

2. Ronald Heifetz, Alexander Grashow, and Marty Linsky, *The Practice of Adaptive Leadership: Tools and Tactics for Changing Your Organization and the World* (Harvard Business Press, 2009), 19.

3. Heifetz et al., *Practice*, 14.

4. Heifetz et al., *Practice*, 14.

5. Heifetz et al., *Practice*, 15.

6. Heifetz et al., *Practice*, 15.

7. Heifetz et al., *Practice*, 15–16.

8. Heifetz et al., *Practice*, 16.

9. Heifetz et al., *Practice*, 16–17.

10. Heifetz et al., *Practice*, 6.

11. Heifetz et al., *Practice*, 32–36.

12. The full account of this process is the subject of Lonergan's major philosophical work, *Insight*. A brief presentation appears in *Method*, 18.

13. This role of self-imaging was drawn to my attention by James Price, who discusses it as "narrative image." James Price, *The Call: The Spiritual Realism of Sargent Shriver* (Los Angeles: SSPI Press, 2023), 137-155.

14. Cameron Harder, *Discovering the Other: Asset-Based Approaches for Building Community Together* (Alban Institute, 2013).

15. Alan J. Roxburgh, *Missional Map-Making: Skills for Leading in Times of Transition* (Jossey-Bass, 2010).

16. John Fuder, *Neighborhood Mapping: How to Make Your Church Invaluable to the Community* (Moody Publishers, 2014).

17. John Bowen, *Evangelism for "Normal" People: Good News for Those Looking for a Fresh Approach* (Augsburg Fortress, 2002), 83–84.

18. O. Henry, "The Gift of the Magi" (1906), Project Gutenberg, text produced by Susan Ritchie, https://www.gutenberg.org/files/7256/7256-h/7256-h.htm.

19. Charles Williams, *Outlines of Romantic Theology*, in *Outlines of Romantic Theology with Which Is Reprinted Religion and Love in Dante: The Theology of Romantic Love*, ed. Alice Mary Hadfield (Wm. B. Eerdmans, 1990), 7–73.

20. Mohandas Gandhi, *Gandhi on Non-Violence*, ed. Thomas Merton (New Directions, 1965), https://archive.org/details/gandhionnonviole0000gand.

21. Talet Ahmed provides an account of Gandhi's influence, while also addressing the complexities in his life. Talat Ahmed, *Mohandas Gandhi: Experiments in Civil Disobedience* (Pluto Press, 2019).

22. Natalia Dubtsova, "From Pulpit to Propaganda Machine: Tracing the Russian Orthodox Church's Role in Putin's War," Reuters Institute, February 6, 2024, accessed September 6, 2024, https://reutersinstitute.politics.ox.ac.uk/pulpit-propaganda-machine-tracing-russian-orthodox-churchs-role-putins-war. For further detail, see the full paper, of which the foregoing is a summary: Natalia Dubtsova, *The Role of the Orthodox Church in Advancing Putin's War Messaging* (Thomson Reuters, 2023), https://reutersinstitute.politics.ox.ac.uk/sites/default/files/2024-02/RISJ%20Fellows%20Paper_Natalia_Trinity2023_Final.pdf.

23. See James R. Price, *The Call: The Spiritual Realism of Sargent Shriver* (Los Angeles: SSPI Press, 2023), and James R. Price and Kenneth R. Melchin, *Spiritualizing Politics Without Politicizing Religion: The Example of Sargent Shriver* (University of Toronto Press, 2022).

24. Price, *The Call*, 13.

25. Price, *The Call*, 13.

26. Price, *The Call*, 14.

27. Price, *The Call*, 17.

28. Price, *The Call*, 69.

29. Price, *The Call*, 21.

30. Price and Melchin, *Spiritualizing Politics*, 12.

31. Price and Melchin, *Spiritualizing Politics*, 17.

32. James MacGregor Burns, *Transforming Leadership: The Pursuit of Happiness* (New York: Grove Press, 2004), 28.

33. Ronald A. Heifetz, *Leadership Without Easy Answers* (Cambridge, MA: Belknap/Harvard University Press, 1994), 22.

34. Heifetz, *Leadership*, 24.

35. Brené Brown, *Daring Greatly: How the Courage to be Vulnerable Transforms the Way We Live, Love, Parent, and Lead* (Avery/Penguin Random House, 2012), 10–12.

36. Brené Brown, *Dare to Lead: Brave Work. Tough Conversations. Whole Hearts.* (New York: Random House, 2018).

37. Heifetz et al., *Practice*, 255–58.

38. Heifetz et al., *Practice*, 270–71.

39. Heifetz et al., *Practice*, 270.

40. Amy C. Edmondson, *The Fearless Organization: Creating Psychological Safety in the Workplace for Learning, Innovation, and Growth* (Wiley, 2018).

41. Heifetz et al., *Practice*, 14.

Chapter 5 How Church Leadership Became Too Big and Lost Focus

1. Marriage was not necessarily understood to be a church thing until the Fourth Lateran Council (1215) encouraged it. Still, society took time to adjust to these expectations. Frances and Joseph Gies, *Marriage and Family in the Middle Ages* (Harper & Row, 1987), 141. Weddings outside, then inside, church buildings occurred in the Middle Ages; however, church weddings were not required for a valid marriage in England until the Marriage Act of 1753. This change in the law was intended to deter people from running away from their families and marrying partners deemed unacceptable by others, as well as to prevent polygamy—which was regarded as both common and easily arranged. Lawrence Stone, *The Family, Sex and Marriage in England, 1500–1800*, abridged ed. (Harper & Row, 1979), 32–33.

2. The theological conception underlying this order is described in Arthur O. Lovejoy, *The Great Chain of Being: A Study of the History of an Idea* (Harvard University Press, 1936). The linkage between civil rule and church order in the Frankish context is addressed in Rutger Kramer, *Rethinking Authority in the Carolingian Empire* (Amsterdam University Press, 2019), 31–57. There is extensive literature on local variations of medieval feudal order. A helpful discussion of the reasons for variation is in Andrew T. Young, "The Political Economy of Feudalism in Medieval Europe," *Constitutional Political Economy* 32, no. 1 (March 2021): 127–143, https://doi.org/10.1007/s10602-020-09324-4.

3. C. N. L. Brooke describes the impact of the Gregorian Reform on priests, as sacramental theology shifts and the priestly function changes with it in C. N. L. Brooke, "Gregorian Reform in Action: Clerical Marriage in England, 1050–1200," *Cambridge Historical Journal* 12, no. 1 (1956): 1–21.

4. Steffen Patzold and Carine van Rhijn, eds., *Men in the Middle: Local Priests in Early Medieval Europe* (De Gruyter, 2016).

5. Kathleen L. Wood-Legh, "Some Aspects of the History of the Chantries during the Reign of Edward III," *Cambridge Historical Journal* 4, no. 1 (1932): 26–50, https://doi.org/10.1017/S1474691300003279.

6. Robert A. Scott, *The Gothic Enterprise: A Guide to Understanding the Medieval Cathedral* (University of California Press, 2011).

7. Scott, *Gothic Enterprise*, 11.

8. Scott, *Gothic Enterprise*, 47–64.

9. Gregory Dix, *The Shape of the Liturgy* (Dacre Press, 1945).

10. Paul F. Bradshaw, "Liturgical Reform and the Unity of Christian Churches," *Studia Liturgica* 44, nos. 1–2 (2014): 163–71, https://doi.org/10.1177/00393207140441-219.

11. Hellmut Lieberg, *Office and Ordination in Luther and Melanchthon*, trans. Matthew Carver (Concordia Publishing House, 2020). Helpful reviews of Luther's understanding of the pastor as preacher appear in H. S. Wilson, "Luther on Preaching as God Speaking," in *The Pastoral Luther: Essays on Martin Luther's Practical Theology*, ed. Timothy J. Wengert (Fortress Press, 2017); and Fred W. Meuser, "Luther as preacher of the Word of God," in *The Cambridge Companion to Martin Luther*, ed. Donald K. McKim (Cambridge University Press, 2006).

12. Lorenzo Valla, *The Treatise of Lorenzo Valla on the Donation of Constantine*, trans. Christopher B. Coleman (Yale University Press, 1922), http://www.archive.org/details/cu31924029363706.

13. A helpful overview is found in Debora K Shuger, *The Renaissance Bible: Scholarship, Sacrifice, and Subjectivity* (Baylor University Press, 2010).

14. A helpful overview is found in Henning Graf Reventlow, *History of Biblical Interpretation: From the Enlightenment to the Twentieth Century*, trans. Leo G. Perdue (Society of Biblical Literature, 2010).

15. Stephen D. W. King includes a thorough and helpful discussion of the meaning of the term "professional" as it impinges on our concerns as he addresses the role of Clinical Pastoral Education in the transformation of the clergy world. Stephen D. W. King, *Trust the Process: A History of Clinical Pastoral Education as Theological Education* (University Press of America, 2007), 1–19.

16. King, *Trust the Process*, 1–19.

17. See, for example, the Midwestern United States as described in Gretchen Townsend Buggeln, *The Suburban Church: Modernism and Community in Postwar America* (University of Minnesota Press, 2015).

18. Scott, *Gothic Enterprise*, 11.

Chapter 6 Under Pressure

1. The Enneagram Institute, "Type 6: The Loyalist," accessed July 10, 2024, https://www.enneagraminstitute.com/type-6/.

2. Brown, *Dare to Lead*, 136–163.

3. Lonergan, *Insight*, 244–47.

4. Lonergan, *Insight*, 247–50.

5. "General Bias" in Lonergan, *Insight*, 250–69.

6. Associated Press, "A New Florida Law Rejects the Term 'Climate Change' in State Statutes," *WFSU Public Media*, May 16, 2024, accessed November 28, 2024, https://news.wfsu.org/state-news/2024-05-16/a-new-florida-law-rejects-the-term-climate-change-in-state-statues.

7. Robin Globus Veldman, *The Gospel of Climate Skepticism: Why Evangelical Christians Oppose Action on Climate Change* (Berkeley: University of California Press, 2019).

8. Douglas Guilbeault, Andrea Baronchelli, and Damon Centola, "Experimental Evidence for Scale-Induced Category Convergence Across Populations," *Nature Communications* 12, no. 1 (2021): 1–7, accessed July 15, 2024, https://doi.org/10.1038/s41467-020-20037-y.

Chapter 7 Finding New Vision for a Church Organization

1. "Manic Monday," side A on *Manic Monday*, Columbia 05757, December 23, 1985, 7" single, written by Prince, a.k.a. Christopher, in 1984.

2. Bradley Morrison, *Already Missional: Congregations as Community Partners* (Resource Publications, 2016).

3. Apologies to those for whom SLOC means Single Line of Code, a computer programming abbreviation.

4. Paraphrasing Ontario Lottery and Gaming's slogan, "Know your limit. Play within it."

5. Douglas Adams, *The Hitchhiker's Guide to the Galaxy*, in *The Hitchhiker's Guide to the Galaxy: A Trilogy in Four Parts* (Heinemann, 1987), 47.

6. Heifetz et al., *Practice*, 49–108.

7. Heifetz et al., *Principles*, 15–16.
8. Heifetz et al., *Principles*, 152–153.
9. Heifetz et al., *Principles*, 154.
10. Heifetz et al., *Principles*, 263–275.
11. Immanuel Kant, "Toward Perpetual Peace: A Philosophical Sketch," in Immanuel Kant, David L. Colclasure, Jeremy Waldron, Michael W. Doyle, and Allen W. Wood, *Toward Perpetual Peace and Other Writings on Politics, Peace, and History*, ed. Pauline Kleingeld (Yale University Press, 2006), 67–109, especially 92, https://doi.org/10.12987/9780300128109.

Chapter 8 Partner, Thoughtfully

1. World Council of Churches, Commission on Faith and Order, *Report of the Third World Conference on Faith and Order, Lund, Sweden, August 15–28, 1952* (SCM Press, 1952), 6, https://archive.org/details/wccfops2.017.

Chapter 9 Considering Closure

1. General Synod of the Anglican Church of Canada, "Statistics 1959-2017," accessed July 12, 2024, https://www.anglican.ca/ask/faq/number-of-anglicans/statistical-archive/.
2. United Church of Christ, "2014 Yearbook," accessed July 13, 2024, https://new.uccfiles.com/pdf/Summary-Stats-1955-2013.pdf. United Church of Christ, *A Statistical Profile With Reflection/Discussion Questions for Church Leaders* (2023), accessed July 13, 2024, https://www.ucc.org/wp-content/uploads/2024/03/2023statisticalreport.v11webUPDATED.pdf.
3. Neuss, *Facts and Figures*, 60. Eames, *Statistics for Mission 2022*, 19.
4. Yearbook of American and Canadian Churches, "The Lutheran Church—Missouri Synod (LCMS)," accessed July 13, 2024, https://www.yearbookofchurches.org/lutheran-church-missouri-synod-lcms. utheran Church Missouri Synod, *2023 Annual Report*, 23, accessed July 13, 2024, https://files.lcms.org/file/preview/annual-report-2023.

Chapter 10 Vision in Unlikely Places

1. Some readers will hear an echo of Rick Warren's thinking about purpose-driven church. There are some similarities between Warren's work and my suggestions in this chapter. The fundamental difference

is that Warren explicitly inhabits the numerical model of church. This defines Warren's anticipated outcomes and, therefore, the strategies that he recommends. Rick Warren, *The Purpose Driven Church: Growth Without Compromising Your Message & Mission* (Zondervan, 1995).

INDEX

adaptive leadership, 51-53, 67-69, 74, 172
ambassadors of reconciliation, xi-xii, xiv, 20, 25, 27, 31, 51, 61-63, 67, 71, 93, 103, 128, 130, 133-134, 137, 139, 143, 153
Anglican Church in Aotearoa, New Zealand and Polynesia, Te Hāhi Mihinare ki Aotearoa ki Niu Tīreni, ki Ngā Moutere o te Moana Nui a Kiwa, 16
Anglican Church of Canada, 9, 11, 16-17, 101, 149, 167, 176
Anglosphere, xi, xiii, 1, 3, 5-7, 11, 13-14, 16, 19, 71, 81, 92, 108, 142, 159
Anxiety, xiii, 57, 87-89, 94, 98, 129, 132
Association of Theological Schools, 142
barque of St. Peter, 23, 170
Beaumont, Susan, xiii, 165
bias, xiii, 33, 37, 52, 59, 70, 90-92, 94-95, 98, 101, 103, 144, 152, 175
Bonhoeffer, Dietrich, 62
Bowen, John, 60, 172
Brown, Brené, xv, 69, 91, 173
Burns, James MacGregor, 68, 173
Christ Jesus, xiv, 10, 20, 25, 70, 100-101, 134, 151, 161
Christian Reformed Church in North America, 14
church growth movement, 4
Church of England, 12, 17, 149, 168
Clinical Pastoral Education, 80-81, 146, 174
conversion (*see*: transformation)
coach (leadership), 56-57, 73, 96
courage, xiii, 10, 19, 33, 39, 41, 52, 56, 61, 69-70. 82. 91, 95-96, 105, 109, 114, 121, 131, 133, 145, 173

decision, xi, 21, 23, 33, 37, 39-40, 49-50, 56-60, 64-65, 68-69, 81, 90-92, 95-96, 130, 133-134, 143, 146, 149, 151-154, 160, 169, 171
Descartes, René, 79
diaconal church, 24, 127, 140, 143
diakonia, 24, 27, 30, 32, 41, 63, 66-67, 74, 84, 170
Dialogue Decalogue, 9, 167
Dix, Gregory (Dom), 78, 174
Doran, Robert M., 37-38, 171
Ecotheology, 7, 9
Enlightenment (historical period), 33, 61, 79, 174
Erasmus, Desiderius, 79
Evangelical Lutheran Church in America, 12, 17, 167
Evangelical Lutheran Church in Canada, 9, 12, 16-17, 101, 167
Evangelism, 9-10, 18, 20, 39, 47-48, 60, 105, 144, 146, 172
Experience, ix-x, xi, xiii, 1, 5, 23, 30, 35, 38, 47, 53, 61, 66-67, 69, 71, 80-81, 87-88, 101, 110, 142, 145, 155, 161
explosions, 31, 46, 48, 61, 64, 67, 87, 90, 101, 132, 161
feelings, 37-39, 49, 66, 110, 124, 154-155, 171
Francis of Assisi, 62, 101
Freud, Sigmund, 32, 37, 170-171
Gandhi, Mohandas (Mahatma), 62, 172-173
Gospel Vision Statement, x, xiii, 67, 83, 94, 97, 99-101, 124-125, 139, 143, 150, 158
Groundhog Day, xiv, 41, 43-47, 49-50, 60, 66, 110, 160, 172

Haughton, Rosemary, 31, 64, 170
Heifetz, Ronald, xv, 51-53, 67-69, 74, 83, 122-123, 133-134, 172-173, 175
Henry, O., 60, 170, 172
Hobbes, Thomas, 79
honesty, xv, 5, 26, 69-70, 128
Holy Spirit, 31, 64, 132, 135, 161
Indigenous people(s), 9, 11, 16, 55, 62, 92, 116, 122-123, 144
interiority, 53, 59-60, 63, 66, 101
judgment, 58, 81, 143, 151, 158, 160
Jung, Carl, 38, 171
Kant, Immanuel, 32, 79, 135, 170, 175
Kirill (Patriarch), 62-63
Locke, John, 3, 79, 165
Lonergan, Bernard, xiv, 32-34, 36-37, 52-53, 60, 67-69, 169-172, 175
Lord's Day Act, 29
Luther, Martin, 60, 78-79, 174
Lutheran Church Canada, 14, 101, 168
Lutheran Church – Missouri Synod, 14, 149, 168, 176
Mann, Charles C., 7, 166
method, 4, 34, 41-42, 52, 68, 79-80, 131, 133, 171-172
Methodist Church in Great Britain, 12, 168
McGavran, Donald A., 4
Melchin, Kenneth, xiv, 41, 63, 66, 173
Nietzsche, Friedrich, 3, 32, 165, 170
nones, 29, 170
numerical growth model, xi, xv, 1, 7-9
presbyteral church, 75-82
Presbyterian Church in Canada, 16-17
Presbyters, xiii, 75-77, 79-81, 83, 85
Putin, Vladimir, 55, 62, 173
Putnam, Robert D., 4-6, 8, 14, 165
Price, James, xii, 41, 63-66, 105, 163, 172-173
resident aliens, 23, 170
Roman Catholic Church, 12, 112, 115, 144

Secularization, xiv, 3, 6, 51, 76, 110, 157, 160
seminary, seminaries, ix-xi, xiii, 9, 15, 18, 26, 52, 56, 61, 70, 72-73, 79-81, 84, 87, 99, 101, 111, 129, 137, 142, 150, 159, 161, 163
Sayers, Dorothy L., 26, 31, 170, 172
self-appropriation, xiv, 10-12, 22, 31-33, 35-36, 39-44, 47, 52-59, 61-63, 65-66, 73, 91, 95-96, 101, 103, 110-111, 127, 131-132, 143, 145-146, 154, 158-161, 169, 171-172
Shriver, Sargent, xiv, 41, 63-68, 74, 132, 160, 172-173
SLOC analysis, 124-125, 133-134, 175
social media, xv, 29, 55, 93-95, 98, 111
Southern Baptist Convention, 14, 16
Spirit, 2, 66-67, 116, 128, 143, 157-158
spiritual direction, xiv, 6, 9-10, 20, 25, 29, 45, 61-67, 77, 81, 83, 96-97, 115-116, 137, 144, 170, 172-173
symbols, 38-39, 171
Swidler, Leonard, 9, 167
teams, 73, 83, 97
Tenzin Gyatzo (Dalai Lama), 62
The Episcopal Church, 12, 17, 167
transformation: includes intellectual, psychic, moral, religious, xi-xv, 1, 10, 19-23, 26, 31-33, 36-42, 45-60, 62-63, 65-70, 72-74, 76, 78-80, 82, 85, 87, 90, 92, 96-101, 103, 105, 110-111, 122, 124, 127-128, 131-132, 134-137, 139, 142-147, 150, 152-155, 157-162, 170, 174
transformational church, 31-50
Trump, Donald, 57
understanding, xiv-xv, xvii, 2, 5, 9, 20, 22-27, 31-39, 4-50, 53-60, 62, 68, 72-73, 79, 85, 87, 90-91, 95-97, 101, 105, 110, 122, 125, 127, 131-134, 137, 144, 146, 152, 154, 160, 169-171, 174

Index 187

United Church of Canada, 12, 17, 101, 167
United Church of Christ, 12, 17, 149, 167, 176
United Reformed Church, 13
Uniting Church in Australia, 13, 168

Valla, Lorenzo, 79, 174
Values, 38, 66, 68, 96, 171
vulnerability, xv, 69-70
Williams, Charles, 61, 172
World War I, 77-78
World War II, 4, 30, 78

www.ingramcontent.com/pod-product-compliance
Lightning Source LLC
Chambersburg PA
CBHW052100300426
44117CB00013B/2214